WELCOME TO BRITAIN

FIXING OUR BROKEN IMMIGRATION SYSTEM

WELCOME TO BRITAIN

COLIN YEO

Biteback Publishing

First published in Great Britain in 2020 by
Biteback Publishing Ltd, London

Copyright © Colin Yeo 2020

Colin Yeo has asserted his right under the Copyright, Designs and Patents Act 1988
to be identified as the author of this work.

ISBN 978-1-78590-577-3

10 9 8 7 6 5 4 3 2 1

A CIP catalogue record for this book is available from the British Library.

Set in Minion Pro

Printed and bound in Great Britain by
CPI Group (UK) Ltd, Croydon CR0 4YY

For my clients

CONTENTS

NOTE ON TERMINOLOGY

First, a few quick words about language. I have endeavoured to make this book an accessible one to non-lawyers and non-specialists. To do so, I have at times played a little loose with my use of technical terms and legal language.

In this book I have referred to 'unauthorised migrants' when describing non-citizens who do not have formal legal permission to remain in the country. Some prefer to use the label 'undocumented migrants' but I feel this confuses lawfulness with proof of status; there are lots of lawful residents of the United Kingdom who do not possess documents to prove their status, as the Windrush scandal (see Chapters 2 and 3) highlighted. This sorry episode concerned those who had arrived in the United Kingdom from Commonwealth countries in the 1950s, '60s and '70s but who, in recent years, were denied access to jobs, accommodation and services because of their lack of documents. The label 'irregular migrants' is also sometimes used, particularly in academic literature, but the meaning of the word 'irregular' is not sufficiently clear to my mind. Other labels include 'illegal immigrants' or 'illegals', but there are two major problems with that terminology. Firstly, no person is inherently illegal; actions might be so but people themselves are not. Secondly, there are many migrants who do not currently possess lawful status but who are eligible for it or who will become so in due course. To describe them as 'illegal' implies their position is clear and irredeemable when it is not. The boundary between lawful and unlawful is notably porous in both directions in immigration law.

Having said I do not consider the word 'irregular' sufficiently clear, I have struggled to find an alternative to the word 'regularisation'. This is a term widely used by lawyers, campaigners and politicians to describe a process by which an unauthorised migrant becomes authorised. It might be through an 'amnesty', which is where status is granted to a significant number of migrants at the same time, or it might be through a more individualised legal process, whereby one single person eventually earns authorised status over time or because of family or other connections.

Some readers may be puzzled to encounter the word 'racialised' for the first time. This term is common in academic writing, but I have rarely seen it used elsewhere. It denotes a group of people who have 'racial' characteristics attributed to them and it is used because the whole concept of race is a colonial invention with no foundation in biology. Race is often used as an alternative to referring to skin colour, but it has a wider meaning because some groups with light skin colours have been racialised too – the Irish in the nineteenth century, for example, or Jews throughout history.

Legal readers will need to forgive me; I have at times been a little carefree with some of the terminology of immigration law. Deportation is a formal legal process under the Immigration Act 1971, usually used against migrants who have committed criminal offences and preventing re-entry. I have sometimes used this word to describe a forced removal from the country that could be described by a different legal process. However, in my view the word 'deportation' better reflects public understanding and is therefore more evocative of what removal from this country really involves. I have also been less than systematic in my use of the terms 'asylum seeker' and 'refugee'. In my defence, in legal terms a refugee is a refugee whether or not she has been formally recognised as such. Likewise, an asylum seeker might be a person who is seeking asylum but may not be recognised as such.

Elsewhere, I have tried to provide context to words with a specific legal meaning where I have first used them. I have undoubtedly included too much context for some and too much jargon for others; I apologise to both sets of readers.

INTRODUCTION

Originally from Nigeria, Modupe Odelola is a doctor. She is not just any doctor, though; having graduated with distinction from the University of Ibadan, she later qualified as a consultant surgeon and senior lecturer at the University of Lagos and Lagos University Teaching Hospital. Following that, she came to the United Kingdom for a two-month clinical attachment, with a view to registering with the General Medical Council and applying to remain as a postgraduate doctor. Everything went well and, duly, she made her application, paying £335 for the privilege of doing so. She met the rules, she was highly qualified (the United Kingdom needing doctors of her calibre) and she fully expected her application to succeed. Yet, for some reason, a decision on her application was delayed – she had applied in January and by March had still not heard back from the Home Office.

Then, at the very end of March, with immediate effect, the Home Office changed the rules under which Dr Odelola had applied. She was no longer eligible and, a few days later, her application was refused under these new regulations. Understandably unhappy with this outcome, Odelola challenged the refusal on the basis that it was unfair: she had come to the UK and made an application in good faith under one set of rules, only for them to be changed while her application was still pending. The British are supposed to pride themselves on their sense of fair play and this was a blatant moving of the goal posts. Dr Odelola's case went all the way to the House of Lords, which was at that time the highest court in the United Kingdom, and over three years after her initial visa refusal, their lordships held that she could have no legitimate expectation that the same rules under which she had applied would be those under which her application would be decided. She had no vested right, no contractual right, no public law right, they said, nor was there sufficient unfairness in her treatment when attempting to overturn the decision. The rules belonged to the Home Secretary and he could change them as and when he wished, even if that was after Dr Odelola had made and paid for an application. The best the judges could do was politely suggest, though not order, that Dr Odelola at least be refunded the fee she had paid. Her appeal was then dismissed.[1]

But that was not the end of the story for Dr Odelola. She persevered and, fourteen years later, she now practises as a consultant surgeon, saving lives at a busy accident and emergency department in Essex. Which begs the question: what was the point of changing the rules and putting her through all that? Her experience typifies the treatment of migrants all across the United Kingdom. Having given up their homes and jobs to migrate, they have to play by multiple sets of complex rules in which they have no say. The rules can be, and indeed often are, changed – at any time, with immediate effect and without any warning. Courts are available to those who can afford them, but we will see that the reality is the judiciary in the United Kingdom is often unable or unwilling to interfere with Home Office decisions. Most migrants who arrive to work, join family members or seek sanctuary are eventually allowed to remain, but, having arrived full of hope, by then many are exhausted, alienated and disillusioned, not to mention considerably poorer. Nevertheless, they are expected gratefully to integrate.

Not all migrants are as persistent or fortunate as Dr Odelola. We will see that since 2010 a panoply of policies intended to deter migrants from coming to the United Kingdom have been introduced in a vain attempt to meet the net migration target set by David Cameron. There is no evidence that these deterrent policies have succeeded in reducing or limiting the number of arrivals, nor in encouraging departures. What the policies have done – from sky-high immigration application fees to effectively preventing migrant children attending university – is permanently handicap the migrants who do seek new lives here. Socially, economically, financially, educationally and otherwise, migrants and their families are deliberately penalised for being migrants. This government-orchestrated discrimination not only disadvantages migrants and their children compared to their peers but also makes their integration into British society harder, not easier. Meanwhile, a large unauthorised migrant population, thought to number between 600,000 and 1.2 million, has developed over many years. This is due to sometimes intentional and sometimes accidental (but always predictable) policy choices by successive governments.[2] I argue here that this is a social and democratic policy disaster, and that we need fundamental reform of our immigration system.

But what would a fair immigration system with broad political and public support look like? Most of us, on whatever side of the political spectrum and wherever we stand on the rights of migrants, can agree that the current system is broken. It does not seem to work for the public. It also does not seem to work for the government or civil servants. And it certainly does not work for migrants themselves. The only people for whom the current system does function are immigration lawyers like me, and it is a very bad sign indeed if something is good for lawyers. It is easy to criticise the current system, but it is difficult to imagine how we might go about reforming it. To avoid the failures of the past we need to understand what those failures truly were, what their impact was, why they came about and how they were operationalised. This book is my attempt to step back, see the wood for the trees and propose some ideas for reducing my future workload.

I argue that we should see newly arriving migrants as citizens-in-waiting. Given that, as I will show, migrants arriving as family members, workers and refugees are ultimately going to be allowed to remain anyway, would it not be better to stop actively obstructing their integration into society? This means ending the failed attempts at deterrence, which do not actually deter migrants from coming but do nevertheless significantly handicap them as they live their lives here. At the same time, immigration and citizenship laws should be reformed in an inclusive way to help the current unauthorised population become full members of the society of which they are already part and prevent a replacement unauthorised population arising in future.

We have a long way to go to achieve any of this. On the face of it, the current 'system' does not resemble a true system at all. A member of the public reading newspaper headlines about the latest immigration controversy; a migrant trying to understand what documents to include with an application; a lawyer attempting to explain the nonsensical requirements; a civil servant puzzling over a conflict between a law and a policy; or a judge trying in vain to discern some sort of purpose to it all: every one of these would question whether there is any intelligent design behind the shambles. Applications by non-citizens to enter or remain in the UK are governed by a cobbled-together conglomeration of incomprehensible and outdated laws, criteria that are set out in constantly shifting so-called 'rules' and apparently randomly privatised services delivered by the lowest bidder. Immigration laws, rules and procedures appear to have evolved chaotically in response to short-term political crises and economic pressures, with very little in the way of strategic planning.

The Home Office, the government department responsible for immigration, was memorably described as 'not fit for purpose' by then Home Secretary John Reid in 2006 and, if anything, its reputation has only deteriorated since.[3] But to see only accident and misfortune is to miss an important point. Politicians and civil servants are not naive or powerless, nor has this ramshackle construction evolved of its own accord. There are architects and engineers behind it all and the broad way in which the present system operates is the result of deeply ingrained thinking, long-term policies and conscious choices. Sometimes those choices may have been decisions not to act, but that in no way reduces responsibility for the predictable consequences of inaction.

Since 1962, successive governments have pursued an exclusionary citizenship policy. It is hard to escape the conclusion that this was and still is intended to preserve the existing ethnic composition of the population. In other words, and not to beat around the bush, the policy is racist. Contorted legal devices were initially deployed to maintain a facade of wide citizenship, but in practice they denied rights of entry to those citizens who were black or Asian. The pretence ended with the creation of new forms of British nationality and the abolition of birth-right citizenship in 1981. Since then, citizenship policy has been repeatedly tightened further by means of wider and tougher character tests, a written examination, dramatically increased costs, new bureaucracy for EU citizens seeking citizenship and the increased use of citizenship-stripping powers. For a short time, during David Blunkett's tenure as Home Secretary, cosmetic attempts were made to present British citizenship as more potentially inclusive in nature, while, in reality, reforms only made citizenship harder to acquire.

This exclusionary approach heavily influences the shape and nature of the immigration system that acts as a gatekeeper to citizenship. The immigration system has also therefore been exclusionary, albeit with very significant exceptions during the decade from 2000 to 2010. Restrictions are imposed both directly, through rules, and indirectly, through complexity and cost. To enforce this approach, the United Kingdom's border has been exported abroad and heavily fortified with fencing, scanners, guards and dogs. These twin policies of externalisation and securitisation have been very effective at keeping unauthorised migrants out but at a huge cost in migrant lives lost. A 'pull factor' is something that, in theory, attracts migrants to one particular destination country over another. Policies allowing migrants to work or claim benefits might be examples, as might fair treatment, a common language and a nice climate. Rather than seriously attempting to enforce removals, deterrent policies intended to eliminate as many of these supposed 'pull factors' as possible were introduced, beginning in the 1990s in the asylum sphere and then later for unauthorised and authorised migrants alike. The 'hostile environment' system of everyday citizen-on-citizen immigration checks, by employers, landlords, banks, hospitals and others, aimed at unauthorised migrants began tentatively in 2006 and was massively expanded from 2012 onwards. Then, a seemingly never-ending series of rule changes targeting authorised migrants began in 2010, including a minimum income threshold of £18,600 for marriage and partner visas and increases to the length of time spent here and the qualifying salary needed to achieve settlement. The purpose of these changes was to break the link between migration and settlement.

Unlike the secure and external border, there is no evidence that any of these deterrent policies have achieved their overt objectives. What research is available suggests that reducing pull factors simply does not work. The result of these policies, combined with what have, in reality, been tokenistic attempts at detention and deportation, has been the growth of a significant population of unauthorised migrants. Finally, what has made all of this possible is a highly centralised immigration system governed by total executive discretion with very weak oversight, whether by the legislature or the judiciary: there is no policy devolution and little to no input from departments other than the Home Office. None of this is accidental. The Immigration Act 1971, which continues to form the bedrock of immigration control today, embodies a deliberate decision to confer huge power – and huge responsibility – on the shoulders of the Home Secretary alone.

Seen in this way, today's immigration 'system' includes lacunae and accidental outcomes, as well as explicitly expressed rules. Or, to put it another way, the law comprises the actual *effects* of the laws themselves, as well as the stated intent. Politicians and policy-makers are responsible for the whole system, including the unintended but often eminently predictable effects.

Returning to the example of resident unauthorised migrants, the growth in their numbers was the foreseeable outcome of multiple facets of citizenship and immigration policy over many years. Politicians have repeatedly stated that unauthorised migrants are not welcome and have continually passed laws criminalising their presence, yet no government has been willing to detain and remove them. A radical and controversial programme of building detention camps and tearing families and communities apart, similar to what we see in the United States today, would have been needed to enforce such ideas. Instead, for example, asylum seekers whose claims are rejected are unceremoniously evicted from their accommodation, while their departure from the United Kingdom is not enforced. The same applies to migrants who overstay their visas. Birth-right citizenship was abolished in 1981 and high fees have been introduced in recent years, both of which prevent children born in Britain from registering as British even when they qualify, and thus making this precariousness generational.

The outcome of choices like this over many years is that the population of unauthorised migrants could now be as high as 1.2 million. It is thought there are around 215,000 undocumented non-citizen children living in the UK today and a further 117,000 young people between the ages of eighteen and twenty-four who were born in the country or brought here as children. The size of this unauthorised population is likely to increase significantly after Brexit for two reasons. Firstly, policy-makers have chosen to require EU citizens currently resident in the UK to apply for a new immigration status. As discussed in Chapter 9 on free movement, it is inevitable that tens or even hundreds of thousands of EU citizens will not do so and will therefore become unauthorised. Secondly, EU citizens not resident in the UK will still be able to enter the country without a visa after Brexit. It is inevitable that some will then remain in the country to work and live without applying for the permission they will need to do so lawfully. They will be unauthorised migrants, as will be their children.

I am not saying for a moment that these unauthorised migrants should have been removed previously or that they should be removed now. Rather, I believe that policy-makers and politicians should face up to the choices they have made. It seems to me self-evidently undesirable that in the UK there should exist a large group of mainly black and ethnic minority non-citizens, who live and work in real communities but who can be easily exploited, with no access to proper healthcare, decent housing or the social safety net. We cannot pretend to ourselves that our society is a fair one while this gross inequality is allowed to fester. As I discuss in Chapter 11, no government is forcibly going to remove as many as one million migrants, many of whom are deeply embedded in our communities. Another way forward is needed.

These various exclusionary policies and practices are founded on the premise that migrants are a threat. Immigrants have variously been regarded as a danger to racial purity, to culture, to religion, to values, to traditions, to solidarity, to security, to public funds, to jobs, to women and more. Some politicians have described migrants in almost biblical language, as a 'flood' or 'swarm' against which (not whom) existing residents need to be protected and shielded. The days are gone when politicians could make explicit reference to race but, as Maya Goodfellow argues in *Hostile Environment: How Immigrants Became Scapegoats*, references to culture, values, traditions and solidarity have become proxies.[4] Major political figures continue to associate migrants with crime and terrorism, despite the evidence showing that migrants commit fewer crimes than existing residents, or the fact that major acts of terrorism on British soil have been carried out by British citizens born and brought up in the country. Even discussing 'migrants' as a group at all seems peculiar, given that they are a hugely disparate range of individuals defined only by not being 'us'.

An opposing view, that migrants should be regarded as an economic opportunity, has become an important strand of contemporary thinking on immigration. However, those migrants who are perceived as desirable tend to be defined as exceptional compared to others; they are 'the brightest and the best'. There is nothing inherently wrong with seeing immigration as an opportunity, but the discourse around economic migration often only serves to reinforce the idea that migrants are a threat in general and too often this way of thinking has degenerated into treating migrants as a natural resource to be managed, mined and exploited.

The first chapter of this book outlines very briefly the mixed history of immigration law and policy since the start of the twentieth century, with a few more historical references thrown in for good measure (on the subject of references, sources for facts, figures and quotations that are not cited here in the introduction can be found in the relevant chapters).[5] Perhaps surprisingly, the twentieth century began with no immigration laws at all and remained remarkably open until 1962. However, a mainstream political consensus to severely restrict immigration rapidly emerged and lasted until around 2000, when Tony Blair's Labour government instituted an active economic immigration policy for the first time in decades. The growth in the number of asylum claims from the mid-1990s onwards, before a rapid and unplanned increase in migration from new members of the European Union from 2004, enabled immigration to be rapidly repoliticised as an issue. Ultimately, it would contribute its part to Labour's loss of office and the subsequent Brexit referendum result just over five years later.

The second chapter takes a long, hard look at the evolution and effect of the net migration target. As the primary driver of immigration policy for a decade, this target was hugely influential. Widely thought to have been announced by David Cameron when he was Leader of the Opposition in January 2010, the idea of introducing a specific numerical limit to immigration actually dated back to the

Conservative Party manifesto of 2005. Once he took over as leader after that election, Cameron was careful never to state a specific number and proposed to apply the limit to non-EU immigration only. This was too nuanced, though, and from 2010 onwards the perception gradually spread that a target had been set, restricting net migration to 100,000, to be applied to all forms of migration, EU and non-EU alike. Cameron had never said nor intended this, yet the perception was so widespread that he and his Home Secretary, Theresa May, felt bound to embrace it.

In the third chapter I will turn to the signature immigration policy of Home Secretary and later Prime Minister Theresa May: the hostile environment. This is a system of laws and regulations requiring private citizens and public servants to carry out 'papers, please' immigration status checks on one another. The primary purposes of this are supposedly to deter unauthorised migrants from arriving and to force those already resident to leave. A secondary purpose is to save money. There is no evidence, however, that it achieves any of these aims, and there has been no attempt to monitor success or failure. In reality, the policy looks more like a moral crusade to make life miserable for unauthorised migrants than a serious attempt to reduce the number of them living in the UK. It has been an unmitigated public policy disaster that brought the Windrush scandal bubbling to the surface and continues to do huge violence to race relations in the United Kingdom.

The last of the thematic chapters, Chapter 4 looks at the complexity and cost of the current immigration system. Described by top judges as 'byzantine' and an 'impenetrable jungle', immigration law grew rapidly from the 1990s onwards. An ever-changing web of treaties, laws, regulations, rules and policies has obscured the meaning and purpose of the law, generating huge volumes of litigation and making it all but impossible for a migrant to navigate the system without a lawyer. Meanwhile, the cost of making an application has shot up to over £3,000 per person in some situations, putting lawful status beyond the reach of many and causing social hardship and disadvantage even to those who are able to find the money from somewhere. Individual changes and tweaks to the rules may seem incompetent or unintentional when taken in isolation, but the trend is clear and therefore deliberate. A simplification project has belatedly been re-launched, but it would be naive to think that the complexity has not become a tool of wider immigration policy.

I will then turn to individual policy areas for different categories of migration. Chapter 5 takes a look at family migration rules and in particular how they have changed since a major reform package in 2012. Families have been torn apart by these rules, with any spouses or partners earning less than £18,600 forced to make an invidious choice between emigrating, splitting apart or living illegally in the UK. Around 40 per cent of the working population of the United Kingdom cannot afford a spouse visa, with women, ethnic minorities, the young, the old and those outside London being particularly disadvantaged. The rules on children are outdated and fail to take account of the preferences of the parents, the child's own opinion or the child's best interests. It is now virtually impossible to sponsor a dependent parent, forcing those whose parents require care either to pay for impersonal treatment abroad or to re-migrate to provide it themselves. Family visits to the UK are unavailable to many because, since the abolition of appeal rights in such cases in 2014, a visit visa refusal is usually now final and permanent. The option of relocating together as a family to a nearby European Union country will also be lost at the end of the Brexit transition period, along with the free movement rights of British citizens. The reforms have been driven by futile attempts to meet the net migration target, a desire to maintain the existing ethnic composition of the population and, at the very least, wilful blindness to the effects on those concerned.

Chapter 6 traces the recent history of asylum policy. Media, political and public hostility to refugees prevents many genuine refugees from reaching the United Kingdom but does not stop them from trying, while deterrence and the elimination of 'pull factors' have proved to be ineffective. The borders have been successfully strengthened, but the price of this security is paid by the refugees who die on their journeys. Over 20,000 have drowned in the Mediterranean since 2014. Following the increase in asylum claims that first began in the 1990s, a culture of disbelief has developed at the Home Office, with the success rate for asylum claims transformed from 87 per cent in the early 1980s to just 4 per cent by the next decade. While there are still major problems with Home Office decision-making, particularly concerning wishful thinking about how politicians and officials would like real refugees to behave as opposed to how they actually behave, nearly 40 per cent of asylum seekers are now recognised as refugees by the department. Once appeal outcomes are taken into account the total is more like 55 per cent. The deterrent policies that make life miserable for asylum seekers and that permanently disadvantage them if they are allowed to remain were designed at a time when it was thought the majority would not be permitted to do so. In reality, the majority of asylum seekers win their cases, so it would make sense to help them start to integrate and rebuild their lives as soon as they arrive. At the very least, asylum seekers should be treated with far more respect and generosity than that with which they are currently greeted when they land on our shores.

The focus of Chapter 7 is economic migration. The points-based system, introduced from 2008 onwards, was the culmination of multiple attempts to inaugurate a positive economic immigration policy and 'modernise' the various routes by which migrants could come to work in the UK. The purpose was to boost productivity, prosperity and public finances and the tests for success were whether the new system would be 'operable, robust, objective, flexible, cost effective, transparent, usable'. It turned out to be none of those things. The Home Office was massively over-ambitious in trying in effect to automate the decision-making process and eliminate subjective judgment entirely. With the change in government after the 2010 election, the department retrenched from a positive economic immigration policy, while it continued to pay lip service to the concept in public. Sweeping subjective judgments were reintroduced but the intricate framework of now obsolete objective rules remained in place. Economic migration can bring real benefits domestically and internationally, but its language is often starkly utilitarian. When migrants are seen as a natural resource to exploit rather than as human beings with their own lives and families, there is a danger that they become a servant class.

Chapter 8 moves on to discuss international students. Ignored for decades before being seen as an opportunity, then more latterly being viewed as a threat, successive governments have swung between seeking to attract international students and trying to deter them from coming. However, the evidence is overwhelming that international students boost local economies and cross-subsidise domestic students and research. As much as 13 per cent of all university income is derived from the high fees that they pay. The efforts to deter foreign students from studying in the UK were founded on faulty data regarding how many students leave the country at the end of their studies and a perception that too many students were somehow 'bogus'. In reality, many were ripped off and then abandoned by the private, unregulated colleges and test centres that the government permitted to flourish in the early days of the points-based scheme. The evidence suggests that 97.4 per cent of international students leave the UK at the end of their studies, while those who do remain add skills and productivity to the economy and diversity to our national life. Students should be saluted, not shunned.

Chapter 9 homes in on EU free movement laws. I take a wistful look back at how ordinary British citizens enthusiastically embraced their European free movement rights and how the country's departure from the European Union was engineered despite this. Euroscepticism began as an esoteric, narrow vision of the meaning of national sovereignty that had little popular resonance. The invention of populist Euromyths and the concept of benefit tourism in the 1990s, combined with the surge in migration from the EU following its expansion in 2004, transformed Eurosceptism into a powerful force. As Prime Minister, David Cameron woefully mishandled the issue. Setting impossible expectations with promises that tightening welfare benefit eligibility rules would magically deter the non-existent benefit tourists, he then pledged to renegotiate the terms of British membership of the European Union with no realistic prospect of being able to deliver on this either. The outcome was Brexit. EU citizens in the UK are now being forced to apply to the Home Office just to remain lawfully resident in the country and it is likely that tens or even hundreds of thousands will be left living here unlawfully when the deadline for applications passes. Meanwhile, British citizens are yet to grasp what departure from the European Union means for visiting, studying, living or retiring in European countries.

Deportation is the subject of Chapter 10. Often more akin to exile and nineteenth-century-style transportation, any criminal sentence of twelve months or more now triggers the automatic expulsion of non-citizens, even for those born in the United Kingdom or brought here as small children. Statutory exceptions have deliberately been so narrowly drawn that virtually no one can rely on them. The problems and difficulties that have arisen with deporting foreign national offenders were never about the law, though. They were the result of incompetence at the Home Office and the setting of impossible expectations by politicians. Any semblance of humane flexibility has been lost as a consequence, yet the number of high-risk foreign national offenders removed has fallen and the number of low-risk EU citizens has risen. Deportation law, procedure and prioritisation all need to be rethought.

Chapter 11 turns to the sharp end of immigration law: detaining unauthorised migrants and enforcing their removal. The number of beds in immigration detention centres was massively expanded by the Labour governments of 1997 to 2010 but even then their number never came close to reaching the capacity needed genuinely to enforce immigration laws. There is estimated to be a population of between 600,000 and 1.2 million unauthorised migrants, all of whom are potentially eligible for removal. Whether a particular migrant is detained and removed is a matter of luck. In this context, any decision to detain is inherently arbitrary. The detention system does not, in fact, enforce immigration laws and there is no evidence to suggest it has any meaningful deterrent effect. I argue that its only real function seems to be either moral or political. Meanwhile, the human cost to those migrants who experience indefinite immigration detention can be awful. While the number of migrants detained every year has started to fall as the Home Office has begun to rethink its approach, the number of vulnerable immigration detainees actually seems to have increased.

Finally, Chapter 12 considers the possible legal meanings of being

'British', the rights and responsibilities of being a British citizen and then the possible routes available to those wishing to become British, whether that be through birth, descent or application, and the growth in the phenomenon of citizenship-stripping. On closer inspection, it turns out that British citizenship is little more than a revocable form of immigration status. For a time, citizenship was linked to migrant integration, but it was never clear whether it was supposed to help facilitate integration or to reward it after the event. Citizenship policy has been driven by the conception of citizenship as a privilege not a right, by the desire to keep numbers of new citizens small and by a related racial dimension. The outcome is a large population of long-term resident non-citizens, some of whom have lawful status and some of whom do not. They are excluded from full participation in national life, for example through being unable to vote in parliamentary elections. Citizenship law and policy should be reformed to ensure that migrants and long-term residents are both able and encouraged to become citizens.

In the conclusion I argue that we cannot and certainly should not go on as we have. We need to move on from seeing immigration as a 'take it or leave it' contractual transaction in which the United Kingdom can dictate the terms of entry and stay no matter how harsh or unfair those terms might be. Instead, we should see newly arriving migrants as citizens-in-waiting who will join and be part of our society. The fact is that most migrants who arrive in the United Kingdom to work, join family members or seek sanctuary will be allowed to stay. It is wrong to disadvantage them deliberately from the start, and wrong to treat them as a disposable servant class. I argue that meaningful change should begin with citizenship policy. Drawing up an explicit rather than implicit policy would be a good start; one that is inclusive, which regards and treats migrants as future citizens and treats them and existing citizens with respect and fairness. This means recognising the existence of the unauthorised population, offering an amnesty (or at least proper routes to regularisation), reforming family migration routes to take account of not just economic concerns but social ones too, and rationalising economic migration routes.

CHAPTER 1

WELCOME TO BRITAIN

Imagine Paddington Bear managed to smuggle himself into today's modern Britain. His experience would be rather different to that portrayed by beloved children's author Michael Bond and recently reprised in two hit films. Stowing away from Darkest Peru and skipping passport control on arrival, Paddington commits the criminal offence of illegal entry. He faces up to six months in prison. Should he manage to avoid detection, he would be classed as an illegal entrant. That is where his problems would *really* begin. The hostile environment designed and built by Theresa May as Home Secretary, then, briefly, as Prime Minister, is intended to make life in Great Britain intolerable for latter-day Paddingtons. The very purpose of the hostile environment is to dissuade migrants from coming here at all, and to encourage those already here to 'self-deport' themselves, as politicians in the United States call the process, and leave.

Yet our traditional self-image as Britons is that we are a tolerant and welcoming nation. For time immemorial, the standard line trotted out by Home Office spokespeople in response to the exposure of wrongdoing by immigration officials – just check almost any newspaper article on the topic in the past twenty years – is that 'the UK has a proud history of granting asylum to those who need our protection'. The subtext to these fine words is that the proud history in question is historical; it is finished. Nevertheless, they cleverly evoke a collective memory of welcoming Huguenot refugees fleeing religious persecution in the seventeenth century; of French aristocrats fleeing revolution in the eighteenth century; of dissidents fleeing tyrants across Europe in the nineteenth century; and of Jewish refugees fleeing Hitler in the twentieth century. The waves of Celts, Romans, Angles, Saxons, Jutes, Norsemen, Normans and Irishmen might come to mind as might more recent successors from the Commonwealth. The warm reception that Paddington Bear enjoys from the Brown family in the 1950s fits right into that now outdated self-portrait.

The reality was always rather more mixed.

THE MIXED HISTORY OF BRITISH WELCOMES

Migration and migrants themselves are often regarded with relative benevolence when hypothetical or historical, but heaven forbid that a migrant should actually try to migrate in the here and now. The Protestant Huguenots who fled Catholic France in the sixteenth century are celebrated today, but they were reviled in their own time. So too were the Irish who fled famine and the Jews who ran from pogroms in the nineteenth and early twentieth centuries. Long-settled European dissidents were interned during the First World War, race riots and even lynchings broke out in Barry, Cardiff, Glasgow, Hull, Liverpool, London, Newport, Salford and South Shields after the war. The 'British Schindler', Nicholas Winton, had to forge British immigration papers to smuggle in Jewish children fleeing the Nazis before the outbreak of the Second World War.[1] The post-war wave of arrivals from Jamaica and other Commonwealth countries were greeted with public and political hostility at the time.[2] The first national Windrush Day was celebrated in 2019 and thus it is only now, decades later, that a belated welcome is being retrospectively imagined for that generation.

Still, there are some examples of the British government and public offering willing welcomes in the past. An estimated 250,000 Belgian refugees were extended shelter during the First World War, although most were forced to leave once it was over. There was also a major resettlement programme for Polish nationals who were unable or unwilling to return to Soviet-controlled Poland after the Second World War and the Polish Resettlement Act 1947 offered British nationality to 200,000 Poles living in the United Kingdom. Polish resettlement ran alongside the post-war European 'Voluntary' Worker Scheme (in fact it entailed significant compulsion), which was aimed at displaced workers across Europe and recruited around 180,000 workers.[3] Britain, in common with many other countries around the world, also offered refuge to Hungarians fleeing the Soviet crackdown in 1956. An estimated 20,000 found new homes in Great Britain. These resettlement exercises welcomed tens of thousands of migrants in a very short space of time and the fact they are now largely forgotten suggests that hostility at the time was limited and integration successful. Notably, these exercises involved white Europeans.

In contrast, the movement of black and Asian British subjects from the New Commonwealth to the United Kingdom was severely restricted from 1962 onwards. Notably, no equivalent controls were introduced for Irish citizens, who were mainly white. An urgent humanitarian resettlement programme in the 1970s involved resettling around 28,000 British subjects to the United Kingdom over several years. They were the Ugandan Asians, persecuted and ultimately expelled by Idi Amin. Some had retained their British status when Uganda became independent in 1962, but even many of those who had acquired Ugandan citizenship had that status stripped from

3

them by Amin. Their arrival has not been forgotten because, to put it bluntly, their skin colour was not white, and they were ruthlessly exploited at the time by controversial 'rivers of blood' politician Enoch Powell and the National Front. In 1979, Cabinet papers show that newly elected Prime Minister Margaret Thatcher resisted an informal UN request that Britain resettle 10,000 Vietnamese refugees 'on the grounds that there would be riots in the streets if they were given council housing ahead of "white citizens". She made clear to her Cabinet colleagues that she had "less objection to refugees such as Rhodesians, Poles and Hungarians, since they could more easily be assimilated into British society".[4]

No matter what the prevailing public or government response to migrants and refugees, though, there have always been at least a precious few in the United Kingdom willing to offer welcome. Churches, temples and mosques have always provided sanctuary and support to migrants who are not entitled to central or local government help. Some individuals open their homes to separated child refugees, offering fostering care. I have met many such amazing people through my own work representing young Afghans over the years. There are charities both large and small that have been set up to help refugees and others. To give two examples, Refugees at Home (www.refugeesathome.org) exists to offer spare rooms to refugees at different stages of the asylum process and Together Now (togethernow.org.uk) makes practical arrangements for family members of recognised refugees to travel to the United Kingdom. Towns and cities across the UK, as different as Bath and Barnsley and as distant as Aberdeen and Abergavenny, have signed up to the City of Sanctuary movement, which aims to build a society of hospitality and welcome. A growing number of people do what they can, motivated by the belief that there is, in the words of murdered Member of Parliament Jo Cox, more that unites than divides us.

THE OPEN ERA

Before the twentieth century there were no legal restrictions on immigration into the United Kingdom. As Robert Winder shows in *Bloody Foreigners*, immigration has been a feature of British life for centuries, although the numbers were previously relatively small. The nineteenth century saw an influx of European migrants responsible for founding quintessentially 'British' brands like Marks & Spencer, Moss Bros, Burton, Schweppes, Triumph cars and motorcycles, the massive ICI chemicals company General Electric, and Harland and Wolff, the engineering firm responsible for the *Titanic*.[5] This era of permissive, albeit sometimes grudging, openness ended with the first real immigration law in the United Kingdom: the Aliens Act 1905. Prompted by a vicious antisemitic campaign in Parliament and the media, it was introduced with the purpose of preventing the entry of Jews fleeing pogroms in Russia and Eastern Europe. Like later immigration legislation, the Act itself was drafted in more neutral, universal language than that, but it carefully afforded the new immigration officers sufficient discretion to achieve its intended aim.

For the next sixty years immigration can be seen as an accidental outcome of citizenship policy, which was itself driven by the foreign policy objective of maintaining British centrality in the rapidly disintegrating empire. British subjects had a right to enter the United Kingdom and there were an estimated 600 million of those across the globe. Before the Second World War, only relatively small numbers exercised this right, and even then, non-legislative steps were taken to restrict the right of entry by making it difficult to prove in practice. Then, although the British Nationality Act 1948 did not directly refer to immigration or a right of entry or residence, it did put citizenship on a legislative footing, thus reinforcing the pre-existing rights of British subjects and in the process making it difficult for later legislators to introduce immigration restrictions. It would look very strange to deny a citizen a right to enter and live in her country of citizenship, after all. Nevertheless, some members of the public and some politicians became increasingly agitated when growing numbers of racialised British subjects and citizens from Africa, the Caribbean and the Indian subcontinent did just that. These countries were widely known as the New Commonwealth, in contrast to Australia, Canada, New Zealand and South Africa, the white-dominated countries of the so-called Old Commonwealth.

The existence of a legal right of entry did not, in reality, stop politicians from trying to undermine it, and various 'informal controls', as they have become known, were deployed to try to reduce the number of New Commonwealth citizens moving to the UK. These measures included pressurising colonial and Commonwealth governments into denying passports to their citizens and ratcheting up the proof required for entry.[6] As it became clear these informal controls were insufficient to keep out racialised people, legislation became inevitable. The result was the Commonwealth Immigrants Act 1962.

THE CLOSED CONSENSUS

Historian Randall Hansen argues that it was surprising it took politicians so long to legislate given that public pressure to do so was high.[7] Hansen's trawl of government archives shows that as early as the start of the 1950s the political class was searching for concrete ways to restrict immigration from racialised New Commonwealth countries. These efforts foundered on a combination of a categorical refusal by key senior parliamentary figures to countenance the restriction of Irish migration; a widespread reluctance to prevent the entry of mainly ethnically white Old Commonwealth citizens;

an unwillingness to introduce an explicit colour bar; difficulties with replacing the citizenship scheme of the British Nationality Act 1948 so soon after its introduction; and the delicate international politics of decolonialisation. Committees were repeatedly appointed and draft legislation was even prepared in 1955 but was discarded. By the early 1960s the desire to restrict New Commonwealth immigration outweighed the attachment to free movement around the Old Commonwealth and the Commonwealth Immigrants Act 1962 was the outcome.

Replacement of the 1948 citizenship scheme was considered but later abandoned, and instead a bizarre mechanism of control was adopted. Citizens of the United Kingdom and Colonies would only have the right to enter the UK – their own country of citizenship – if their passport had been issued under the direct authority of the British government. Those whose British passports had been issued by colonial governments would lose their right of entry, meaning that different citizens with the same notional status had very different rights. At the same time, the Irish continued to enjoy unrestricted rights of entry and a voucher scheme for skilled workers was expected to maintain access to the United Kingdom for Old Commonwealth citizens. Britain went from having an extremely open immigration regime to an extremely closed one almost overnight, at least for racialised groups, and has been described as operating a 'zero immigration' policy for the next forty years.[8]

Inward migration did continue in these decades, but this was almost exclusively by family members joining those already living in the UK, not what might be called primary immigrants. When it transpired that the East African Asians, as they became known, had retained or acquired a right of entry, this was rapidly closed down in the follow-up Commonwealth Immigrants Act 1968. The

Immigration Act 1971 ended the remnants of preferential treatment for Commonwealth citizens over non-Commonwealth ones and consolidated the power to make new immigration rules in the hands of the Home Secretary, subject only to nominal parliamentary scrutiny. The British Nationality Act 1981 eventually re-wrote the citizenship laws, ending the fiction of universal Commonwealth citizenship, creating the formal status of 'British citizen' for the first time and also creating new lesser classes of British nationality that did not carry with them a right to live in Britain.

After 1962 both the major parties signed up to the idea that immigration should be severely restricted in order to promote the acceptance, integration or assimilation of those migrants who had already arrived. This is not to say there were not controversies, variations on or discussions concerning immigration issues; rather there was broad mainstream agreement that immigration should be restricted and it was not a significant party-political issue. That party-political consensus started to break down as the numbers of asylum seekers started to rise from the early 1990s onwards. Net migration began to rise rapidly from 1997 (see chart opposite), although this was not initially as a result of any change to immigration policies. From around 2000, though, the New Labour government started to pursue an active economic immigration policy for the first time in decades and then, for reasons of foreign not immigration policy (see Chapter 9), no controls were imposed on citizens of Eastern European and Baltic countries that joined the European Union in 2004. Immigration was re-politicised by the British National Party in the late 1990s, then by the Conservative Party in the run-up to the 2005 election and finally by the UK Independence Party after 2009. By the time the Conservative Party entered government in 2010, immigration had become a major issue of political debate and positioning. Whereas immigration was barely mentioned in party manifestos in 1997, by 2010 it was impossible for a political party not to have both a position and a set of policies on the subject.

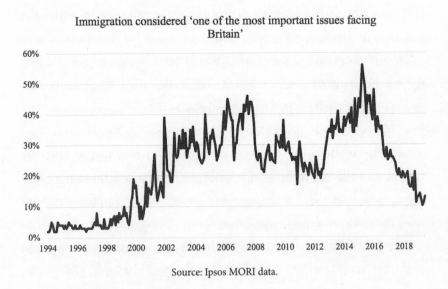

Immigration considered 'one of the most important issues facing Britain'

Source: Ipsos MORI data.

A HOSTILE ENVIRONMENT

When David Cameron accidentally set a net migration target in 2010, discussed in the next chapter, he signalled an intention to return as far as possible to zero immigration. Indeed, Cameron specifically invoked the levels of immigration of the 1990s when discussing net migration. The country and the world had changed since that era and much of the rest of this book documents the ultimately futile attempts to turn back time by Cameron and his Home Secretary, then successor, Theresa May. Standout features of these years included the introduction of a system of citizen-on-citizen immigration checks known as the hostile environment, discussed in Chapter 3; new barriers to acquiring lawful status or citizenship, discussed in Chapters 4 and 12; major reform of family immigration routes, discussed in

Chapter 5; the hollowing out of the points-based system, discussed in Chapter 7; and the vilification of international students, discussed in Chapter 8.

The single biggest immigration policy development during this time was entirely accidental: Brexit. In the past, decisions with profound but unintended implications for immigration policy were taken for unrelated reasons. The British Nationality Act 1948 was a matter of imperial pride, while the decision not to impose transitional controls following EU accession was driven by foreign policy. But Brexit was the reverse, as immigration policy seemed to be remoulding Britain's entire place in the world. As discussed in Chapter 9, this was the result of setting public expectations that could not possibly be met because the mechanisms chosen to implement them were always going to be ineffectual.

The new conventional wisdom during the Cameron period was that any credible politician needed to be tough on immigration. In this context, media stories about inconvenience to migrants or hard-nosed decisions by officials would help rather than harm a minister's reputation. A trickle and then a flood of outraged news stories about the rejection of applications by EU nationals for permanent residence and citizenship after the Brexit referendum vote in 2016 showed that public attitudes were more nuanced than had been thought.[9] Those personally unfamiliar with the immigration system began to ask why their friends and neighbours were being treated so abysmally by immigration officials. The fact that white, middle-class professionals were affected gave the issue more traction in the media and with the general public than would have been the case if the victims had been racialised or poor. Soon, opinion polling showed that concern over immigration as an issue began to plummet.

There then followed a string of horrifying stories telling of long-term residents who had arrived in Britain from the Caribbean decades previously as children – later dubbed the Windrush generation by campaigner Patrick Vernon – being denied life-saving healthcare, being sacked from their jobs and being evicted. These were people who had lived lawfully in Britain for decades but who did not possess any proof of their status: a decision had been made in the 1970s to automatically grant status, by operation of law but without documentary proof, to those Commonwealth citizens who already lived in the UK. Lawyers call this a 'declaratory' approach and the advantage at the time was that everyone eligible was automatically lawful, but it also meant that they did not necessarily have the evidence to prove it. Decades later, with the introduction of the hostile environment, those who still did not have proof – and unless they had travelled abroad, they would never have needed it – found themselves denied housing, benefits, healthcare and threatened with deportation. The Home Office simply refused to believe people who said they had been resident for decades, even where they had years of National Insurance contributions and their children had been born here. It was primarily one journalist, Amelia Gentleman, who researched and wrote these articles, but the space for the stories to be told and heard had been created by the earlier accounts EU citizens and a new narrative that the Home Office was a failing institution. Prior to that, there had been little or no media or public interest.

Theresa May, who as Home Secretary had driven forward the restrictive reforms, had moved on to become Prime Minister. It was May's successor at the Home Office, Amber Rudd, who was engulfed by the scandal. Rudd was forced to resign after denying that immigration officials had worked to removal targets when, in fact, they did exactly that and had done for years.

On taking up the bloodied reins at the Home Office, Rudd's

successor Sajid Javid rebranded the 'hostile environment' as the slightly less threatening 'compliant environment'. The change of tone was not accompanied by any official change in policy, although some of the measures most likely to affect unintended victims, such as automatic closure of bank accounts, were suspended (see Chapter 3). Although Theresa May was able to survive the Windrush scandal, she could not weather Brexit and formally resigned as Prime Minister on 24 July 2019 to make way for Boris Johnson.

JOHNSON AND BEYOND

In 2018 the government belatedly published a White Paper proposing a new immigration system for post-Brexit Britain. It proposed that the status quo established by Theresa May as Home Secretary would be maintained, except that free movement for EU citizens would be ended and they, along with all other migrants, would be subject to a slightly streamlined version of the existing immigration system. This was perhaps no surprise, as the White Paper was published with Theresa May still at the helm as Prime Minister, although admittedly very much in her latter days. There was no suggestion that the system of citizen-on-citizen immigration checks would be dismantled, the family immigration rules reformed or citizenship policy widened.

May's replacement by Johnson threw these plans into doubt. One of Boris Johnson's defining characteristics, and perhaps his greatest strength, is what some might call his moral flexibility – though others might call this lack of principle. At the time of writing it is impossible to discern what immigration policy, if any, Johnson might pursue in office. So far, he seems to offer all things to all factions.

Those in favour of a more liberal approach to immigration issues might take heart from Johnson's disavowal of the net migration target.

Although this means nothing by itself, it would nevertheless be an essential precondition to any change of culture in official attitudes to migrants and migration. He has previously advocated in favour of an amnesty for unauthorised migrants and has often presented himself as social liberal (although so too did David Cameron, it might be noted). To shield himself from detailed questions about his future immigration policy, Johnson has pledged to introduce an 'Australian-style points-based system'. On inspection, the limited details of a new plan published in February 2020 suggested relatively minor amendments to the existing system I describe in Chapter 7. The salary level for recruiting skilled workers would be dropped a little, the application process would be streamlined and a limited route for unsponsored workers would be re-opened. A capped route for unskilled agricultural labourers was confirmed but no similar routes for other sectors of the economy were proposed. The one concrete change at the time of writing had been to increase and then scrap the cap on the number of exceptional or global talent visas, but seeing as the cap has never even come close to being hit, this is hardly a radical departure from the past.

The image we hold in our minds of Britain as a welcoming country is a comforting mirage. Significant inward migration took place after the Second World War but was never a matter of deliberate policy. The British public were hostile, and politicians of all hues legislated repeatedly in the 1960s, 1970s and early 1980s to restrict immigration. Similarly, after 2004 immigration from the expanded European Union was essentially an accident, and Brexit was the resulting backlash. This is not to say things cannot get worse, though. Since 2010, the post-war consensus of limiting immigration but also preventing and suppressing race discrimination has been quietly abandoned. The first part of that equation has entirely usurped the second. Because of the net migration target discussed in Chapter 2, and by means of the hostile environment policies discussed in Chapter 3, we have seen the introduction of a raft of policies actively encouraging race discrimination in day-to-day life. Meanwhile, other aspects of immigration policy discussed in this book have deliberately dampened the life outcomes for migrants who settle here, in a vain attempt to deter them from coming in the first place. The twin shocks of Brexit and the coronavirus pandemic that was taking hold as this book went to press give us an opportunity to change direction and embrace a more equal, fair and respectful approach to those migrants who make this country their home.

CHAPTER 2

NET MIGRATION: THE ACCIDENTAL TARGET

onventional wisdom tells us that the origins of the hostile environment – and arguably also one of the major contributors to Brexit – lie on a rather uncomfortable-looking cocktail chair in a TV studio in January 2010. It was on this chair, during an interview with the BBC's Andrew Marr, that then Leader of the Opposition David Cameron reiterated a three-year-old Conservative Party policy to cap immigration and said he aspired to reduce net migration from 'hundreds of thousands' to 'tens of thousands'. This interview somehow morphed into a universally received understanding that a solid, solemn pledge had been made to reduce net migration to below 100,000, known as 'the net migration target'. This net migration target became unofficial government policy and was to be hugely influential, driving the adoption of a range of harsh immigration policies that were intended to reduce arrivals and increase departures. It infected all aspects of immigration policy and decision-making.

In reality, David Cameron never intended to set a firm net migration target. The whole episode, which came to define Cameron's government, determined immigration policy for the next decade and contributed significantly to Brexit. It was an example of woolly words being hardened by headline writers into a solid pledge.

WHAT WAS THE NET MIGRATION TARGET?

Net migration is a measure of inward migration minus outward emigration. To put it another way, net migration is the overall change in population due to inward and outward migration over a given period. In the United Kingdom, the given period is one year, because the definition of 'migrant' that is used in compiling the statistics is a person who moves to another country for a period of at least one year. The figures also include British citizens returning from abroad or leaving for other countries. Back in the 1970s and 1980s, net migration was negative, meaning more people were emigrating from the UK than were migrating in. From the mid-1990s, net migration has been consistently positive, with more people arriving than leaving each year. In the 1990s the figure was in the order of 'tens of thousands' but from 1997 onwards it started to rise, increasing to a number continually over 250,000 per year, coinciding with the period immediately after the expansion of the EU in the mid-2000s. This then fell below 200,000 for three years from 2012 before rising sharply again, as can be seen in the chart below.

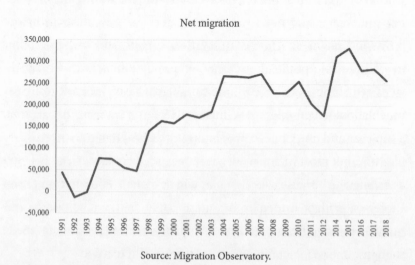

Net migration

Source: Migration Observatory.

To a politician, the attraction of focusing on net migration, rather than solely on inward immigration, is that the policy can be presented as one of overall population management, rather than one of keeping foreigners out – with the connotations of racism and xenophobia that might be implied. The net migration figures are also by their nature lower than those for immigration, because the number is calculated by deducting emigration from immigration. It might be thought that lower numbers would be seen as less alarmist to members of the general public. But this perhaps naively assumes that if a person was worried by immigration figures of, say, 200,000 per year, that person would not also be worried by net migration figures of, say, 100,000 per year. This is all a matter of political positioning, which may seem to be of paramount importance in the short term. Eventually, though, as events were to prove, the net migration target was a tactician's gambit for winning an election rather than a strategist's plan for governing effectively and retaining power.

The disadvantages of setting a net migration target are legion. To start with, net migration is a terrible way of measuring changes to population or what most members of the public understand immigration to be. It takes no account, for example, of population change through births and deaths, so it is hard to see that it is really about what amounts to a 'sustainable' population. Because the equation includes British citizens returning from abroad, the final figure also does not really say much about actual migrants either. If two British citizens return from a gap year and one Chilean student leaves then net migration would be plus one, but most members of the public would consider that to count as minus one because a foreign national departed. As migration expert Professor Bridget Anderson has pointed out, if the definition of 'migrant' is adjusted from a person moving for a period of four years rather than just one year, net migration has been negative for many years.[1]

The statistics on which the net migration figures are based are not as reliable as a politician who bets his entire reputation on them might hope. The basis for calculating net migration is not, as a rational person might expect, simply counting them in and counting them out. For starters, counting them out is impossible as formal exit checks for those leaving the UK were scrapped in 1998 and have never been fully reintroduced. Instead, the numbers are based on the International Passenger Survey. This sounds awfully formal but really it just involves a handful of people hanging around at airports and ferry terminals on certain days (not nights) in tabards with badges. They randomly ask a few passengers willing to talk to them why they are leaving the UK and when they plan to return. The percentage of travellers questioned is 0.34 per cent of the over 240 million who pass through UK ports each year, and the survey identifies between 3,000 to 4,000 long-term migrants who say they are moving residences – emigrating to Australia or returning home to Sri Lanka, for example. This small sample is then extrapolated, meaning that it is multiplied up on the assumption that those sampled are representative of the whole.[2]

I was once accosted at Gatwick Airport by a former colleague brandishing a clipboard as I attempted to depart on holiday with my wife and two very young children on one of the busiest days of the summer holidays. The timing was hardly ideal, but it was too late to duck away by the time I realised what was happening: he was now working for the International Passenger Survey. It is not hard to imagine that there might be problems with a system that relies on such a small sample size: a degree of self-selection by passengers (the busy or shy ones just refuse to be interviewed) and accurate self-reporting (some people might lie) being just a couple. To put it mildly, it is not an accurate way of measuring total population movement. Indeed, the net migration figures come with a 'large margin of error', as the

Oxford-based Migration Observatory team of researchers put it, and the figures have twice been retrospectively amended because better information subsequently suggested that the original figures were wrong.[3] Indeed, in 2019, the Office for National Statistics downgraded the classification of net migration statistics from 'national statistics' to 'experimental statistics' because they were not considered sufficiently reliable.[4]

There is almost nothing that a government can do to control outward emigration, short of crashing the economy and thus sending citizens abroad in search of work. There is also little if anything that the governments of European Union countries can do about inward EU migration. After the UK joined what was then the European Economic Community in 1973, imposing a quota on European migration would have been illegal under European law. It is primarily the economy that governs EU migration, as the vast majority of the union's citizens move across borders to find work. If Britain's economy were to outperform the economies of other EU countries, for example, citizens of those countries might well be incentivised to move to Britain in search of work. This is exactly what was to happen from around 2012 onwards, as Britain recovered from the global economic crash faster than some other countries in the union.

Other types of inward migration from outside the EU might be possible to control in theory, but the social and economic consequences of doing so need to be carefully considered. From 1962 onwards, the cross-party, mainstream political consensus was that immigration needed to be limited if good race relations were to be maintained – but there had never before been a policy of aiming to limit immigration to a particular level. Policy-makers and civil servants with particularly long memories might have recalled the total failure of informal controls to limit Commonwealth immigration in the immediate post-war period.[5] To truly restrict immigration, quotas or caps would be needed. While caps had previously been used, their history was not really an auspicious one. A voucher system for migrant workers was introduced by the Commonwealth Immigrants Act 1962, but the number of vouchers available was slashed in 1965 from 40,000 to just 8,500.[6] Then, after the Commonwealth Immigrants Act 1968 shut the doors on the East African Asians, a special voucher scheme was introduced to allow in a very small number every year, until it was finally abolished and replaced with citizenship rights by David Blunkett as Home Secretary in 2002.

The idea of imposing quotas on skilled economic migration is therefore plausible, but it is always likely to be unpopular with the business community as well as amounting to a form of economic self-harm. Preventing unskilled workers arriving may be more attractive to a policy-maker, who may envisage any number of resulting favourable headlines. But in 2010 there was no immigration route for non-EU unskilled workers anyway. Because foreign students pay far, far higher tuition fees than domestic students, limiting the numbers of such students via a quota system would cut off a crucial source of funding for higher education; besides, there is no public pressure to do so. Application quotas would also be very problematic for family immigration; they might be a fair way of deciding which lucky individuals get Glastonbury tickets, but would it really be fair and reasonable that a first-come-first-serve, when-they're-gone-they're-gone system may prevent the entry of a spouse, child or parent, just because others had applied before them? Setting a quota for refugees is likely to be portrayed as heartless, not to mention that it would require the radical step of withdrawal from the Refugee Convention, the international treaty ratified by 145 countries around the world that determines who is and who is not a refugee.[7]

To make matters worse, from a savvy politician's perspective, the statistics on net migration are published quarterly, meaning that the issue recurs in the media at least every three months. It is rather hard to defuse and entomb an issue when it has to be wheeled out in public every three months. For all these very good reasons, there had never been an overarching immigration policy that aimed for a certain level of immigration. Now that a specific numeric limit had been introduced, however, it turbocharged the subject's political importance. Ministers and civil servants had to try to find ways in which to meet it. Arrivals needed to be discouraged and departures encouraged. The reality was that unless the quotas were to be imposed in the strict ways laid out above, the only way to do this was to crash the economy and make the UK a less attractive place to live. Yet crashing the economy is hardly a sure-fire way of winning elections – at least in normal times.

THE ACCIDENTAL TARGET

So, net migration is inherently very difficult to manage without doing so indirectly, through a politically suicidal economic policy. Even the migration routes that can be directly affected by domestic immigration rules involve some very serious trade-offs, as we have just seen. David Cameron could certainly be criticised for his short-term thinking, but he was no fool; this is why I believe he never intended to set a net migration target in the first place.

Returning to Andrew Marr's cocktail chair, at the time of Cameron's interview the former Archbishop of Canterbury, George Carey, had recently attached his name to a controversial report calling for immigration to be reduced, opining that the population of the UK was growing too quickly.[8] Given the media coverage attracted by the report and Carey's remarks, it was unsurprising that Cameron was asked by Marr whether he agreed. In response, Cameron started to talk about pressure on public services but was soon pressed by Marr as to whether the previously announced 'cap on the numbers coming into this country' would involve a specific figure. Cameron responded that he would like to see net migration in the 'tens of thousands rather than the hundreds of thousands'[9] and Marr follows up again, asking whether there would be a 'specific figure, a real cap that you will announce and stick to?' Cameron notes that there should be 'a clear annual figure that people should see', which would be announced each year. No specific number was given there and then.

By omitting to qualify Marr's question about an overall cap on immigration, and by moving the discussion on to net migration, Cameron had accidentally implied a new policy of setting an overall cap on net migration. According to *Spectator* editor Fraser Nelson, it was not intended to be a deliberate, hard-edged net migration target at the time.[10] Nevertheless, the interview was covered in the *Daily Telegraph* the next day with a headline reading 'David Cameron: net immigration will be capped at tens of thousands'. The article was more nuanced when read in its entirety, but the write-up still suggested a commitment that under a Conservative government, 'net immigration would be kept in the "tens of thousands", rather than the current rate of "hundreds of thousands"'.[11] It is probably not going too far to suggest that the *Telegraph* headline ended up driving a fundamental transformation of British immigration policy.

There was quite some history to the Conservative Party policy of a cap on immigration, as Andrew Marr will have known very well when he decided to press Cameron on the point during the interview. The concept of an unspecified 'overall annual limit on the numbers coming to Britain' had featured in the party's manifesto for the 2005 election, along with a related pledge to withdraw from the

Refugee Convention.[12] It was perhaps a response to David Blunkett's politically unwise statement as Home Secretary in 2003 that he saw 'no obvious limit' to the number of skilled migrants who might enter the country, nor did he believe there was a maximum population that could be accommodated.[13] The Conservative Party commitment in 2005 was a hard cap applying to EU, economic, family and human-itarian immigration. No actual number for the proposed cap was announced in the manifesto, but the policy attracted accusations of racism and xenophobia.

When David Cameron took over as Conservative Party leader following that election, he set about re-positioning his party as more modern and liberal. He attempted to move on from having a crude absolute limit on all immigration and in 2007 gave a speech on the subject of population growth. Cameron suggested it was not *immigration* as such, but high *net migration* that was the problem, because it was pushing up the total population to 'unsustainable' levels. As a solution, he proposed 'explicit annual limits on non-EU economic migration, set at a level substantially lower than the current rate.'[14] No specific numbers were proposed. The policy was more refined and more realistic than the previous party position, as it did not require withdrawal from the Refugee Convention and it did not suggest that EU migration either could or should be limited.

However, it transpired that Cameron had been a little *too* successful in moving the discussion from immigration to net migration. In solving the short-term problem of the political positioning of the Conservative Party, he had created a new long-term problem for governing. The headache that was to haunt both Cameron and his Home Secretary Theresa May, who would be responsible for imple-menting the impossible pledge, was that such a limit would have no impact on EU migration nor on emigration, which would prove to be significant contributors to overall net migration in the coming years. If the problem was net migration, then a limit on non-EU migration could never be the solution. As the economy improved, more EU citizens arrived and less UK residents departed; or, in other words, net migration rose.

The hamstrung approach set out by Cameron in 2007, of vaguely aspiring to reduce overall net migration by means of setting an immigration cap on non-EU migration, eventually featured in the Conservative Party manifesto for the 2010 election: 'We will take steps to take net migration back to the levels of the 1990s – tens of thousands a year, not hundreds of thousands.'[15] The means of achieving this policy remained the same as that proposed in 2007: 'Setting an annual limit on the number of non-EU economic migrants admitted into the UK to live and work.' There was no specific, unambiguous net migration target here, only a commitment to 'take steps' to reduce net migration to somewhere in the 'tens of thousands'.

Cameron was to return to the immigration issue in another major speech in 2011. This time he could not have been clearer: 'No ifs. No buts. That's a promise we made to the British people. And it's a promise we are keeping.'[16] By late 2011 the BBC was reporting that the government had 'pledged to cut net migration to tens of thousands by 2015', and that the promise was being spectacularly missed. 'Tens of thousands' proved to be too wordy for journalists and headline writers, though. By early 2014, the figure of 100,000 seems to have emerged as received wisdom in the media.[17]

A further hardening of words found its way into the Conservative Party manifesto in 2015, which declared, 'We will keep our ambition of delivering annual net migration in the tens of thousands, not the hundreds of thousands.'[18] Far from 'taking steps', this was arguably the strongest, clearest expression so far that the party not only had a target for net migration but fully intended to stick to it. Indeed, there was nothing really to be lost by this stage; everyone already thought that there was such a target anyway, no matter whether one had actually been set or not. Nevertheless, in 2017 the Conservative Party manifesto reverted once more to the ambiguous language previously used, returning to the hamstrung approach of mentioning net migration but suggesting it could be achieved with a limit on non-EU immigration: 'It is our objective to reduce immigration to sustainable levels, by which we mean annual net migration in the tens of thousands, rather than the hundreds of thousands we have seen over the past two decades. We will, therefore, continue to bear down on immigration from outside the European Union.'[19]

The accidental net migration target became central to Theresa May's identity as Home Secretary then Prime Minister. Meanwhile, the *actual* policy of limiting non-EU migration was basically forgotten from 2010 onwards, no matter what the manifestos said. A cap on skilled workers was imposed but no similar caps were introduced for family or humanitarian immigration. As we will see in Chapter 6, David Cameron even agreed, under huge pressure, to a refugee resettlement scheme that increased the numbers of refugees arriving in the UK by 20,000 over a five-year period. Had the government been serious about meeting the net migration target, this increase in humanitarian migration would need to have been balanced out with a reduced quota for other types of migration.

This was never seriously on the cards. The accidental net migration target could only ever be met through chance, if at all, because the government, for the very good reasons we have examined here, was not willing to impose a strict quota on families, students, refugees or other categories of migrant. Rather than resile from the impossible policy, however, May and Cameron felt it was better to at least look like they were trying. The result was an all-out assault on immigration in which not just migrants but lawfully resident and even British citizen ethnic minorities became collateral damage: the hostile environment.

CHAPTER 3

HOSTILE ENVIRONMENT: PAPERS, PLEASE

Towards the end of *The Great Escape*, the famous film of 1963 depicting a mass escape by British prisoners of war, we watch with a sense of dread as a young Gestapo officer works his way down a train carriage inspecting the documents of the passengers as he goes. '*Ihre Pässe, bitte*,' he casually demands of two key British characters, Bartlett and MacDonald. 'Your passports, please.'

As a young immigration lawyer at the turn of the millennium I was taught that this was not the British way. Unlike other European countries, we have sea borders and check immigration paperwork on entry. We did not need or want continental-style identity cards or any bureaucratic checking that papers are in order, I learned. Identity cards had been introduced in the United Kingdom during both world wars but were scrapped again afterwards. Clement Attlee's Labour government initially tried to retain identity cards after the Second World War, arguing they were needed for access to state services such as rationing, the NHS and welfare benefits. But following the very public conviction of Liberal Party member and former councillor Harry Willcock for refusal to produce his identity card to the police, the system was scrapped in 1952 by a Conservative government. History appeared to repeat itself when a Labour government introduced a new system of identity cards with legislation in 2006, which was then scrapped by the Conservative–Liberal Democrat coalition government in 2010. Or so it seemed at the time, anyway.

One of the key elements of the hostile environment has been introducing citizen-on-citizen 'papers, please' checks into ordinary life, for employment, accommodation, banking, driving, healthcare, marriage and more. If you think this sounds a lot like a system of identity cards, you would not be far wrong. It *is* a lot like a system of identity cards, except that it is also far more complex; there is no single document available to use as convenient proof and some people are more likely to be challenged than others because the system is tied to immigration status rather than identity. The policy has increased discrimination against ethnic minorities, members of the Windrush generation have been turfed out of jobs, homes and hospitals, while young Britons have had to apply for passports, not to go on holiday but to live in their own country. After Brexit, the tens or even hundreds of thousands of EU citizens who miss the application deadline will feel the effects.

ORIGINS OF THE HOSTILE ENVIRONMENT

The term 'hostile environment' has a backstory. We have seen that Theresa May used the words while she was Home Secretary in 2012, but they were already in use within the Home Office, security services and police many years before her arrival, and had even been used by previous Labour immigration minister Liam Byrne. Initially the hostile environment was a term that related to terrorism. It was the label used to describe the post-9/11 policy, both indirectly and directly attacking terrorism, and was to be contrasted with the previous 'soft' or 'safe' environment. The idea was that it was hard to arrest, prosecute and convict actual terrorists themselves, but it might be easier to target them indirectly by cutting off financial and other support from sympathisers and donors. The same principle of indirect influence and the label 'hostile environment' were later applied to serious and organised crime. And then, as David Cameron's government sought means by which the net migration target might be met, to immigrants.

The key moment in the development of the hostile environment for immigrants was the creation in 2012 of a secret inter-ministerial group in government, initially called the Hostile Environment Working Group.[1] A wide range of ministers from across government were involved, including those acting for care services, employment, housing, schools, justice, health and transport. The idea was to make life in the UK intolerable for those who were unlawfully resident by cutting them off from the necessities of life and preventing access to public services. This was to be achieved by requiring the production of immigration papers in all walks of life. And here lies the origin of the problems experienced by the Windrush generation: the government wrongly equated absence of papers with absence of permission. While it was true that those unlawfully in the UK would not have immigration paperwork, it does not follow that all those who did have a right to be here would be in possession of their documents. The working group came up with a wide range of new regulations and data-sharing agreements between government departments, so that if a person was deemed to lack evidence of status by one branch of government, like the NHS or the police, that information would be shared with various other branches of government too. The culmination of the group's efforts were the Immigration Acts 2014 and 2016.

These Acts were not the first pieces of legislation to introduce privatised, outsourced immigration checks, but they did expand them drastically into new areas of everyday life. The first example on the statute book of privatised immigration controls had been the Immigration (Carrier's Liability) Act 1987, which imposed a fine on airlines and ferry companies if they carried a person without the correct immigration documents. In effect, this forced the companies to carry out their own checks before allowing passengers on board. If the papers turned out to be good-quality forgeries, the penalty would be nevertheless waived if a check had been carried out. This was followed by the introduction of a similar set of rules for employers by the Asylum and Immigration Act 1996, with the key and rather stark difference that the sanction would be a criminal conviction rather than a simple fine. If a company was found to be employing an illegal worker and had not carried out immigration checks, the employer could be prosecuted. Such prosecutions were almost unheard of, though, probably because they were so draconian. The Immigration, Asylum and Nationality Act of 2006 introduced a new system of civil penalties that was much more like the original carrier sanctions scheme. Again, the system imposed a fine if the employer was caught employing an illegal worker without having carried out an immigration check. While it was not a legal obligation to carry out such checks, a wise employer who wanted to avoid the risk of a fine would still carry them out diligently. To avoid accusations of discrimination, which would likely be well-founded, an employer would have to carry out such checks on all members of staff irrespective of their race or background.

The level of fines for employers was originally set at a maximum of £2,000 per illegal worker. Over the next few years this was increased to £5,000, then to £10,000 and finally in 2014 to a massive £20,000 per worker. The penalties would have remained hypothetical without 'boots on the ground' raids on business premises by immigration officials, though. Operation Mayapple began in 2012 and involved high-profile immigration enforcement action in workplaces in and around Brixton, London, which is famous for being an ethnically diverse area where the Windrush generation had first settled after the Second World War. Images and videos of the raids were posted by the Home Office on various social media channels, including YouTube, Twitter and Flickr. Most have now been deleted or lost to the ever-shifting sands of the internet, but some were still available even at the time of writing. In these videos, minority ethnic workers can be seen being dragged from high street shops by uniformed immigration officials in stab vests, while a second cameraman also records events for posterity in the background. At the time, the Home Office claimed that a total of 2,000 Indians, Pakistanis, Nigerians, Chinese, Bangladeshis and Brazilians were rounded up as part of the operation. Although it has been speculated that Australians might be the number one immigration offenders in the United Kingdom, it was notable that none were reported to have been arrested in the operation. The number of these raids soon increased sharply, with the number of penalties recorded almost trebling between 2012 and 2016. Over the same period, the total value of fines handed out multiplied by around five times to almost £50 million.

With all this publicity and substantial financial penalties becoming a real possibility, workplace culture began to shift. Checking the immigration papers for new and existing employees became a routine part of human resources department policies up and down a country that supposedly prides itself on its aversion to identity cards. In contrast to the highly visible workplace raids, there was at first no fuss and no publicity when black employees were quietly given the shove by employers behind the scenes following these checks. Few cases ever reached the courts because it was very hard indeed for a person without immigration papers to challenge their dismissal. Worse still, legal aid was effectively ended for immigration cases in 2013. Victims just had to cope as best they could – if they could. Some ended up reliant on the charity of friends and family, while others had no choice but to become homeless.

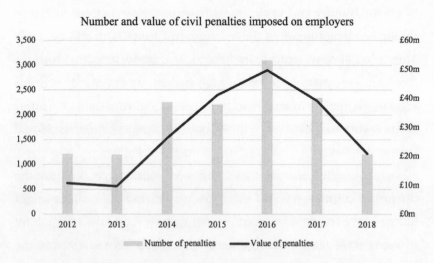

Number and value of civil penalties imposed on employers

Source: Home Office illegal working civil penalties quarterly reports, compiled.

One case that did reach the courts, though, was that of Mr Baker,[2] a Jamaican who had lived in the UK since childhood. Everyone agreed that he had the right to live and work in the UK, but unfortunately, he had no current paperwork to prove his status. His employer, a bus company in London, wrongly believed that it was under a legal duty to dismiss him if he could not prove his status and was notably under pressure from the newly increased financial costs of employing illegal workers. The company invited its employee to a meeting on 24 February 2015, where he was asked for evidence of his right to work. Mr Baker explained that his Jamaican passport had expired back in 2000 and he had no current papers. Promptly, he was sent home with a list of documents and told that he would not be paid until he could produce one of them. A company manager arranged for Mr Baker to be lent £350 to apply for the required documents and he duly requested a new Jamaican passport. The passport alone was insufficient, however, as a new stamp was also required from the Home Office to replace the old one, which would come in at a cost of several hundreds of pounds. The whole process was deemed to be taking too long for the employer, who dismissed Mr Baker on 3 July 2015. Mr Baker was fortunate to find lawyers to represent him for free and, two years later, on 5 October 2017, he eventually won his legal challenge for unfair dismissal. As is often the case with a court victory, this will have been small consolation given the stress and misery Mr Baker had suffered in the process.

Just how often similar situations have been played out up and down the country without a victim fortunate enough to find legal aid and take the case to court we will never know. A small number of cases were later reported when journalists belatedly started to show an interest following *Guardian* reporter Amelia Gentleman's pioneering work on what would become known as the Windrush scandal. But still, there will inevitably be many examples that remain unknown. Mr Baker's employer was unusually generous in offering a loan and waiting for so long; other employers either refuse to employ the person in the first place or simply dismiss them immediately. Mr Baker was also unusually lucky in finding lawyers willing to take on his case for free.

Along with this practice of civil penalties laid out above, the other main plank of the early system of citizen-on-citizen immigration checks was the concept of sponsorship, introduced by the original British points-based system in 2008. The sponsorship system was introduced through changes to the Immigration Rules without the need for an Act of Parliament and it is still in force today. Despite frequent calls by certain politicians to introduce an 'Australian-style points-based system' following Brexit, we actually already have at least a nominal points-based system in place and have done since 2008. In fact, it is literally called 'the points-based system' in the Immigration Rules.[3] Under this system, employers and education providers wanting to employ or educate foreign nationals are required to pay the Home Office for a 'sponsor licence'. These licences come with onerous conditions and they can be (and are) withdrawn if those conditions are breached. In fact, in 2017 a total of 605 employer licences were revoked and in 2018, the last full year for which figures are available at the time of writing, the total fell to 265, perhaps reflecting something of a softening of approach following the breaking of the Windrush scandal early in 2018.[4]

Under this system, which is still in operation today, it is impossible for a foreign national to obtain a UK visa to work for a company that does not have a licence or for them to study at an unlicensed institution. Lecturers have to report students who miss a certain number of lectures, and employers must dismiss and report any employee who has a certain number of unauthorised absences. There is a clause in these licences that imposes a rather vague duty of co-operation, 'including in connection with the prevention or detection of crime, the administration of illegal working civil penalties and/or the apprehension or prosecution of immigration offenders'. This is a general duty, not just in connection with the migrants sponsored by the institution concerned. From time to time, for instance, I travel to events at universities where my travel is paid for; on other occasions I have delivered lectures and written research reports. The stringency of the passport checks I have undergone even where I am merely claiming travel expenses or working as an unsponsored contractor has been surprising to me, and I am an immigration lawyer. Failure to comply to the above-mentioned duty means loss of the sponsor licence – and the consequences can be existential.

London Metropolitan University discovered the importance of this co-operation when their licence was revoked on 29 August 2012, just as the academic year was about to begin. The Home Office accused the university of 'serious systemic failure' in its management of foreign sponsored students. Around a quarter of the university's 2,000 foreign students were found not to have permission from the Home Office to study there, a 'significant proportion' were said not to speak a good standard of English and in more than half of cases the university could produce no records to show that the students were turning up to lectures. The effects of the licence revocation were calamitous. The 2,000 foreign students already studying were given just sixty days to find a new course at a new institution or otherwise leave the country, and several hundred students, who had already paid the enormous fees to begin their courses in the new academic year, had their visas cancelled. London Met said the loss of the licence left a £30 million hole in its budget, equivalent to around 20 per cent of their total income for the year.

Nine months later, though, the licence was eventually restored. No doubt eager to stay in the Home Office's good books, London Met was tight-lipped about the cost to the university of the period of suspension. They were certainly pleased to get the licence back, telling *The Guardian* that it was 'excellent news' and thanking international students for their 'patience and support over the last nine months'.[5] It is hard to imagine that the university could have continued to exist at all had the licence not been reinstated.

The duty of co-operation extended to employers as well as universities. In July 2016, managers at posh burger chain Byron arranged a fake meeting for the migrants they employed in central London. Different cover stories were told to different members of staff: some thought it was about a new recipe, while others were told it was about the dangers of the medium and medium-rare cooking of burgers.[6] In reality, the meeting was for the sole purpose of enabling immigration officers to detain, arrest and remove staff members working without the proper paperwork. 'Nobody move, we're immigration, stay where you are,' the officers were reported to have said as they burst in. Thirty-five nationals of Brazil, Nepal, Egypt and Albania were arrested, sent to various immigration detention centres around the country and then removed. Some of the employees were said to have used fake papers to secure employment, which would normally be expected to exempt an employer from a fine. Byron found themselves at the centre of a debate about how far employers were required to co-operate with the Home Office; whether it had been legally obliged to act as it had; whether it had been strong-armed into action by the Home Office with threats to cancel the company's licence (a sort of 'nice business you've got there, shame if we were to force you to sack half your workforce' kind of idea); whether it had effectively plea-bargained for reduced fines from the Home Office (the maximum £20,000 fine per worker can be reduced if the employer co-operates); or whether it had been over-enthusiastic in aiding the government of its own accord. The incident provoked protests and a boycott, although this seems to have done no lasting damage to the business in the long term.

It is not just high street chains and big employers who need to worry. Hundreds of take-aways, restaurants and corner shops have been targeted by immigration officials and publicly named and shamed in the process. Even individuals, sometimes rather prominent ones, have found themselves in trouble over these 'papers, please' checks.

Take for instance Patricia Scotland, who was a very well-respected

Queen's Counsel barrister before being appointed to the House of Lords as a Labour peer in 1997. In 2007 she was promoted by Prime Minister Gordon Brown to the position of Attorney General, the government's senior legal adviser, responsible for overseeing criminal prosecutions in England and Wales. However, in 2009, she was fined £5,000 for failing to conduct proper 'papers, please' checks on her cleaner, Lolo Tapui.[7] Baroness Scotland claimed that she had checked the woman's papers but admitted she had failed to keep copies as required by law. Shadow Home Secretary Chris Grayling called for her resignation and said that employers could not be 'inadvertently innocent'. Baroness Scotland kept her job. Not so Lolo Tapui, who was later jailed for eight months for fraud, possession of a false identity stamp and overstaying her visa. She was later removed to her native Tonga. It emerged at her trial that Lolo Tapui had been paid £95,000 by the *Mail on Sunday* to tell her story and that publicist Max Clifford had pocketed a £19,000 commission.[8]

Baroness Scotland was thought to be the first individual to be fined under the civil penalties scheme for employers. But she was not the last politician to fall foul of them. In 2014 Mark Harper was forced to resign, and once again because of a cleaner. What made this incident so notable was that he was then the minister for immigration, piloting new immigration legislation through Parliament and having been responsible for the notorious 'Go home' vans that were sent out to patrol diverse areas of London, as well as the dramatic increase in enforcement activity against employers. The migrant concerned in this case was a Colombian national named Isabella Acevedo, who earned £30 per week from Harper. She was actually self-employed, meaning that Harper had not technically broken the law and was not liable for a fine. 'I should hold myself to a higher standard than expected of others,' Harper's resignation letter nevertheless piously intoned. Harper ended up getting his officials at the Home Office to verify Acevedo's status, notably a course of action that was not open to most employers.

The consequences were rather different for Acevedo. While Harper was to return to office just weeks later, Acevedo was arrested at her daughter's wedding in a conspicuous enforcement raid shortly afterwards and was later removed from the United Kingdom.[9] Trenton Oldfield, a family friend who was present, told *The Guardian* that immigration officers 'swept into the room when we were just about to start the ceremony … We don't know where they came from. They must have been waiting in the building.' The timing and manner of Acevedo's arrest – it seems unlikely that it *had* to be at the wedding venue, and it was hardly discreet – make you wonder whether revenge played some part in the arrangements.

If an Attorney General and an immigration minister could be caught out by these checks, what chance do other individuals or small businesses stand? Over the past five years a total of around £200 million in penalty charges has been levied on employers.[10] It is thought many small businesses have gone bankrupt as a consequence. If the purpose of this project was to protect the rights of home-grown workers, bankrupting small employers across the country is an unusual way to achieve that end.

IMMIGRATION ACTS 2014 AND 2016

The 'papers, please' checks imposed on employers were proving onerous, even to well-resourced companies, and the Scotland and Harper incidents only highlighted the difficulties of compliance for individuals. Nevertheless, the Immigration Acts 2014 and 2016 expanded the hostile environment system from employment into new territory: landlords, banks, building societies and the Driver and Vehicle Licensing Agency (DVLA).

Firstly, a virtually identical system of civil penalties to the one already in place for employers was introduced for landlords, described in legislation as the 'Right to Rent' scheme. Until the Immigration Act 2014, it had never crossed anyone's mind that they might need a 'right' to rent. It is one of a new batch of fake 'rights' that are used to separate 'us' from 'them' and which, in reality, represent restrictions on liberties that had previously been taken for granted.[11] Every single landlord in the country, from large commercial companies to those with a single property or even just a lodger, would have to check the immigration papers of a potential or existing tenant against a list provided by the Home Office and refuse tenancy to or evict any tenant whose papers did not match those listed. In the event of confusion, a landlord could even call a Home Office helpline to check the immigration status of the person concerned. The scheme was reinforced with a new criminal offence that landlords and agents might commit by knowingly renting to a person without permission, and a new system of accelerated eviction where the Home Office served a notice on a landlord. The eviction provisions allowed landlords in some cases to evict without a court order, leaving individuals, including children, entirely at the whim of the Home Office and the accuracy of the information held in its databases.

In her 2012 interview announcing the hostile environment, Theresa May said, 'If you're going to create a hostile environment for illegal migrants … access to financial services is part of that.'[12] Although the 'Right to Rent' scheme has attracted the most attention, it was arguably the financial measures in the Immigration Acts 2014 and 2016 that were the flagship changes. The 2014 Act prevents people from opening bank accounts if they do not have permission to live in the UK. Since then, every bank or building society has been required to check the residence status of each new potential customer with a specified anti-fraud organisation or data-matching authority. The 2016 Act then developed these rules even further, requiring banks and building societies to make checks on existing account holders and to notify the Home Office if the individual may be a 'disqualified person' (or, in other words, an unauthorised migrant).

Not being able to open a bank account is one thing; having your existing account closed is quite another. It may well render you destitute, homeless and jobless. And what if the Home Office made a mistake and closed the account of a person who was actually a lawful resident? As we will see, this was a real possibility, and yet the law was implemented anyway, albeit that it was quickly suspended.

The Immigration Acts 2014 and 2016 also strengthened the duty for marriage registrars to report suspected sham marriages and increased the notice period for all marriages from fifteen to twenty-eight days, for the explicit purpose of enabling Home Office investigation; we will take a closer look at these changes in Chapter 5.[13] In addition, the DVLA was granted a new power to revoke driving licences when they had been issued to a person who did not have leave to remain in the country. Where a licence was revoked and the person continued to drive anyway, perhaps unaware of revocation, this would amount to what lawyers call a 'strict liability offence', or the idea that lack of knowledge is no excuse. Finally, just as Uber and similar services were increasingly rendering traditional taxi regulations redundant, reams of regulations – literally hundreds of pages – were introduced to amend various of these archaic laws. Local authorities were then obliged to check the immigration status of both new and existing private and black cab taxi drivers, revoking licences where required.

So far, we have considered just the changes where Acts of Parliament were needed. In other walks of life, the checks could be and were introduced by secondary legislation, bureaucracy and data-sharing agreements between departments.[14]

PUBLIC SERVICES AND CIVIL SOCIETY

One of the key battlegrounds of the hostile environment has been over access to the National Health Service. The debate over charging foreign nationals for use of the NHS dates back to its very birth. Labour politician Nye Bevan had been responsible for driving through the reforms that created the NHS, and he addressed these issues head on as early as 1952:

> How are we to distinguish a visitor from anyone else? Are British citizens to carry means of identification everywhere to prove they are not visitors? For if the sheep are to be separated from the goats both must be classified. What began as an attempt to keep the Health Service for ourselves would end by being a nuisance to everyone.[15]

Bevan went on to point out that the cost of looking after visitors who fall ill could not amount to more than a 'negligible fraction' of the total NHS budget, that reciprocal systems could be agreed with other countries and, anyway, foreign nationals were themselves often paying VAT, income and National Insurance taxes that contributed to the NHS budget. For many years, Bevan's arguments held sway. Eventually, though, legislation was introduced in 1977 permitting the charging of non-residents for NHS services.[16] The first regulations enabling this to occur were introduced in 1982 and further legislative changes were made in 2006 to little effect. In reality, very little, if any, money was recovered via this method. To do so would be inconvenient, costly and for very little purpose; it would be a classic example of a hammer being used to crack a nut. The total cost of what some describe as 'health tourism' (deliberate rather than accidental use of the NHS by foreign nationals who are not entitled to it) is estimated as 0.3 per cent of the total NHS budget.[17]

But cracking nuts with hammers is a signature feature of the hostile environment. New regulations were introduced in 2015, and strengthened in 2017, to force hospitals to carry out immigration checks and impose upfront charges for treatment to those who were not eligible for free care. Data-sharing between the NHS and Home Office was then formalised in a memorandum of understanding that took effect on 1 January 2017. This allowed for the transfer of limited non-clinical patient information about immigration offenders between the NHS and the government.[18] It was reported even before the formal agreement in the first eleven months of 2016, that 8,127 requests for patient information had been made by the Home Office.[19] The arrangement was scrapped in the face of a legal challenge by Migrants Rights Network in 2018, although it was expected that a new, more limited arrangement would be introduced at a later date.[20]

In 2016 the Home Office persuaded the Department for Education to start collecting nationality data from school children, even though all children in the United Kingdom are entitled to schooling, irrespective of nationality or immigration status. Activists such as the organisation Against Borders for Children immediately raised suspicions about this new requirement. They were concerned that the data would be shared with the Home Office for immigration enforcement purposes. Their fears were justified. The Department for Education later admitted that the details of individual children on the national pupil database in England and Wales – their names, recent addresses, school and earliest and latest attendance dates – had been passed to the Home Office eighteen times over four years. Unusually, in response to the outcry, the government reversed course, and in April

2018, the Department for Education announced that it would end the collection of nationality and country of birth data in schools.[21]

It may or may not surprise the public to know that the police have played a very limited role in the enforcement of immigration laws for decades. There are myriad immigration offences on the statute books, but prosecutions are rare and convictions even rarer.[22] This approach was a matter of conscious policy on the part of the police. Former senior police officer and Liberal Democrat peer Brian Paddick has written of everyday immigration enforcement by the police that 'Such was the damage these arrests were causing to police relations with the black community that a policy decision was made that the police would no longer actively seek to enforce immigration law but would assist immigration officers when they needed it.'[23] But this was to change in 2012, with the launch of Operation Nexus in London.

Initially, Operation Nexus was a joint working arrangement between the police and the Home Office, aimed at suspected criminals and gang members who were also foreign nationals living either legally or illegally in the UK. The objective was to remove those individuals from British society by deporting them rather than bringing them to trial and imprisoning them. Deportation is a relatively straightforward process with a lower standard of proof than is required for a criminal case. The project evolved over time and was then rolled out nationally, with the result that immigration officers were embedded at police stations to interview not just alleged perpetrators of crimes but also victims.[24] In response to a Freedom of Information request in April 2017, the Metropolitan Police confirmed that it passes on individuals' personal details where there are concerns over immigration status, even when such people are the victims or witnesses of crime.

The tentacles of the hostile environment were now reaching beyond the government. A number of homeless charities, alleged to include St Mungo's, Change, Grow, Live and Thames Reach, were drawn into running joint 'sweep' operations with immigration and local government officials and passing location information on rough sleepers to the Home Office.[25] European nationals were specifically targeted in one operation, which was later ruled to be unlawful by the High Court,[26] and hundreds of thousands of pounds in funding was provided to various religious and community groups to promote 'self-deportation' by destitute migrants.[27]

The general public was also encouraged to get involved. 'I want everyone in the country to help with this,' David Cameron said in a major speech on immigration in October 2011, 'including by reporting suspected illegal immigrants to our Border Agency through the Crimestoppers phone line or the Border Agency website. Together I do believe we can reclaim our borders and send illegal immigrants home.'[28] And now there is indeed an Immigration Enforcement Hotline, as well as an online reporting form that concerned citizens can use if they want to shop a neighbour, colleague, tenant or former lover. Citizen denunciations were once a feature of Soviet societies, but there are now around 50,000 such reports made every year by members of the public here in the UK. Yet their accuracy is questionable. An internal Home Office review commissioned by firm Deloitte in 2014 politely suggested that the 'intelligence' generated was 'not the most efficient way for [Immigration Enforcement] to direct its activity.'[29]

Even Members of Parliament have been keen to get in on the action. In 2017, the Home Office recorded seventy denunciations from MPs concerning their own constituents, while in 2018, after a certain amount of public outcry, the number of MP tip-offs actually went up.[30] Migrants, whether lawful or not, are constituents under the British parliamentary system, even if they do not necessarily have a right to vote in general elections. But with tightening immigration rules meaning more and more people are affected by visa problems, and cuts to legal aid effectively removing access to lawyers, immigration issues have grown in recent years to form a major part of many MPs' constituency work. Normally, information from a constituent to their Member of Parliament would be considered confidential, for obvious reasons; as Conservative MP Nigel Evans puts it, 'People need to have absolute knowledge that when they come to an MP for help they will be safe to talk without fear of retribution.' Indeed, a constituent who seeks support from an MP would presumably be looking for assistance to resolve his or her position in the UK, rather than just staying below the radar. Being cued up for a dawn raid by the immigration authorities is hardly likely to help with that.

The hostile environment has been a disaster. The system encourages race discrimination; the financial costs of the red tape needed to set it up have been huge; the wrong people have been catastrophically affected; there has been no discernible decrease in unlawful immigration; and even where the 'right' people have been punished, the public have baulked at the dire consequences.

COLLATERAL DAMAGE

The intended victims of the hostile environment are publicly referred to as 'illegal immigrants'. The reality is that all citizens and UK residents have been affected, albeit some more than others. The impact has been hardest felt by ethnic minorities, who have suffered additional racial discrimination as a result.

If you are white, male, middle-aged and middle-class then you are less likely to be getting married, opening a bank account for the first time, seeking NHS treatment, moving between jobs or buying your first home. Being asked to prove that you have the right to be in Britain will be a minor annoyance at most. No, you are more likely to be asked to prove your immigration status if you are black or minority ethnic, young, poor or female. And if you are black or minority ethnic, being asked to prove your right to be in Britain turns from the inconsequential bother of the white man into a sinister question of whether or not you belong.

To make matters worse, the design of the hostile environment encourages over-zealous over-enforcement. There are penalties for failure to implement these immigration laws, no prizes for applying them correctly and no sanctions for being over-enthusiastic. As academic Paul Daly has written of the Right to Rent scheme, the danger is that this approach encourages a 'systemic overenforcement by landlords who have difficulty in understanding the laws they are required to enforce and who, quite rationally, err on the side of caution'.[31] Right from the conception of the scheme, the fear has been that this caution would manifest itself as racial discrimination, with some landlords being reluctant to rent to black and minority ethnic tenants for fear of being fined if they turn out to be illegal.

It was reportedly then Prime Minister David Cameron himself who insisted that the hostile environment be extended to landlords. Eric Pickles, who was Communities Secretary at the time, has supported the story, telling journalist May Bulman that he thought the idea was 'ill-conceived – utterly wrong'.[32] Pickles hit the nail on the head: 'If you're a landlord, how the heck do you know what various documents look like? And wouldn't you say to yourself, "Well heck look, this person's got dark skin or a funny sounding surname, the safest thing is not to rent to them?"' Pickles aired his concerns directly with Cameron at a ministerial meeting. A forensic dissection of the development of the Right to Rent policy by Wendy Williams, published as part of her 'Windrush Lessons Learned Review' report in March 2020, showed that it was not just Pickles who was concerned. Other ministers,

Liberal Democrats and Conservatives alike, expressed concern, and Grant Shapps MP, then housing minister, submitted a paper that stated the Right to Rent proposal was 'strongly not recommended'.[33]

The vast majority of landlords are private individuals with limited resources and little to no understanding of equalities duties. Recruiting landlords as in-country border guards would self-evidently risk race discrimination occurring on the ground, while tenants would have no effective avenue of complaint. However, this was either not obvious to all, or otherwise it was considered a price worth paying. Cameron's response at the key ministerial meeting was apparently to slam his red folder on the table and storm out of the room. The Prime Minister eventually got his way and the proposal became law, subject only to a requirement tagged on by the Liberal Democrats that the scheme be trialled in a pilot test.

The pilot began in the West Midlands in December 2014. The Home Office commissioned research into the risk of discrimination, and while the researchers found minority ethnic tenants were no less likely to be offered a tenancy, the research team did find that minority ethnic tenants were more likely to be asked for their immigration papers, and that some landlords displayed potentially discriminatory behaviour or attitudes.[34] The same research revealed that British citizens without a passport, older people without photo ID and younger people on low incomes were also at risk of being prejudiced by the scheme, as were lawful migrants and 'any foreigners'. Even before the evaluation was finished, though, David Cameron inadvertently revealed it for a sham by announcing shortly after his general election victory in May 2015 that the scheme would be rolled out nationally.[35] Independent research by the Joint Council for the Welfare of Immigrants (JCWI) later showed that the predicted prejudicial impact was real. The charity conducted a mystery shopping exercise, with the results showing significant discrimination against a lawful settled migrant compared to a British citizen.[36]

The issue ended up in the High Court in 2018. Mr Justice Martin Spencer considered the evidence from JCWI, housing charities Shelter and Crisis, the Residential Landlords Association, the Chief Inspector of Borders and Immigration and others, and concluded that the scheme was inherently discriminatory on the basis of race and nationality. Not only did it merely provide the occasion or opportunity for race discrimination, he said, but it actually caused landlords to act in a discriminatory way when otherwise they would not. 'As I have found,' he concluded, 'the measures have a disproportionately discriminatory effect and I would assume and hope that those legislators who voted in favour of the Scheme would be aghast to learn of its discriminatory effect.'[37] Rather than taking this on board, though, the government chose to appeal the decision; the outcome is awaited at the time of writing.

THE WRONG VICTIMS

If a policy depriving residents of jobs, homes and money is going to be introduced, one would hope that it would at the very least be implemented using the best available data, with strong failsafe mechanisms in place to reverse any potential errors. It would, you would have thought, be a disaster if innocent individuals ended up being forced into penury and out of the country as a result of incorrect information. That is, of course, precisely what happened.

Oliver Letwin, who as a Cabinet minister sat on the hostile environment ministerial committee, later told journalist Amelia Gentleman, 'We assumed that the one thing that the Home Office would know is whether someone was here lawfully.'[38] In reality, however, Home Office data on the immigration status of residents of the United Kingdom is often wrong. Officials in the department probably already knew that their information was unreliable, but public confirmation was provided in 2013, when a contract was awarded to the private company Capita to track down 174,000 suspected unlawful residents on the Home Office database. Capita was to be paid according to its results and therefore felt incentivised to scare people into leaving the country. As soon as the company started sending out threatening text messages, though, it became clear that lawful residents, and even British citizens, were somehow included on the database.[39] Capita dismissed the number of complaints it subsequently received as 'negligible', but that was not how those wrongly targeted felt. Furthermore, in 2016 it emerged that hostile environment bank account checks were throwing up incorrect results as much as 10 per cent of the time. In these cases, people were wrongly being refused permission to open a bank account. Officials admitted that relevant changes to a person's status might not be entered on the appropriate database 'until some months after the event, and that data was often entered in the wrong field, commonly as free text'.[40] Incredibly, this did not prevent the government from implementing the next stage of its banking checks, where the existing bank accounts of those believed to be in the UK illegally would be closed.

As well as getting the facts wrong on multiple cases it *does* know about, there are also many people living in the United Kingdom of whom the Home Office is not aware. The vast majority of them are lawful residents and many of them are British citizens, they just do not have documents yet – perhaps because they did not really need them until the hostile environment was launched. There is no population database or register for the United Kingdom and nor is there a central register of British citizens. There are plenty such citizens who have never applied for a passport, for example. The most recent census showed that 17 per cent of UK residents (about ten million people), the majority of whom are likely to be British citizens, do not have passports. There is simply no reason for the Home Office even to know of the existence of these people and, traditionally, it would be considered none of the government's business to know about them.

There are also plenty of foreign nationals living in the UK who are unknown to the Home Office. Some have been resident for decades and were granted status many years ago, before Home Office computer records began, while others are unknown because the department has no record of EU citizens who have not yet applied for UK residence under the post-Brexit EU Settlement Scheme. Either way, these people (who have not done anything wrong) are all potential victims of the hostile environment. One of the fundamental flaws in the whole conception of the hostile environment scheme is that, even though it is intended to affect unlawful residents, it is actually aimed at undocumented residents.

This leads us to the most prominent victims of the hostile environment: the Windrush generation. Broadly speaking, this is a label coined by campaigner Patrick Vernon to describe lawful long-term residents from Commonwealth countries. Many either migrated to the UK themselves when they were in effect considered British citizens or are the children of those who did so.[41] Typically, they are lawfully resident because they were granted 'Indefinite Leave to Remain' status many years ago, sometimes automatically by law and sometimes in the form of a stamp in a long-expired passport. For decades, the only challenges made to their right to be here were from outright racists. But as the hostile environment geared up from 2012 onwards, such challenges started to come in thick and fast from an ever-wider range of people, businesses and institutions. We saw what happened to Mr Baker earlier, when he was dismissed by his company for being unable to prove his right of residence. Unfortunately, he was not alone.

Back in 2014, Fiona Bawdon researched and wrote a report entitled 'Chasing Status' for the Legal Action Group.[42] The report highlighted the plight of thousands of long-term UK residents who find themselves unable to prove their immigration status, despite having lived in the country legally for most of their lives. Bawdon called these residents 'surprised Brits', because they felt British, and many thought they actually were British citizens, and yet they had been caught out by the new hostile environment laws. Based on twelve interviews with long-term residents, one of the cases included was that of Aubrey, who arrived in the UK from Jamaica as a boy in 1973. A working single father then aged fifty-six, Aubrey had been suspended from his job without pay. He needed to make an expensive immigration application to obtain new proof of his status, but the application would take up to six months, during which time he would be without pay or welfare benefits. Lasith, another interviewee, had arrived from Sri Lanka in 1964, aged ten, to join his parents. He had lived, worked and raised his own five children here, all entirely lawfully. Yet, after being fired from his job for failing to produce proof of his right of residence, he received a letter from the Home Office telling him he had twenty-eight days to leave the country. Bawdon estimated at the time that there were over 10,000 such cases and she proposed several reforms to ease the situation of those affected, including setting up a special unit to process their cases. The Guardian ran an article about the report but the Home Office response was dismissive.[43] There were no plans to set up any such special unit, a spokesman said, and 'it is up to anyone who does not have an established immigration status to regularise their position, however long they have been here'.

At the time, there was no other interest outside the immigration law and campaigning community. The 'Chasing Status' report seemed to have sunk without trace. After the Brexit referendum in 2016, though, the media found a new appetite for stories critical of the Home Office, following a string of articles about generally white, middle-class EU migrants who were facing difficulties proving their permanent residence. *Guardian* journalist Amelia Gentleman soon started to investigate the cases of destitute black and Asian residents. Realising that the people she was meeting must be just the tip of the iceberg, Gentleman began to unearth a shocking series of similar examples.[44] As Bawdon had shown and predicted two years before, lawful residents were finding themselves turfed out of jobs and homes, denied life-saving NHS care and threatened with deportation to countries they barely knew. Their claims to be living lawfully were falling on deaf ears, with immigration officials demanding written evidence from 'official' sources of their residence for every single year of the multiple decades they had lived in the UK.

In one of my own cases, I acted for a musician from Jamaica who had arrived in the 1980s but was now being refused by the Home Office because he was missing evidence of residence for a short period of several months in the 1990s. He easily won his appeal because judges, unlike immigration officials, are willing to accept evidence from witnesses and unofficial sources; in this case from flyers from gigs the man had played back in the '90s, which a friend had fortunately kept. This attitude, that it was somehow the fault of long-term residents for failing to obtain documents they did not previously need, went right the way to the top. 'Albert Thompson', who, following the conclusion of his legal battles, now goes by his real name of Sylvester Marshall, was denied cancer treatment by his local hospital, despite lawful residence of forty-four years.[45] His case was eventually raised with Prime Minister Theresa May in 2018, who wrote in response: 'While I sympathise with Mr Thompson ... we encourage him to make the appropriate application [and provide evidence of] his settled status here.'

Some, indeed, had 'self-deported' and left the country. Gentleman visited Jamaica to interview some of those affected. Joycelyn John had arrived in the UK in 1963, aged four, and was lawfully resident. However, there had been a mix-up with her papers and by 2014 she had been wrongly classified as unlawfully resident in the country. She lost her job, was unable to find a new one and ended up home-less. John then agreed to a so-called 'voluntary' departure to Grenada in late 2016 – though, in reality, there was nothing voluntary about it at all, given that her only alternative was to sleep on the streets. In another case, Colin Smith (not his real name) had been detained and formally deported in 2013, following a fourteen-month sentence for a relatively minor offence. But this should never have happened, as Windrush-era Commonwealth citizens were legally protected from deportation by the Immigration Act 1971. Others, like Vernon Vanriel, ended up trapped outside the UK. Vanriel had arrived in the UK with his family in 1962 and lived here until 2015, when he visited Jamaica. Refused a visa to return, when Gentleman met with him, he was living destitute in a wooden shack. Joe Robinson had experienced a similar fate. Having arrived in the UK aged six, he vis-ited Jamaica for his fiftieth birthday with his family. He was refused boarding for the return flight and it took him two years for him to be able to sort out his situation and return.[46]

The Windrush scandal finally received the attention it deserved in April 2018. Immediately before a Commonwealth heads of government meeting, Prime Minister Theresa May had refused to meet with a del-egation of twelve Caribbean high commissioners to discuss the situa-tion of long-term residents facing immigration difficulties. An article about this diplomatic snub appeared on the front page of *The Guardian* and suddenly, as Gentleman writes, 'ministers who had shown no interest were falling over themselves to express profound sorrow'. Home Secretary Amber Rudd was forced to appear at the Commons despatch box to make the first of two comprehensive admissions that the Windrush generation had been treated 'appallingly'. Theresa May herself was forced repeatedly to apologise, although her initial efforts could be labelled weak attempts of the 'sorry-not-sorry' variety. Very belatedly, the special unit that Fiona Bawdon had advocated in 2014 was set up, along with a compensation fund for those affected.

Still, the fundamental flaw in the design of the hostile environment persists: it targets the undocumented, not the unauthorised. The problem is an inherent one and, as discussed in more detail in Chapter 9, the system will have major consequences for EU citizens once the Brexit transition period ends and free movement rules are fully abandoned. The majority of lawful residents living in the United Kingdom without status papers (i.e. undocumented migrants) are citizens of European Union countries who entered the UK under free movement rules. In fact, immigration officials are literally forbidden from stamping the passports of EU citizens entering and leaving the UK and they have no idea why an EU citizen might be entering the UK, nor for how long he or she will stay.

Brexit therefore represents a huge challenge; no one knows how many EU citizens live in the UK, but estimates go as high as four million. During the referendum, these people were promised by the official Leave campaign that their position would be automatically – and magically – protected, but this has turned out to be untrue.[47] When EU law ceases to apply in the United Kingdom, all of those millions of EU citizens and their family members from outside the UK will need to have applied for and received new immigration status under

UK law. If they do not apply by the deadline, they will become unlawfully resident. No registration campaign around the world has ever achieved a 100 per cent success rate and experts predict that as many as hundreds of thousands of EU citizens will miss the deadline.[48] Some will be elderly residents in care homes, some will be young children, others will not speak good English. Some may be afraid of applying and some will have believed the Leave campaign promise that their rights would be protected. Some will just be disorganised or unaware; after all, a lot of people miss the deadline for filing their tax return every year, even though they get fined for doing so. Some may refuse on principle.

No matter what their reasons, the effect of being exposed to the hostile environment will be the same. Their jobs will be lost, their bank accounts closed down, their tenancies terminated and their access to the NHS and welfare benefits ended. The consequences for any individual caught out in this way will be calamitous.

THE RIGHT VICTIMS

The hostile environment is intended to deny work, money, housing and public services to unauthorised migrants in order to force them to 'self-deport' and leave the country. In order for this approach to work, however, the policy must achieve three things. Firstly, the right people have to be affected (and we have already seen that in fact many of those affected, sometimes catastrophically, have been the wrong people – i.e. lawful residents). Secondly, their life must be made miserable. And thirdly, this must have the effect of forcing them to leave. We will soon turn to whether enforced and voluntary departures from the UK have actually gone up in the era of the hostile environment, but in the meantime, it is necessary to question the human impact of this denial of life's basic requirements.

The testimonies gathered by Amelia Gentleman from affected members of the Windrush generation are heartbreaking. They tell of the human cost of the hostile environment: poverty, isolation, ill health, homelessness, despair, forced exile from the country and even suicide. Yet, it is important to recall that this is the whole purpose of the hostile environment; ministers claim that they are sorry that some of the 'wrong' people were affected in this way, but the fact remains that these effects were supposed to be felt by the 'right' people.

Consider the impact of immigration checks, combined with up-front charges for NHS care, combined with data-sharing with the Home Office. What are the consequences if some residents of the UK and their children, whether they are here lawfully or unlawfully, are unable (or, for fear of the possible consequences, unwilling) to access doctors? Some conditions are personal and non-contagious, such as cancer. Rather than such a condition being caught early and treated, the victim may die prematurely. When Kelemua Mulat was denied urgent cancer treatment, it was a personal tragedy for her. The decision was reversed some six weeks later after a media outcry, but she died a year afterwards.[49] There are also reports of very ill patients wrongly being turned away by hospitals and pregnant women being afraid to seek antenatal care for fear of the immigration consequences, with obvious risks to their own health and the health of their babies.[50] As has been starkly illustrated by the coronavirus crisis, other illnesses are contagious and have wider public health implications. It is critically important that vaccination rates are very high amongst the public, for example, and that transmissible conditions such as HIV, tuberculosis or new diseases like Covid-19 are identified and treated. By denying healthcare to afflicted people and making them scared of going to the doctor, it can be argued that the hostile environment represents a risk not just to individuals but to public health in general.

Inculcating a fear of the authorities is problematic in policing, as well as in public health. Good, effective policing relies on trust and community consent, but both are being corroded by the discriminatory way in which some communities perceive they are targeted. Commenting on Operation Nexus, the joint working operation between the police and immigration authorities (see Chapter 3), in 2013, Rita Chadha, chief executive of the Refugee and Migrant Forum of East London, said:

> What we are seeing now is that they are targeting all crimes and low-level criminality. This is going to stop victims coming forward in the black and ethnic minority communities because they fear they will be targeted by Nexus. If you have a woman suffering domestic violence in a household of overstayers she is not going to come forward. This is totally going to mess up local policing and any trust communities have in the police.[51]

The societal price of the hostile environment is the creation of an illegal underclass of foreign, mainly minority ethnic workers and families. These people are highly vulnerable to exploitation and have no access to the social and welfare safety net that protects not just British citizens as individuals but the very fabric of our society.

DOES THE HOSTILE ENVIRONMENT ACTUALLY WORK?

The stated purpose of the hostile environment is to drive down inward migration to the UK by making it as disadvantageous, risky, expensive and inconvenient as possible to come here. The policy is also intended to encourage migrants already in the UK to leave, by administering many into irredeemable illegality (as we will see in the next chapter) and making their lives as marginal and difficult as possible. Given the impact of the hostile environment on the lives of citizens, its breadth across government and the cost of implementing it, we might expect that the success or otherwise of the policy would be carefully monitored. But it is not. Ministers and civil servants are just not that interested in the question of whether the system actually works or not.

In his inspection report on the hostile environment, David Bolt, chief inspector of borders and immigration, found that 'there was no evidence that any work had been done or was planned in relation to measuring the deterrent effect of the "hostile environment" on would-be illegal migrants'.[52] Furthermore, 'no targets had been set by ministers for voluntary returns or net migration and there was no pressure to deliver specific outcomes'. Revealingly, the inspectors were told by civil servants that, even if there was research to show that the hostile environment was not effective, the policy would still not be abandoned: 'This was because it was the right thing to do, and the public would not find it acceptable that illegal migrants could access the same range of benefits and services as British citizens and legal migrants.'

Similarly, a separate report by Bolt's inspectors on the Right to Rent programme targeting landlords found that 'overall, the scheme is yet to demonstrate its worth as a tool to encourage immigration compliance (the number of voluntary returns has fallen). Internally, the Home Office has failed to coordinate, maximise or even measure effectively its use. Meanwhile, externally it is doing little to address stakeholders' concerns.'[53]

Even as late as February 2020 the government had still failed to commission any research into whether the hostile environment has any effect on migrant behaviour. In her 'Windrush Lessons Learned Review', Wendy Williams revealed that a research proposal 'to increase our understanding of the behaviour, attitudes and motivations of immigration offenders' had been submitted to ministers in January 2018, but was yet to be approved. Williams looked particularly closely at the Right to Rent scheme, which has been repeatedly flagged as presenting a clear risk of discrimination. She concluded that, although an intention to attempt in future to track the outcomes for people subject to 'compliant environment' sanctions had been declared, 'to date there has been nothing to indicate any such assurance or monitoring has been put in place for the Right to Rent scheme'.[54]

Although the architects and engineers of the hostile environment seem remarkably nonchalant about whether the policy does what it was supposed to, there is some evidence available for us to take a look for ourselves. The Home Office publishes immigration statistics every quarter and the data suggest a fall in both enforced removals and voluntary returns away from the UK since the hostile environment was first announced in 2012:

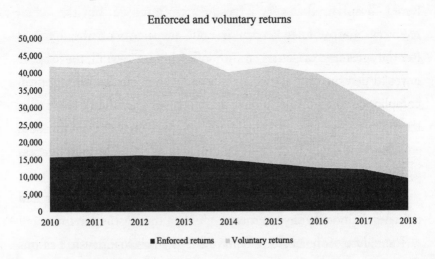

Enforced and voluntary returns

■ Enforced returns　　■ Voluntary returns

Source: Home Office quarterly immigration statistics year ended September 2019, table Ret_01.

Another measure of success would be if the hostile environment saved money for the taxpayer. The idea was, in part, that those who were not entitled to public services would no longer receive them, which would thereby reduce costs. It was also expected to reduce the need for expensive, unpleasant and resource-hogging enforced removals, involving dawn raids, detention and charter flights, because life would be so hard for illegal immigrants that they would 'self-deport'. However, all this ignores the costs of implementing the policy itself and creating the systems to routinely check immigration status that are required alongside it. In reality, the costs of introducing the hostile environment have been huge and the savings illusory.

Sometimes the costs are obvious and upfront, as with the creation of the sinister-sounding Interventions and Sanctions Directorate at the Home Office. Its purpose is 'the indirect enforcement of immigration control through third parties'. It has existed since June 2013 and was reported to have a staff of 146 in 2016 and a budget of £5.5 million in 2015/16.[55] It might be thought that this team was self-financing due to the income from sanctions imposed on employers and landlords. Barely. It is true that very large fines are imposed, but the actual recovery of those fines is small in comparison. Very few employers pay the fines they are charged with, often because the employer goes out of business and sometimes because they successfully appeal. Other costs to the Home Office are effectively hidden because they end up inflating other, existing internal budgets, as with the additional workload caused by the massive increase in referrals for investigation by marriage registrars discussed in Chapter 5. This makes it hard to measure the true cost to central government of implementing and policing the hostile environment.

The nature of the hostile environment as a privatised system of immigration controls means that the costs of its administration fall largely on public services, private citizens and companies. It is impossible to quantify easily the financial burden borne by private individuals and companies, and therefore ultimately, if indirectly, by the British public. But it must be huge. The NHS may well be spending more on conducting checks on potential patients than it recovers in charging them fees as a consequence, for example. Professor Martin McKee, professor of European public health at the London School of Hygiene and Tropical Medicine, gave evidence in February 2017 to the House of Commons Health Select Committee. He told the committee that his research team had just completed a study in which they submitted Freedom of Information requests to every hospital trust in England to ask them how much they spent collecting money from overseas patients and how much they recovered. It was found that 'most of them were spending more money than they were recovering. They had a very low level of recovery, but as time went by they found they were often trying to recover from people who were entitled anyway'. It may seem to be a matter of common sense to many members of the public – and perhaps ministers and civil servants too – that preventing foreign nationals accessing public services will save money. But setting up and enforcing a system of 'papers, please' checks is very expensive. Designing and creating the required systems has upfront costs, and operating those systems costs staff time that must also be paid for. It seems that these costs, which end up being absorbed into existing budgets where they squeeze service delivery even more, may well outweigh the savings.

The hostile environment is supposed to discourage illegal immigration but there is no evidence to suggest it works. No targets were set, no evaluation has been commissioned and the expense of implementation may very well be greater than the very limited savings generated. The closer we look at it, the less the hostile environment seems to be evidence-based policy-making, and the more it resembles a moral crusade.

CHAPTER 4

COMPLEXITY AND COST: NO WAY TO RUN A WHELK STORE

'*The history fills me with such despair at the manner in which the system operates that the preservation of my equanimity probably demands that I should ignore it, but I steel myself to give a summary at least ... I ask, rhetorically, is this the way to run a whelk store?*'

LORD JUSTICE WARD[1]

The byzantine complexity of the UK's immigration law has become legendary. It is good for business for immigration lawyers like me; not only migrants but also their families, employers, universities and landlords all now need our help. Yet it is a terrible way to run a country and it can lead to slight and innocent mistakes that may cause dire consequences. Even lawyers and judges – those of us who are the most initiated in the ways of the law – have repeatedly struggled to understand and interpret sloppily drafted and continually amended laws, leading to widespread calls for reform.

One of the greatest judges of modern times and senior law lord Tom Bingham wrote that one of the fundamental principles of the rule of law is that it 'must be accessible and so far as possible intelligible, clear and predictable'.[2] The reasons for this should be self-evident. Just as it is impossible to play a sport fairly without knowing the rules, so too it is impossible to live life fairly without knowing the law, or at least being able to find out what it is should you wish to do so. But immigration law is anything but accessible, intelligible, clear and predictable. Nicholas Easterman put it characteristically bluntly in a set of decidedly unofficial comments at a Bar Council event in 2017. 'Immigration law is a total nightmare,' said the full-time immigration judge. 'I don't suppose the judges know any more about it than the appellants who come before them.'[3]

HOW MUCH IMMIGRATION LAW IS THERE?

First of all, immigration law is voluminous. There is a lot of it. It consists of several layers and each layer is packed with various different laws, each doing different things. Indeed, the sheer weight of paper required to print it all out would make immigration law inherently hard to get to grips with to begin with, even if it was all beautifully and clearly drafted. Which it is not – as we shall see in a moment.

At the top of the pile there is a lot of relevant international law. The Refugee Convention, the European Convention on Human Rights, trafficking and statelessness conventions, EU law and various international trade agreements all have an impact on the rights of migrants. All of these international legal instruments have been interpreted in various different court cases around the world and it is possible that any number of these might potentially have relevance elsewhere, because judges in different counties like to try to follow the same approach as one another for laws that apply in different jurisdictions.

Next, there are the Acts of Parliament, or what lawyers call primary legislation at a national level. There are a lot of these as well, with Acts of Parliament from 1971, 1988, 1999, 2002, 2004, 2006, 2007, 2008, 2009, 2014 and 2016 all still being relevant today. There are also other bits of legislation that are not mainly concerned with immigration, but which nevertheless have an impact on immigration cases, like the Crime and Courts Act 2013. All of these pieces of legislation are substantial. The Immigration Act 2016 alone is 234 pages long, featuring nine parts, ninety-six different sections and fifteen schedules. The Immigration Act 2014 is 137 pages long, with seven parts, seventy-seven sections and nine schedules. The Borders, Citizenship and Immigration Act 2009 is fifty-five pages long, has four parts, fifty-nine sections and, mercifully, just one schedule. But you get the picture. There is a lot of law.

That is barely the start of it, though. Below the primary legislation lies secondary legislation. This consists of regulations, rules, orders and statutory instruments, all of which are drawn up by civil servants and made law by ministerial fiat under powers delegated to ministers by the main Acts of Parliament. In 2018 alone, there were seventeen pieces of full secondary legislation with the word 'immigration' in the title, from the Immigration (Health Charge) (Amendment) Order 2018 to the Immigration (Provision of Physical Data) (Amendment) (EU Exit) Regulations 2018. This was fairly typical, if a little on the low side, as there had been eighteen such statutory instruments in 2017, twenty-three in 2016 and twenty-five in 2015. And this does not include changes to the main set of rules governing entitlement to a visa, known simply as the Immigration Rules. The current set of these rules was introduced in 1994 and at that time ran to some eighty pages. Today, the same document weighs in at over 1,000 pages. In fact, a 2018 study by journalists at *The Guardian* found that there had been 5,700 changes since 2010 and that the rules had more than doubled in size in that time.[4]

It gets worse, of course. The Immigration Rules do not contain all or indeed most of the policy that is to be implemented by officials on the ground. The policy is separately set out in – if I may say so – rather dense and diffuse guidance on the Home Office website. There are thousands upon thousands of pages of it. There are the 'Immigration Directorate Instructions', the 'Immigration Enforcement General Instructions', the 'Nationality Guidance', the 'Modernised Guidance' and plenty more. Some of it sets out legal and procedural rights. For example, it is far from unknown for immigration officials to cut a few corners when making the arrangements to remove a migrant on a particular flight; I have myself had to make weekend telephone calls to High Court judges for injunctions preventing such removals. The process officials are supposed to follow if there is a legal challenge is set out in a part of the 'Immigration Enforcement General Instructions' called 'Returns Preparation', in a section called 'Judicial Reviews and Injunctions', at the time of writing in its nineteenth version. That document is sixty pages long, if you can find it.

AS AMENDED

As well as there being an awful lot of immigration law, and perhaps because of this, it is also sometimes virtually impossible to find the current, latest version of any given regulation. Lord Neuberger, former president of the Supreme Court, told the Australian Bar Association in July 2017:

One access aspect of the rule of law which is sometimes over-looked is access to the law itself, in other words access to statutes, secondary legislation and case law. It is of course a fundamental requirement of the rule of law that laws are clearly expressed and easily accessible. To put the point simply, people should know, or at least be able to find out, what the law is.[5]

The problem is caused partly by repeated amendment, re-amendment and further amendment of those amendments for all these Acts of Parliament, statutory instruments and sets of rules. This is a particular problem in immigration law because politicians have passed so much of it, seemingly in the belief that this will somehow reassure rather than alarm the public. All of the various Immigration Acts not only set out new free-standing provisions of their own but also amend the provisions in previous Acts of Parliament. It is like trying to match an old black-and-white infant school photo with a live adult; the original versions of the Acts are almost unrecognisable compared to the modern, more mature iterations.

The original Acts of Parliament are readily available online at the website legislation.gov.uk. But this is no use at all in immigration law. It is essential to be able to access the current, amended versions of the law and these are not always available – or at least not reliably. Lord Neuberger, in his 2017 speech, went on to say that the government's updating service was 'lamentable' and that it 'should not cost much for the UK government to ensure that its legislation website is kept up to date, so that current legislation is freely available to everyone'. Things have improved somewhat since 2017 but there has always been a delay in adding new changes, and at the time of writing key sets of regulations remain out of date on the government website, meaning there is no practical way for citizens or migrants to work out what the law affecting them actually says. As a practising lawyer, it is vital that my advice is accurate and correct; my clients would rightly be rather unimpressed if I made a legal mistake. I personally feel unable to trust the government website, instead making use of an expensive private service from one of the major legal publishing houses.

BEYOND MORTAL COMPREHENSION

Even if you can work out which of the myriad laws is the right one to look at, and you are then able to find the latest amended version, good luck working out what it means. Specialist lawyers and judges alike struggle to make sense of the many provisions of immigration law. They are badly written, the words are ambiguous, different laws contradict one another and the structure is sometimes nonsensical. And, most bafflingly of all, some of the most important sections of the Immigration Rules are set out in a non-sequential structure. Let me try to explain how preposterous this is; but for me to do so, you need to step into my world for a moment.

Let us take look at Appendix FM of the Immigration Rules, which sets out the visa requirements for the family members of British citizens. It is arguably the single most important part of the Immigration Rules and it is vital that the guidelines are clear. But it is here of all places that the civil servants drafting the rules decided to abandon a practice dating back at the very least to the Ten Commandments. Numerical sequencing was good enough for God but not for the Home Office, apparently. The appendix begins not with paragraph number one but with GEN.1.1. Logically enough, this is followed by GEN.1.2 and so on. But then, after GEN.3.2, we reach paragraph EC-P.1.1. The next paragraph is *not* EC-P.1.2 but rather S-EC.1.1. and continues in sequence all the way up to S-EC.3.2. After that comes E-ECP.1.1 and so on, through an interminable jumble of letters apparently generated by a toddler hitting a keyboard repeatedly and at random: R-LTRP, S-LTR, E-LTRP and more. This is all incomprehensible enough, you might think. But the real problem comes when you notice that one paragraph often cross references another. R-LTRP.1.1 says, amongst many, many other things, that one of the requirements for limited leave to remain in the UK as a partner is that 'the applicant meets the requirements of paragraphs E-LTRP.1.2-1.12. and E-LTRP.2.1-2.2'. But how will you find out what these other paragraphs say when there is no numerical or alphabetical sequence? Is it forwards or backwards from where you are now? One has to swim directionless through the alphabet soup until serendipity strikes.

Even if you can decipher this up-ended Scrabble board, it turns out that the rules in Appendix FM are secretly supplemented by equally important and mandatory requirements elsewhere. It is a system that puts Kafka to shame. Immigration lawyers know this from experience, and if they look hard enough, because paragraph GEN.1.4. sort of hints at it. The chances of a first-time reader spotting and understanding this, though, are basically zero. To put it as simply as possible, Paragraph E-ECP.3.1 of Appendix FM says that an applicant 'must provide specified evidence, from the sources listed in paragraph E-ECP.3.2., of a specified gross annual income of at least £18,600'. But, unless you read the whole, interminable document from the start, how are you supposed to know that the words 'specified evidence' are in fact an oblique reference to a completely different appendix, Appendix FM-SE, where a whole new set of mandatory requirements are imposed? This includes the rule that the earnings must date back for a continuous period of at least six months and that only certain documents in a certain format can be used as evidence. Electronic bank statements can only be used, for example, if 'accompanied by a letter from the bank on its headed stationery confirming that the documents are authentic or which bear the official stamp of the issuing bank on every page'. Many bank branches, however, refuse to provide such a letter or stamp because it is an unusual request and they are concerned that once out of their sight the documents could be tampered with.

You don't just need to take my word for it. The judges are also unimpressed. I keep a little collection of judicial *bon mots* complaining about how awful immigration law is and will share with you just a few examples. If we start at the top and work down, Lord Sumption, considered by some the finest legal mind of his generation and appointed directly as one of the twelve judges of the United Kingdom's Supreme Court, has said that the Immigration Act 1971 'has not aged well' and is 'ill-adapted to the mounting scale and complexity of the problems associated with immigration control'.[6] Other judges have hit upon various metaphors to try to convey the complexity they are faced with in immigration cases. Lord Justice Jackson in one case suggested that the 'provisions have now achieved a degree of complexity which even the Byzantine emperors would have envied'.[7] In another he compared immigration law to 'an impenetrable jungle of intertwined statutory provisions and judicial decisions'.[8] Lord Justice Beatson plumped to use the urban environment for his description: 'The architecture of the Rules is not the grand design of Lutyens' Delhi or Haussmann's Paris, but more that of the organic growth responding to the needs of the moment that is a feature of some shanty towns'.[9] Similarly, Lord Justice Underhill has said that he has 'great sympathy for applicants trying to find their way through the maze of immigration and asylum procedure (quite apart from the shameful complexities of the substantive law), which is all the more difficult if they are unrepresented'.[10] In a later case his metaphor was more graphic: 'The web of Rules and Guidance has become so tangled', he wrote, 'that even the spider has difficulty controlling it.'[11]

It is important to remember that all of these cases cost a small fortune to bring to court, having to go through multiple steps in the legal system. In another case, Lord Justice Beaton points to the real-life consequences of this mess:

> The detail, the number of documents that have to be consulted, the number of changes in rules and policy guidance, and the difficulty advisers face in ascertaining which previous version of the rule or guidance applies and obtaining it are real obstacles to achieving predictable consistency and restoring public trust in the system, particularly in an area of law that lay people and people whose first language is not English need to understand.[12]

You do not have to be an expert in reading between the lines to detect the judicial frustration infusing these quotes.

THE PRICE OF JUSTICE

Migrants have to pay a small fortune to set foot in this legal mine-field. The upfront visa application fee for a spouse or partner is over £3,500, only £2,000 of which is returned in the event of a refusal. An extension application costing over £1,000 must then be made after two and a half years, and a settlement request after five years costs nearly £2,500. The total cost across five years is around £7,000, and that is before the cost of a lawyer to help with all these applications.

The cost of a settlement application for indefinite leave to remain has skyrocketed over the past decade. Fees for in-country applications were only introduced in 2003; before that they were free. Initially, the level of the fees was set to recover the costs of processing the applications, although they were soon increased to include some element of profit for the Home Office. In 2010, the fee already stood at a historic high of £810. Since then the fee has been nearly tripled by the Home Office, to £2,389 at the time of writing, and that is before the immigration health surcharge (otherwise known as the NHS surcharge) of £2,000 for a five-year visa is added. (At the time of writing it was announced the health charge would increase to £3,120 for a five-year visa from October 2020.) The real cost of processing these applications at the Home Office is much lower, though, standing at £243 in 2019.

The costs for migrants who can only qualify under the 'private life' rules, meant for those with a connection to the UK and considered in the next chapter, are particularly punishing. And they are intended to be so; these routes only exist grudgingly. Each private life application under the limited leave routes costs £1,033 plus the immigration health surcharge of £1,000. Three applications will be needed to qualify for settlement, meaning a total of £8,488 at today's fee levels. In addition, the cost for a child is the same as for an adult. A family of four would thus need to find money for fees of £33,952 over a ten-year period.

The Home Office also does not stop at charging fees to make applications. To simply send an email to the Home Office, a charge of

£5.48 is now levied, while a call to the department's telephone helpline costs £1.37 per minute. Then, there is no guarantee that the emailer or caller will actually receive any help. The private contractors used by the Home Office to keep migrants at arm's length capitalise on their contracts by limiting the number of free appointments and charging for 'optional' extras like uploading documents and 'premium' appointments for faster-than-normal decisions.[13]

The astronomical fees are part of a government drive to create 'a fully self-funded borders and immigration system'. The Home Office line states, 'It is only right we recover the costs of running our immigration system by making sure that those who benefit directly from it contribute appropriately – so the expense to the UK taxpayer is less.' In reality, this means lawful migrants paying immigration and citizenship fees, while also contributing taxes through VAT and, where they are working, through National Insurance and income tax, then also being forced to pay for the costs of carrying out customs checks on incoming lorries, patrols in the English Channel and the deportation of foreign criminals. This double taxation imposes a heavy burden on migrant families, meaning they have less disposable income than their peers. The effect on children, particularly where their parents cannot afford to include them in immigration applications, is unconscionable. As one young person explained to the authors of a report by campaign group Let Us Learn, 'I couldn't do a lot of things other children did. It was the little things that really added up. Not having new shoes. Going to bed hungry. I was always anxious things would go wrong.' For some, though, this adds up to a lot more than the little things; it means being stuck in unsuitable accommodation or, even worse, it means debt, evictions and constant instability.[14] The government is forcing many migrant families into poverty – with all the misery that accompanies it – as the price of living in the UK.

SIMPLIFICATION

The introduction of the points-based system in 2008 marked an inflection point for the growing tangle of rules. As a result of a sudden proliferation of appendices, rules and guidance, the detail of the requirements for entry to the UK went from just about discernible to almost unknowable. And untangling a knot can be difficult. In 2017, the Law Commission, the official body tasked with legal reform, was asked by then Home Secretary Amber Rudd 'to review our immigration laws with a view to simplifying them'.[15] The report was produced in January 2020 and partially accepted by the Home Office a couple of months later just as the coronavirus crisis was beginning. Arguably rather optimistically, the Home Office said it intended to completely rewrite and reissue the whole of the Immigration Rules by January 2021.[16]

Simplifying and rewriting the Immigration Rules would be very welcome indeed, but still this would not address the stream of primary and secondary legislation that spews forth from the government so frequently. There was a Simplification Bill drawn up between 2007 and 2009, intended to consolidate the legal framework for immigration law and doing away with the Immigration Act 1971 and its successors. But the effort was eventually abandoned. There were all sorts of significant problems with the proposals, not least that many believed the exercise was seen by the government of the day as an opportunity to reduce rights and enhance executive powers. But at least the effort was made. Indeed, adherence to the Law of Holes (when in a hole, stop digging) would be a welcome start. Under a new system, politicians could stop introducing new immigration legislation, and if changes must be made, these alterations could be subject to proper consultation. Just as a pharmacist would prescribe Imodium to stem one sort of incontinent, unstructured flow, in this instance I would prescribe the medicine of parliamentary process; requiring the Home Office to submit changes to Parliament for votes and amendments might do something to slow the passage of new rules and improve the quality of those that do pass.

THE SPIDER'S WEB

The trend towards tortuousness began as a result of haste and incompetence. On the face of it, straightforward bad legal drafting by relatively junior and inexperienced civil servants appears to be behind much of the mess. Rumour has it that a single official was responsible for cooking up the non-sequential paragraph-labelling idea for Appendix FM, thinking that it would be a breakthrough in simplicity of use. But we can be sympathetic, to some extent: the frequency and volume of changes to the rules insisted on by ministers had made it difficult for new rules to be slotted in between existing ones and to maintain sequential numbering. This is not the fault of civil servants; it is the responsibility of the politicians who allocate insufficient resources and time and yet insist on change after change after change in an already complex area of law.

Often the changes politicians have insisted on in immigration law are really about the outcomes of individual cases that, either alone or collectively, achieve media notoriety. It is headline-driven lawmaking whereby general rules are drafted with a view to avoiding yesterday's news stories. The pattern begins with the introduction of complex rules that are intended to eliminate the need for supposedly unreliable, potentially inconsistent human judgments on individual cases. When the outcomes are then inevitably not as expected, the rules are repeatedly tweaked. Ministers and officials fail to realise that the problem lies not in the detail of such rules but in thinking that complex real-life situations can be predicted and satisfactorily determined without human input. One particularly bad example can be found in the ragbag of knee-jerk reactions that is the Asylum (Treatment of Claimants etc) Act 2004. Section 2 of the Act attempted to criminalise arrival in the UK if the migrants came without a passport or where that paperwork had previously been held but had later been destroyed. A 'reasonable excuse' clause needed to be inserted, which was defined in the negative as not including deliberately destroying or disposing of a passport, unless the person had 'reasonable cause'. But 'reasonable cause' then also needed to be defined and was labelled as not including certain reasons. Eventually the whole section was rendered largely ineffective by the courts because of the failure to define 'passport' properly;[17] though not before hundreds of genuine refugees had been prosecuted, convicted and imprisoned under this labyrinthine provision, only to later have their convictions quashed, following considerable physical and emotional expense.[18]

My own view is that the continued layering of new complexity on old has, along with increased costs and reduced remedies, come to be opportunistically embraced as a way of meeting the net migration target. While overall immigration policy was driven by this target, it was actually seen as undesirable for migrants to be able to understand and therefore abide by immigration law. If they could not apply in the first place, or if they made simple mistakes leading to rejected applications, that only served to keep the numbers down. Even once within the UK, the intricacy, cost and sheer impenetrability of the system forces some migrants and their families to the margins and out of the net migration figures, a process fellow immigration lawyer Jo Renshaw has described as being 'administrated into illegality'.[19] The opacity of the rules served as a useful smokescreen, obscuring the road to a successful application, and as a financial filter against incoming migrants, as it was only those who could afford a good lawyer who could successfully navigate the rules.

When I started out as an immigration lawyer at the turn of the millennium, making a spouse visa or a work permit application was relatively straightforward, and it was even possible for members of the public to do this themselves. It was like using an accountant to file a tax return: optional for most people, although those with spare cash might prefer to pay a professional to do it. Since then, the Immigration Rules have become so complex that it is now virtually impossible to succeed in making an application without a lawyer.

CHAPTER 5

FAMILIES AND FRIENDS: YOU CANNOT HUG SKYPE

Kylie and Ryan have been married for nearly ten years and have three children together. The last time I spoke to them, Flynn was six, Foster was three and Donovan was eleven months old. Kylie is a British citizen, Ryan is a citizen of the United States and the children are citizens of both countries. Kylie lives with the children in Omagh in Northern Ireland. She and Ryan had lived together for nearly ten years in the US, after meeting at a hostel in Ocean Beach, San Diego when Kylie was travelling. When they decided to move to the United Kingdom, they had thought it would be straightforward for a genuine couple with children, like them, to live together. But they were wrong. Ryan is still in Wisconsin and at the time of writing they had been involuntarily separated for just over a year. They have no idea how they will be able to live together as a family in the future and their upcoming ten-year wedding anniversary will be spent apart. As things stand, the children will grow up knowing their father only as a face on a screen.

When new rules on family immigration were introduced in 2012, the Home Office estimated that there could be as many as 140,000 families affected in this way by 2020.[1] But the government went ahead anyway. If a family member could be prevented from coming to the

UK, then this was a contribution towards meeting the net migration target. If a British citizen was forced out of Britain, all the better, as this was an even greater contribution towards the net migration target, given that net migration counts both immigration and emigration. As we will see, separated families and exiled British children are not some sort of accidental by-product of the policy; they *are* the policy. Breaking families or forcing them abroad is exactly what policy success looks like under the net migration target.

THE PRICE OF LOVE

The reforms to family immigration routes introduced by Theresa May in 2012 have exiled or separated thousands of British families in which one partner has the lack of foresight to be a foreign national. The key reform was a massive increase to the minimum income that a British citizen needs to earn in order to sponsor a foreign spouse. Previously, the level had been set at around £5,500 per year, not including highly variable accommodation costs. It was more than trebled to £18,600 in 2012 and the money now has to be earned for a minimum period of six months before an application can be made. If you are fortunate to have significant savings, you can instead rely on those, but you have to demonstrate a bank balance of as much as £62,500 held in cash for a period of at least six months; this is completely unattainable for most British citizens with a low income.[2] On top of that, the reforms stated that the period before a spouse or partner can qualify for settlement was increased from two to five years; the language requirements were toughened up; the cost of visa applications more than doubled; and devilishly complex new rules were introduced that virtually forced applicants to hire expensive immigration lawyers.

A salary of £18,600 is a lot of money, particularly if you are young or female or a carer or work part-time or live outside London and the south-east or are from an ethnic minority. Or if you are two or more of these things. On average, all these groups are likely to earn lower incomes. The figure is also considerably higher than the national minimum wage, which at the time of writing worked out at about £17,000 per year for those fortunate enough to receive holiday pay. The past or potential future earnings of the foreign partner themselves do not count towards meeting the total unless he or she is already living and working in the UK. Overall, around 40 per cent of British citizens working full- or part-time do not earn enough to be able to sponsor a foreign partner.[3] And all this has consequences.

In 2015, the Children's Commissioner estimated that there were, after only three years of the new system, already as many as 15,000 children growing up in 'Skype families', where one of the parents was ineligible to live in the UK and instead had to stay in touch via Skype or similar technology.[4] The number can only have grown since then and a simple extrapolation of the Children's Commissioner estimate would suggest around 40,000 children affected by 2020. The Home Office's own advance prediction of the number of couples affected was in the range of 108,000 to 142,000 by 2020.[5] And in 2018, the expert number-crunchers at Oxford University's Migration Observatory looked at whether it was possible to calculate the number of affected families, concluding that it was likely to be 'in the tens of thousands'.[6]

Imagine you are British and, like any number of people, you met your partner at a university or college in the UK, where they were attending as a foreign student. Or maybe you just met socially in Britain, when he or she was on a short-term work visa. Or perhaps you met abroad when you were travelling or working in another country. If you have any children together, they will automatically be British whether they are born in the UK or abroad.[7] You would probably have realised that there might be rules that must be met in order for you to live together in the UK as a family, but you may well not have known the details. Then you find out about the £18,600 minimum income requirement. As a young person, it is hard to find a salary paying £18,600 outside of London. And if you are working a minimum-wage job, it does not matter how hard you work; it is likely that you will never be able to afford to live in your own country with your partner.

Returning to Kylie and Ryan, this is the situation they faced. Jobs earning £18,600 are hard to come by in Omagh, Northern Ireland, even if Kylie were somehow able to juggle full-time work with being a single mother to three young boys. She would probably need to work in Belfast, which would be a four-hour round commute. Moving to Belfast would be impractical, because who would look after the children during the working day if she moved away from the rest of her family? This also assumes that she would even be able to find a job paying sufficient wages in Belfast. Initially, Kylie's hope had been that Ryan could come to the UK on a visit visa to look after the children, allowing her to go to work so she could then sponsor him for a proper spouse visa. But Ryan was detained and turned around by immigration officials in Dublin when he flew in for a ten-day visit on his thirty-third birthday in 2019. Luckily, he and Kylie had planned to surprise the children, who knew nothing of the anguish their parents faced. To make matters worse, Kylie cannot return with the children to the United States because Ryan, who was discharged from military boot camp after injuring his ankle, now works in construction and does not earn enough to sponsor her for a green card. So, they live apart, the visa rules of both their countries meaning their children must grow up without one or other of their parents.

Like Kylie and Ryan, those affected by the 2012 rules either have to live abroad, if another country will accept them and they can make a living there, or else separate and face trying to keep in touch at a distance. There is no exception for Brits returning with family members from work abroad, as many have found to their surprise and cost.

For example, meet Stuart, another Brit, who qualified as a teacher in Scotland but moved abroad in search of opportunity and adventure. He undertook voluntary service overseas in Malaysia and worked in Kenya and the Middle East, amongst other places, before eventually arriving in Turkey. There, he was introduced by a colleague to Laila, who worked in the textiles industry buying for British companies like Marks & Spencer, Debenhams and Selfridges. She spoke good English, had studied in London herself and worked with lots of British businesspeople. They married and had two children together: Barry, now aged nineteen, and Lara, now aged twelve. Getting tired of increasingly overcrowded Istanbul many years later, worried by the political situation in the country and mindful of the desirability of a British education for their British citizen children, they decided it was time to move to the UK. Stuart went first, finding a house to buy on the west coast of Scotland and a teaching job. It paid more than the minimum required, and when I spoke to him he said he had thought it would be simple to get the visa for Laila. She discovered otherwise. As it is necessary to hold such a salary for half a year before sponsorship, the couple had to spend six months apart before they could even apply, otherwise the Home Office would not accept

Stuart's income as valid. Visa officials then sat on the application for a further three months before granting it. Laila felt humiliated, her friends and family assuming that Stuart had abandoned her and the children. All that time, Stuart was separated from Laila and their children, and the family had to bear the expense of running two households.

That was back in 2017, and Laila's extension application was approaching when I spoke to the couple in 2019. The minimum income rule applies not just to the initial visa application but also to the extension that must be made after two and a half years, as well as the settlement application at the end of five years. With Stuart and Laila both having lost their jobs in the meantime, it was going to be difficult, perhaps impossible, to qualify. They had money in the bank and some pension funds from their jobs in Turkey, but it would be necessary to call on the generosity of friends and family to get them over the line.

Another couple I spoke to when researching this book were also dreading their coming extension application. Caroline and Carlos met in Ecuador in 2015. They married over there and when Caroline, who is British, fell pregnant, she moved back to the UK to work, build up some savings and give birth. She thought her stay would be temporary and she would head back out to Ecuador soon afterwards. Carlos, for his part, comes from a well-off family, had studied in both the UK and the USA, has a degree and would easily be able to support the family. Yet still, it all started to fall apart after Thomas was born. Suffering from what she now realises was postnatal depression, Caroline found that she did not want to leave the UK. Carlos had come over on a visit visa for the birth and eventually they decided to apply for him to stay. With Carlos not allowed to work, no money between them and facing huge application fees and lawyer costs, they ended up living off credit cards in a caravan in a friend's garden. To make things worse, their application was initially refused by the Home Office, before their appeal was eventually allowed no less than another year later, after a thirty-minute hearing. That was two and a half years ago. Although Caroline was now back on her feet and working as a freelance television producer when I spoke to her, she still felt a constant sense of anxious dread at the prospect of having to go through it all over again every two and a half years until Carlos could finally apply for settlement ten years later.

Where a couple are separated by these ruthless rules, you might hope that they at least could visit one another. But Carlos was very fortunate indeed to get his visit visa. Normally, UK visit visa applications by the foreign partner of a British citizen to join them in the UK are refused, often because officials assume that the partner will then break the rules and refuse to leave at the end of the visit. Indeed, this is what happened when Ryan tried to visit Kylie; he was interviewed by immigration officers and they refused him entry, detained him overnight and put him on a plane back to the United States the next morning. Any face-to-face visits in such cases would need to be conducted abroad, not in the UK. That is a challenge, given the British citizen might well only have limited holidays and needs to earn not spend money to meet the minimum income requirements.

Where a family does apply and is turned down, it is typical for civil servants to note in the refusal letter that family life can be maintained via magical 'modern means of communication'. It is a phrase familiar to all immigration lawyers and judges and it is universally considered to be a joke in very poor taste. It may be that the civil servants who use the copy-and-pasted phrase in their refusals really believe what they say. Maybe they think that a toddler and their father can meaningfully engage on Skype, tell each other about how their day has been and tenderly articulate their love for one another. More likely, it is a fig leaf for a refusal that everyone knows will split the family apart. It is a lie that officials use to insulate themselves from the real-world impact of the rules they must enforce as part of their job. As one family law judge noted, rather more realistically, 'You can't hug Skype.'[8]

The Home Office will say that affected families are not 'forced' apart because they can always go and live in another country. First-ly, that is not necessarily the case. This assumes that the unspecified 'other country' will have rules more generous than the UK's, and that the family will qualify to live there. As Kylie and Ryan have found in their experience with the US green card system, this is by no means always the case. Secondly, it seems very strange public policy to force families abroad as the cost of their staying together. Any children will automatically be British and have an absolute right to enter the UK later in life, despite having been raised and educated abroad. It is hardly a good way to integrate the next generation of British cit-izens. Such exile is also unlikely to be short-term, because it will be harder to find a high-paying job from abroad and, as we have already seen, many families *have* to split apart if returning from abroad. In order to move to the UK at the same time, the British sponsor would need to have been earning at least £18,600 for at least six months abroad and have a job offer for a future role in the UK paying at least that sum.

As with many immigration policies, one is left with the impression that short-term politics outweigh responsible government.

WHAT IS LOVE?

The minimum income requirement is the most controversial of the requirements for a spouse or partner visa, but it is far from being the only requirement. If the couple are not in a formal marriage or civil partnership, they will need to prove that they have lived together for two years or more. The other criteria include that both partners are over the age of eighteen; that the couple are not 'within the prohibited degree of relationship' as the rules put it; that any previous marriage or civil partnership has been formally dissolved and the relationship is not a polygamous one; that the applicant passes the English language test and that the relationship is a genuine one. In fact, it has to be 'genuine and subsisting', each member of the couple must have 'an intention to live permanently with the other' and they must have met in person. These rules are set out in the rather Jane Austen-esque 'eligibility' and 'suitability' sections of the Immigration Rules. These are rules concerning the nature and quality of a relationship.

How do you prove to an official in a tower block in Croydon who you will never meet that your relationship is a genuine one? And what is a 'genuine and subsisting' relationship, anyway? Is it one founded on the Western notion of romantic love? Or are arranged marriages allowed? What about relationships formalised because the couple need a visa in order to live together? Or a relationship where one of the parties hopes to gain something, like money, status or a visa? Appendix FM-SE of the rules sets out precise documentary requirements for every permissible source of income. Other than requiring a formal marriage or civil partnership certificate in spouse applications, it is, however, silent on how to prove a relationship genuine.

There is guidance available to Home Office staff about what to look for and what documents to expect, but even if a person thinks to look for such guidance, it is virtually impossible to find on the gov.uk website unless you know *where* to look.[9] Thus, a couple who want to apply for a visa are basically left clueless as to what evidence might make or break their case. Unless they use a lawyer, of course, but that costs yet more money. The idea seems to be that a 'genuine' couple will not need help or guidance to prove their case. But the reality is that plenty of these 'genuine' couples naively believe that officials will not assume they are lying from the get-go. They do not understand the culture of disbelief and the pressure officials are under to refuse applications. This is an understandable but potentially very costly mistake to make.

The well-hidden guidance referred to above tells those of us in the know about the approach the Home Office will follow when determining whether or not a couple is 'genuine'. It starts well, by stating the assessment 'is not a checklist or tick-box exercise'. However, it then nevertheless sets out a checklist of six things that might count in a couple's favour – and twenty-two things that might count against them. Being in a modern, secular relationship really helps, as does the length of relationship, cohabitation, having children together, sharing a mortgage, visiting each other's home countries and being able to produce documentary evidence to prove all these things. No doubt they are all positive considerations, but what about a religious couple who did not live together before marriage? Or a couple in an arranged marriage? These relationships are to be subject to 'additional scrutiny', according to the guidance.

Even these checklists of factors only tell part of the story. What documents might a couple submit for inspection by an official to actually prove cohabitation or that a relationship is 'genuine and sub-sisting', for example? Where the couple have actually lived together it should be fairly straightforward to prove cohabitation, assuming that they both ended up with their names on utility bills, bank statements and the like. Sometimes one of the partners runs the 'life admin' and only their name appears on official documents, which can be a real problem. Proving the *quality* of relationship is far harder still. Law-yers advise sending in photographs taken together on family holi-days and at social occasions, printed copies of WhatsApp, Skype or text message communications, statements from the couple and from family and friends and even receipts or travel tickets in their names, putting them together in the same place at the same time.

Where the migrant spouse or partner has a poor immigration history, refusal is virtually guaranteed no matter what evidence is submitted. This might happen where, for example, the migrant has overstayed a visa, then popped up again later to apply to stay as a partner, or even where he or she followed the rules by leaving the country to re-apply for entry. Some might say it is fair enough that a migrant is refused future entry in these circumstances; but this knee-jerk response ignores the impact on the British partner and any children. The decision letter will argue that photographs can be faked, that statements and letters of support are lies, that commu-nications are self-generated and that travel to each other's countries does not mean that the couple were visiting each other. The subtext is often that the migrant spouse or partner is simply after a visa, not a relationship, and that the British-based spouse or partner, often a woman, is a naive innocent who has been duped and needs to be protected from the predatory foreign male by vigilant immigration officials. Sometimes both parties are accused of being in on the deception, in which case the Home Office and politicians label it a sham marriage.

Immigration rules specifically aimed at 'marriages of convenience' date back to 1977 and marriage registrars have been obliged to report suspected sham marriages since the Immigration and Asylum Act 1999.[10] The Immigration Act 2014 went further still by introducing a new mechanism for the Home Office to object to a marriage. The department estimated at the time that there were as many as 4,000 to 10,000 such sham marriages every year.[11] The evidence basis for this surprising assertion was simply non-existent, though. At around the same time, then immigration minister James Brokenshire stated that the Home Office had intervened in 1,300 sham marriages the previous year. It later transpired these were not *proven* sham marriages, but were simply cases where the Home Office had, rightly or wrong, intervened. And, unfortunately, immigration enforcement teams crashed a lot of perfectly genuine weddings. In reality, only a handful of prosecutions and convictions occur every year.

As a result of these new investigation powers – which inconvenienced everyone getting married to some extent by imposing additional checks and extending the notice period, and led to a lot of ruined wedding days for innocent migrants and their British or EEA citizen spouses – the Home Office also created a great deal more work for itself. Civil servants had estimated that 35,000 marriages per year would be referred to the Home Office for consideration and 6,000 actual investigations would follow per year.[12] However, actual referrals and investigations turned out to be much, much higher. Around 50,000 referrals per year were being made by 2016, around 12,000 of which were delayed by seventy days for Home Office investigation.[13] We have no idea how much all this extra work cost the registrars or the

Home Office. The declared purpose of the new system and the reason for these costs was detecting and preventing sham marriages, but, again, we have no idea how many more, if any, real sham marriages have been detected as a result. One outcome was that it became harder for *all* migrants to get married in the United Kingdom; but whether this was an unfortunate side effect or formed part of the general deterrent approach to family migration we will probably never know.

Where a relationship is under suspicion, the couple may be summoned to an in-person interview if they are applying for a visa from within the UK. In comparison, applications made from abroad are often just immediately refused, with face-to-face interviews by officials virtually unheard of now. Where an interview does occur, the couple will be separated and quizzed simultaneously in different rooms and by different officials. Pre-arranged questions will be asked about the couple's morning routine, the layout or furnishings of the bedroom at home, recent social activities, their various relatives and their career history. It is a po-faced, existential version of the old *Mr and Mrs* game show, but where the ultimate prize for correct answers is the chance to live together in the United Kingdom, and incorrect answers lead to deportation. The slightest variation in a couple's answers is pounced upon as material to justify a refusal, as is failure to know obscure details of the partner's extended family or educational qualifications. The fact, so widely known that a game show was built on the premise, that many entirely genuine couples also give incorrect replies to such questions is irrelevant; these are exercises in finding excuses for refusal.

A couple under this degree of suspicion will be unable to live together in the UK and will either have to give up on the relationship or move abroad.

CHILDREN

If you are a parent, you are unlikely to want to voluntarily separate yourself from your children. For a country to succeed in attracting migrants like mature students and skilled workers, therefore, that country also needs to allow those migrants to bring their families with them. However, as we have seen with spouses and partners, every child permitted to enter the country is another person tipping the net migration scales further away from the target. The hostility of British politicians to migrant children is not new, though; the difficulties of bringing children to the United Kingdom pre-date the net migration target by over half a century. The current rules are outdated, they fail to put the best interests of children first, they unnecessarily separate children from their parents and they urgently need reform. Yet, while keeping migrants out continues to be the driving force of immigration policy, there is no incentive for the government to make any changes; the current rules are quite effective in keeping the numbers down, and not just the numbers of children. After all, the more children are denied entry, the more adult migrants will be encouraged to stay away too.

The basic approach followed by the UK rules is that, where one parent comes to the UK and the other remains alive and abroad, a non-British child will usually have to stay abroad. It does not matter if the parents agree that the child should relocate to the UK, or even whether the relocating parent has legal custody of the child; as far as the Home Office is concerned, it is not up to the parents.

There are only two exceptions. The first is called the 'sole responsibility' rule. Home Office guidance to officials defines this as meaning, 'One parent has abdicated or abandoned parental responsibility, and the remaining parent is exercising sole control in setting and

providing the day-to-day direction for the child's welfare.' Any decisions about the child's upbringing must have been made under the
sole direction of the applying parent 'without the input of the other
parent or any other person'.[14] Where parents have split up and the
parent remaining abroad has any level of involvement in the child's
upbringing at all, this makes it impossible for the child to accompany
a parent relocating to the UK, even where that parent has sole legal
custody and provides most or even all of the financial support for the
child. If the parent remaining abroad is making maintenance payments but is unable or unwilling to look after the child, that is insufficient as far as the Home Office is concerned. Even where the parent
abroad has entirely vanished, the rule remains very hard to meet
when the active parent travels to the UK alone and then applies for
the child to join him or her later. If a grandparent or relative provides
care while the parent is gone, this will often doom an application to
failure, irrespective of what the child or the parent thinks, because
the Home Office will argue the parent is not solely responsible.

The second exemption is where there are 'serious and compelling
family or other considerations which make exclusion of the child
undesirable and suitable arrangements have been made for the
child's care'. This test is even more vague than the first. Home Office
guidance to officials is not much help either, but it does say that the
'circumstances surrounding the child must be exceptional in relation
to those of other children living in that country'.[15] Whatever that
means, it is clearly not an easy test to meet.

When Amber Murray, an American citizen, was appointed assis-
tant professor in Geography at Oxford University in 2018, she was
reported to be 'ecstatic'. She has two daughters, aged four and nine,
with her Cameroonian husband. Murray came to the UK ahead of

her family to set up their home, but her application for her daughters was refused on the basis that they could stay with their father in Cameroon. The fact that the parents agreed in writing that the children should live with their mother was irrelevant to the visa officials deciding the application.[16] The case of Dr Wesam Hassan was even worse. An Egyptian doctor starting a PhD at Oxford University, she had a nine-year-old son with her husband; he worked as a humanitarian coordinator for the UN in Yemen. However, Yemen was designated a 'non-family station' because of the conflict there, so no rational person could suggest the boy should live there with his father. Nevertheless, the application was refused.[17]

These cases are the tip of the iceberg and were only reported by journalists because of their post-Windrush new-found interest in immigration stories, and because those concerned fit the narrative of being 'good migrants'. My colleagues and I deal with refusals like these day in, day out. Personally, I have lost count of the number of cases I have worked on where children were refused entry despite it being obviously in the child's best interests to join their parent in the UK.

This wilful blindness to the welfare of children reflects a wider malaise at the Home Office. Officials are legally obliged, by Section 55 of the Borders, Citizenship and Immigration Act 2009, to consider the best interests of children within the United Kingdom. For the duty to protect and promote the best interests of children to really mean anything, officials would need to be able to exercise positive discretion based on individual assessments and move beyond the outcomes dictated by the unseeing rules. The reality is that the duty is routinely ignored. Refusal letters will sometimes pay lip service to the obligation, and Home Office policies do refer to it, but decisions rarely if ever turn on what would be best for the affected children.

In an inspection of Home Office treatment of child refugees in 2018, for example, inspectors looked at a sample of refusal letters. The inspectors found that these letters 'simply stated that it was in the child's best interests "to be reintegrated" into their own country'. It was noted that this appeared to be a 'formula' that was 'drawn from a template'. In one of the twelve cases checked, the relevant paragraph was clearly a 'cut and paste' from another decision because it referred to the wrong country of origin.[18] And this was not just a matter of form over substance. Of the twelve children concerned in these cases, none were recognised as a refugee by the Home Office, but nine had lodged appeals, six of which had been allowed by the time of the inspection report. One of the remaining three had been dismissed and two remained outstanding. The error rate in initial decision-making on child refugees was essentially 50 per cent, then. To put this into perspective, officials would get decisions right just as often if they randomly sorted cases into two different piles and designated one of them the 'grant' pile for no other reason that they preferred the look of it.

The failure to consider seriously the impact of immigration decisions on children is not limited to asylum casework. We have already looked at the impact of the 2012 Immigration Rules on families, where Skype families now exist because officials have repeatedly not considered the impact of their decisions on children. In these cases, the rules on money and income would seem to trump everything else. An inspection on decision-making under the family rules revealed that not one of a sample of thirty-seven applications for entry involving a child even referred once to the best interests of that child.[19] The same inspection found that caseworkers had given specific consideration to the impact of refusal on the affected child in only one amongst a sample of twenty-one relevant refusals of further leave or settlement.

In another examination of children's citizenship applications, inspectors found that, in the twenty-eight refusal decisions made on the basis the child was not of sufficiently 'good character' (see Chapter 12) between July 2017 and August 2018, only two made reference to the best interests of the child concerned.[20] Decisions to detain migrants who are parents are also often made without any reference to the best interests of affected children, leading in one example to a child nearly being adopted and an award of £50,000 compensation.[21] Unsurprisingly given all of this, when the Children's Commissioner for England and Wales reported in 2017 on the welfare of children subject to immigration control, she discovered that most found the immigration system 'adversarial, confusing and stressful', and their treatment at its hands 'dehumanising and disrespectful'.[22]

The effect of an immigration decision on a child can be life-changing, yet for Home Office officials this is barely even an afterthought.

PARENTS AND GRANDPARENTS

The introduction of the minimum income requirement was not the only reform to the family immigration rules in 2012. Arguably the cruellest change was an alteration to the rules governing the entry of elderly parents, though in the sanitised and bureaucratic language of the Home Office, they are known as 'Adult Dependent Relatives'. In effect, the changes to the rules made it all but impossible for elderly relatives to enter the UK. The year before the rules were changed, over 4,000 applications were made and 2,300 visas were issued under this route. These numbers were not particularly large. However, the year after the change, only 723 applications were made and just thirty-seven visas were issued. Those numbers were tiny.[23]

Those of us who are fortunate enough to have our parents live to a ripe old age will eventually need to look after them, as they once looked after us. Some dread the prospect, and no one claims that it is easy, but most accept that it is part of the cycle of life and are committed to doing the best job they can. Some, the so-called sandwich generation, will need to juggle care responsibilities for children as well as parents, and most will need to carry on working.

Carmen came to live in the UK in 2007 and became a full British citizen. Her mother, though, still lived alone in South Africa. Carmen watched with growing alarm and sadness as her mother's health deteriorated, developing a degenerative back disease, osteoarthritis and fibromyalgia. By 2013, Carmen's mother could barely bend down or lift objects, was unable to stand or walk for long periods, suffered constant pain and disrupted sleep and struggled to cook, clean or look after herself. She was also suffering from depression and anxiety. Carmen investigated how she could bring her mother to the UK to live with her so that she could properly look after her, but quickly found that the rules had changed in 2012 to make it virtually impossible for her mother to get a visa. Carmen would need to prove that her mother required 'long-term personal care to perform everyday tasks' because of 'age, illness or disability'; that, even with Carmen's assistance to find it, there was no adequate care available in the whole of South Africa; or that such care was unaffordable.[24] The problem was that Carmen had a good job as an accountant in the UK, so could not claim that care was unaffordable. For he mother to obtain the visa, Carmen would somehow have to show that adequate care could not be provided anywhere in the whole of South Africa, for example through a care home or by paying a carer or team of carers privately. To do so would be to prove a negative, which any logistician will tell you is impossible.

Carmen was able to find a good team of lawyers, who will have advised her that it would be expensive to apply and that even if she did the chances of success were low. She decided to go ahead anyway; the application was refused. The Home Office rejection letter said she could not prove that care was not available in South Africa and that Carmen could leave the UK to look after her mother. The first judge to hear the appeal agreed with Carmen and overturned the decision but the Home Office then appealed. The second judge sided with the Home Office. In turn, Carmen appealed to the next highest court: the Court of Appeal. It is in the Court of Appeal's judgment that we can read all about the case.[25] Carmen's appeal ultimately failed, leaving her to face the choice of going back to South Africa to look after her ailing mother or leaving her mother in the hands of private carers.

This is the cruel choice that many have been forced to make since the new rules were introduced in 2012. For partners, children and parents alike, refusing entry to one person, family member or not, is a contribution towards meeting the net migration target. Forcing their British or settled family member to leave is even better.

The standards applied by Home Office civil servants often lead to monstrous decisions. In another case I dealt with myself, the parent of a settled migrant had visited the UK repeatedly over the years but had not done so for some time. Her son knew that she was getting forgetful, but when she arrived, he realised that she was suffering from dementia and that it was growing rapidly worse. With several family members providing an admirable 24/7 regime of care in the UK, he assumed that the Home Office would see sense and allow her to live out her few remaining days with them in comfort and security. Not so. The application was refused, and it took an appeal to get the decision overturned. Another case I dealt with involved an autistic child applying to join her mother in the UK under the same set of rules that applies to parents. Again, the Home Office refused the application and it took an appeal for the decision to be reversed.

There is an unofficial presumption of refusal in family immigration cases and it leads to inhumane decisions. Each refusal is a contribution towards meeting the net migration target, though, and there is no sanction against those who make these cruel decisions when they are shown to be unlawful and are overturned on appeal.

FAMILY VISITS

If you migrate from one country to another, you leave many family members behind. You will also usually want your new family to stay in touch with your old family. Such links are important to many people in many cultures and are a way of reminding the next generation of their background and heritage. And the only real way for this education to happen is through face-to-face visits. You visit them, and they visit you. Such trips are particularly important for the key milestones in life, like births, graduations, marriages and funerals.

To come to the UK for a holiday from a country where low incomes are widespread and the population is mainly racialised, first you must apply for a visit visa. Without that visa, you will be refused boarding on the airplane in the first place, as otherwise the airline that allowed you to board will be fined £2,000. Visitors from rich, predominantly non-racialised countries do not require a visa before boarding; they can ask for the visa when they arrive at passport control. Around 150 million passengers travel through British ports and airports every year – a number that includes British citizens coming and going. This is a staggering volume of people for the immigration authorities to manage and it is one that increases year-on-year as more and more people travel around the world. Around 2.4 million of these passengers travel on a visit visa, the majority of which are intended for tourists who do not have a family link to the UK. Comparatively, only around 300,000 to 400,000 visas are issued specifically for the purpose of visiting family members.[26]

Where one of these family visit visas is refused, it will always be disappointing. A father might be unable to attend his son's graduation, for example. A mother may not be present to help her daughter after the birth of her first child. An older brother may miss the funeral of a younger sister. A bride and groom may find that key family members are for ever absent from their wedding-day photographs.

To be fair, it is hard for immigration officials to get decisions right. They have a matter of minutes to look at an application and either grant or refuse. Does the person have a 'good' reason for visiting the UK? Are the documents forged? Have they got a job or family to return to? An unknown number of people come to the UK each year as visitors and then overstay their visas, failing to return home by the time it expires. Immigration officials assume that migrants from poor countries and those who are themselves poor, or those who are young and mobile or who lack 'family ties', are more likely to break the rules than established travellers with a history of complying with the rules in the past. The problem is that everyone starts out young and it is difficult to become an established traveller if you get refused a visa every time you try.

Since 2015 the Home Office has been using what it calls a 'streaming tool' to automate the risk analysis of visa applications, classifying them in a traffic light system as red, amber or green. An official still reviews all the applications but will apply differing levels of scrutiny according to the given colour. And it has an impact: less than 4 per cent of 'green' applications are refused compared to over 50 per cent of 'red' applications. But, as the chief inspector of borders and immigration has warned, there is a risk that the streaming tool leads to 'confirmation bias' on the part of officials, who might tend unconsciously to disregard any evidence that contradicts the streaming rating, and attach more weight to evidence that supports it. In effect, it becomes the 'de facto decision-making tool'.[27]

Campaigners have asked the Home Office what information, evidence or other factors are taken into account by the algorithm behind the 'streaming tool' but the government has refused to say.[28] The suspicion is that certain groups of people are disadvantaged based on generic markers such as age, nationality or whether they have travelled before. Another word for this approach, though, is 'discrimination'. There is certainly evidence of different standards being applied. We might expect the refusal rate to be higher for countries with a lower GDP, whose citizens therefore have a greater incentive to break immigration laws after entry. However, we would also hope that the same standards of decision-making would apply no matter what country or region a person comes from. The chief inspector of borders and immigration found that while in 32 per cent of cases globally officials were failing properly to consider the evidence, that figure rose to 37 per cent for applications from Africa and to 50 per cent for applications from the Gulf, Iran and Pakistan.[29] There can be no conceivable excuse for this.

This is why appeals matter. An appeal to an independent judge makes officials accountable and allows UK family members to attend court in an attempt to persuade the judge that the visit is genuine. Yet such appeals were abolished in 1993, and at the time a young shadow Home Secretary said this:

When a right of appeal is removed, what is removed is a valuable and necessary constraint on those who exercise original jurisdiction.

That is true not merely of immigration officers but of anybody. The immigration officer who knows that his decision may be subject to appeal is likely to be a good deal more circumspect, careful and even handed that the officer who knows that his power of decision is absolute. That is simply, I fear, a matter of human nature, quite apart from anything else.[30]

The speaker's name was Tony Blair and the right of appeal was duly restored by the New Labour government in 2000. The success rate for family visit appeals fluctuated over the following years, but in 2010 it was as high as 45 per cent.[31] The right of appeal was nevertheless abolished again, this time by Theresa May in 2013. Since then, there has been no proper accountability for immigration officials and the refusal rate is thought to have crept upwards.[32] An unknown number of wedding guests, mourners, proud parents and grandparents have wrongly been refused entry with no right of appeal. And once their passport is marked with a visa refusal, the chances of a future visa application being approved falls dramatically. In effect, a refusal of a visit visa is often a permanent bar on entry.

FRIENDSHIPS AND PRIVATE LIFE

It will come as no surprise that a government that attaches so little value to family life attaches even less weight to friendships and other community ties. In parallel to the reform of the family rules in 2012, the rules on other ties to the United Kingdom were also toughened up. This was presented at the time as targeting foreign criminals, who were supposedly abusing Article Eight of the European Convention on Human Rights to remain in the UK on the most tenuous of grounds. This right protects a person's private and family life, but it is what is called a qualified right, meaning that it is not absolute and has to be balanced against other considerations. As we will see in Chapter 10, a notorious cat story that came to symbolise this supposed abuse of rights was in fact untrue. Migrants with deep-rooted ties to the United Kingdom have been caught up in the reforms and even those born in the United Kingdom or brought here as children find they do not qualify. Decisions in this field of work can seem very harsh indeed, with people who are British in the eyes of everyone except the law finding they have to leave everything they know behind and build a new life for themselves in a foreign country they barely recognise.

There are five main private life routes set out in the rules, based on ties to the UK. The first is the ten-year route to permanent settlement, which requires ten continuous years of lawful residence. Any gaps between visas, for example those caused by a slightly late visa renewal application that is subsequently granted, will be pounced on by officials to justify refusal. The second is the thirty-year route, which is the only route to becoming permanently settled if so much as one single day of a person's stay has been unlawful. On this route, the person is eligible to apply for temporary status after twenty years, and that status then has to be renewed every two and a half years for a further ten years until the person can finally apply for permanent settlement. The qualifying period was fourteen years in total until 2012. Whether you overlook a visa extension deadline or you smuggle yourself into the country illegally and remain hidden for twenty years, you have been unlawfully resident for at least one day and therefore this is the route for you. The third option applies to children who have been resident in the UK for at least seven years and where the Home Office considers it unreasonable for the child to leave the country. The rub, however, is in the second leg of this test: officials almost always consider it reasonable for the child to leave, no matter how long the child has lived in the country. The fourth route is for young people between the ages of nineteen and twenty-five who have spent at least half of their life in the country. A young person aged twenty-four who was brought to the United Kingdom at thirteen and was schooled and brought up in the UK, all of whose friends are here and who has little memory of her country of nationality, will be refused because the maths says that just over half of her life has been spent abroad. The fifth and final route is for any migrant over the age of eighteen where there are 'significant obstacles to the applicant's integration into the country to which he would have to go if required to leave'. This test is interpreted by immigration officials as insurmountable for the applicant.

In one of my cases, for example, a 44-year-old Lebanese man with Down's syndrome had lived happily in the United Kingdom for seventeen years, cared for and supported by his brothers, who unlike him had lawful status. His parents in Lebanon had died in the meantime. Despite the obvious difficulties someone with Down's syndrome would face living independently in what had become to him an unknown country, the Home Office refused his application to remain. Instead, he could reintegrate in Lebanon, they said, with his brothers sending him money from the UK.[33] In common with the many other cases attracting negative publicity, the Home Office eventually reversed the decision; but only because of the publicity.

The cost of the applications is huge. For some it is simply unattainable. And as we saw in the previous chapter, for those who do somehow find the money, it can still be financially and emotionally crippling.

SIDESTEPPING THE RULES

These inflexible rules on family and community ties were originally introduced in order to relieve officials of the moral dilemmas immigration cases invariably involve. It is one thing for a politician to say that it is in the public interest for immigration to be lower, or that economic considerations should trump moral or social ones. It is quite another for an official to try to balance these abstract concepts against the very real and immediate impact that their decision has on the life of a migrant and his or her family members. Ministers were unhappy with the outcome of individual balancing exercises undertaken by officials and judges – too many cases were succeeding in their view – and their response was to attempt to pseudo-automate the decision-making process through the reforms of 2012. In common with the changes to economic migration routes that we will turn to in Chapter 7, the effect of purging human discretion from migration decisions was also to eliminate common sense.

A telling anecdote emerged from the Conservative Party conference in 2019.[34] Former immigration minister Mark Harper recounted an example of a person abroad wanting to visit a dying relative in the UK. The case had been referred to him because, in his view, it was impossible for immigration officials to make judgement calls on supposedly complex cases like this. He instructed officials to grant the visa. But actually, it is perfectly possible for officials to make judgement calls; this was not really a complex case and, as the Institute for Government has observed, there is no other department in which the minister would be expected to make day-to-day caseworking decisions on, for example, whether to terminate a person's benefits.[35] It is illuminating that in cases like this one, which are referred to ministers due to media attention, the response is almost invariably to grant the requested visa. Faced with the real, human consequences of the rules they made, ministers often decline to follow them.

Theresa May was never explicit about what she expected those affected by the family immigration reforms of 2012 to do. Should they work harder or get higher-paying jobs in order to meet the rules? With 40 per cent of the working population ineligible to sponsor a spouse or partner from abroad, the rules of capitalism suggest this was never going to be possible for everyone. Blaming the poor for their own poverty has always been some people's response. Or should British citizens avoid falling in love with foreign nationals in the first place, or perhaps terminate such relationships before they become serious? This seems unrealistic at best. At worst, it looks like an attempt to preserve the existing ethnic composition of the population, at least amongst the poor. In any event, there were many family units already living together in 2012, who would inevitably be affected. Should they move abroad into exile? Forcing British citizens to leave their own country as the price of keeping their family together certainly seems harsh, and the impact on the affected British children even more so. Or should families just dissolve, forcing couples to split up and children be brought up by just one of their parents? Even the most ardent anti-immigration advocate would surely agree that this is an unacceptable outcome.

My experience of working with those affected by these harsh rules is that such families do not simply accept their own annihilation. They fight and they struggle to stay together. It is incredibly stressful, it can be very expensive and it is not guaranteed to succeed; those who do stay in the UK despite being unable to meet the rules always live in fear of final refusal and a dawn raid.

Some have tried to sidestep the rules. One path is to rely on the various 'exceptional circumstance' exemptions in the Immigration

Rules themselves. It was almost impossible to succeed on these very narrow grounds until the Supreme Court upheld the main rules in a case in 2017 but forced the Home Office to widen the exceptions.[36] Even now, though, if a couple is childless it remains virtually impossible to succeed, and even cases that do involve children are still refused.

Another route is to move to another European Union country with family members, live there a while and then return to the United Kingdom relying on family-friendly EU law rules. This is sometimes known as the Surinder Singh route, after a European Court of Justice case of that name from 1992.[37] The Home Office considers this a loophole and has repeatedly introduced new rules and regulations to prevent families making use of it. It has been the only way for some families to live together in the United Kingdom, but it will disappear, along with the other free movement rights of British citizens, at the end of the Brexit transition period when the UK finally leaves EU law behind.

The Conservative Party likes to present itself as the champion of communities and families. However, the rules introduced in 2012 tear both apart. Back in 2010, while still Leader of the Opposition, David Cameron said that he wanted his government to be 'the most family-friendly government we've ever had in this country and that is about everything we do to support families and it's about supporting every sort of family'.[38] But clearly he did not mean families that include a foreign national.

CHAPTER 6

ASYLUM: SANDBANKS AND CROCODILES

'The Secretary of State ... considered your account of crossing the Zaire River by canoe at night to be totally implausible. The Secretary of State is aware of the size, strength and considerable dangers posed by the river such as shifting sandbanks and crocodiles.'

So wrote an official at the Home Office in the early '90s, in an example cited by charity Asylum Aid in their report 'No Reason At All'.[1] That was in 1995, before the internet transformed the way we live, and the canoeist in question struggled to prove that the Secretary of State did not know what he was talking about. These days, a simple search on Google quickly reveals multiple pictures of people in canoes on the Zaire (or Congo) River. And there are no crocodiles in sight. From where had the official landed on the idea of the sandbanks and crocodiles? Were these hazards derived from an old geography textbook, a guidebook or perhaps from novelist Joseph Conrad? Or were they entirely imaginary, invented to justify a literally pre-judged refusal of asylum? There is something about the language and tone ('totally implausible ... considerable dangers') that suggests this was no *reason* for refusal, but rather an excuse.

One evening in 2012, I was called to a house in south London by members of a religious community who wanted me to advise one of their members. The community had been badly persecuted in their country of origin and the man claimed to have been shot in the head before managing to flee. It later turned out that the bullet was still lodged in his skull, and he had an X-ray to prove it. He was there that evening, walking and talking, and he showed me the X-ray himself. I am no doctor, but it looked a lot like an X-ray of a bullet in a skull to me. Obviously, he had been rather lucky to take a bullet to the head and survive, although it might also be said that, on a more fundamental level, he had been pretty unlucky to be shot at in the first place. He was due to have the bullet removed the next day at hospital and the following week he would be interviewed by the Home Office.

It might reasonably be thought that a man from a persecuted religious minority with an X-ray of an actual bullet in his head stood a pretty good chance of getting asylum. But it was my job to think like a Home Office civil servant so we could prepare the case as best we could. And all of the rest of us there that evening had seen apparently very strong cases refused.

To begin with, my client would need to show proof that he was a refugee, and to do that, he would have to pass two tests. The first is whether he is believed. Officials at the Home Office like to refer to this as being 'credible' rather than 'truthful', as it is much more acceptable to say a person is 'not credible' than to say they are a liar. When an asylum claim fails, this is almost always the reason why: because the asylum seeker is considered to be 'not credible'. Then, the second test my client would need to pass would be to show that he meets the legal definition of a refugee, as set out in the Refugee Convention. This definition requires that a person has a well-founded fear of being persecuted for reasons of race, religion, nationality, membership of a particular social group or political opinion, is outside their own country and would be unable to obtain protection within their country if they were to return.

The level of probability that a refugee needs to show of being persecuted is low, and this is the case for two reasons. Firstly, it has always been recognised that it is difficult for a refugee to prove his or her case; repressive regimes rarely document their own crimes or allow them to be documented by others. Even if there was some documentary proof you could have brought with you, if you were a refugee would you have thought to do so or would you just have fled when you had the chance? Secondly, the consequences of making a wrong decision are also recognised: these are life-and-death cases. The words 'being persecuted' have now acquired a particular legal meaning, but broadly they mean 'serious harm'. This might consist of serious one-off harm, like torture or rape. But lesser injury also qualifies if repeated over a long period. The persecution must also be experienced for one of the five reasons stated above, or else the person is not legally a refugee. For example, those fleeing drought or natural disaster might be referred to as refugees in news reports, but they are not technically refugees under the Refugee Convention.

Returning to my client in south London, the X-ray had no name on it and could have belonged to anyone; there was nothing concrete to link it to the man in front of me claiming it was of his. It seemed miraculous that he had survived; perhaps, I had to consider, too miraculous to be plausible to a civil servant. There was no proof that the man had been shot for the reasons he claimed, and he might have been shot by accident or because of a personal dispute with a neighbour or while carrying out a bank robbery. There were no press accounts of the event in question, while it might be expected that an attack of that nature would be reported. My client's problem could perhaps be interpreted as a localised one, and he might be expected to relocate elsewhere in the very populous country from which he came. Then, even if he was believed, the person who shot him was unknown, and as far as we knew not a state official; perhaps my client would be expected to seek protection from the authorities on his return. An official was likely to ask why he could not go to the police for protection in his own country rather than fleeing all the way to ours.

We talked through the additional evidence he might be able to obtain and what medical evidence we could request from the doctors. I questioned him about what had happened to see if it all made sense, to determine whether he sounded 'credible' and to assess him as a witness. How would he perform in a Home Office interview, a notoriously hit-and-miss and sometimes very confrontational environment, in which the interviewer may insist that the account is told in reverse, starting at the most recent event and working backwards from there?

Happily, he was granted asylum in the end. But what makes some officials so sceptical and even cynical about asylum seekers' stories?

THE CULTURE OF DISBELIEF

The advent of the internet has altered the way that asylum claims are decided – gone are the days of using *Lonely Planet* guides and dog-eared photocopies of old Amnesty International annual reports – but the fundamental scepticism of officials at the Home Office has changed little. In 1999, Asylum Aid published a follow-up to its previously mentioned report, entitled 'Still No Reason At All'. Amnesty International then issued 'Get it Right: How Home Office decision-making fails refugees' in 2004. The UN High Commission for Refugees has been working with the Home Office to improve the quality of decision-making since 2004, and in the Quality Integration Project First Report of 2010, for example, they criticised the 'poor assessment of credibility by Case Owners when establishing the material facts of an asylum claim'.[2]

Asylum Aid returned to the theme in 2011 with 'Unsustainable: the quality of initial decision-making in women's asylum claims'. The UK Lesbian and Gay Immigration Group also published 'Failing the Grade: Home Office initial decisions on lesbian and gay claims for asylum' in 2010 and followed up with 'Missing the Mark' in 2014. Medical charity Freedom from Torture for its part released 'Lessons Not Learned: The failures of asylum decision-making in the UK' in 2019. The fact that these reports continue to be published and continue to criticise what has become known as the Home Office's 'culture of disbelief' tells us that problems remain.

I was working as a legal adviser at the Oakington immigration detention centre near Cambridge in 2000 when one asylum seeker was told in his official Reasons For Refusal letter that his claim was, and I quote, 'a pile of pants'.[3] In another infamous example, a Home Office caseworker confused guerrillas with gorillas, earnestly writing, 'Information from the World Wide Fund for Nature confirms that guerrillas are not native to that part of the country and in any event there are few recorded incidents of primates attacking humans unless their natural habitat is disturbed or their young threatened.' This is an extreme, absurd example, but mistakes about countries, names and dates abound in these refusal letters. Meanwhile, and in spite of making such basic mistakes themselves, the letters continue to shamelessly seize upon the slightest of inaccuracies within migration applications.

In 2010, a whistleblower revealed that asylum officials in Cardiff were humiliating colleagues who granted asylum by placing a stuffed gorilla they called the 'grant monkey' on their desks.[4] Another official was reported to have boasted that he forced boys who said they had been forcibly conscripted as child soldiers to lie down on the floor and demonstrate how they shot at people in the bush. I have myself had conversations with Home Office staff who claim, with straight faces, that they can decide cases on instinct, as if asylum claims were some sort of movie poker game. One, who seemed to have quite an interest in firearms, would ask witnesses how to reload a Kalashnikov rifle. Another, who was gay, said they relied on their 'gaydar' when deciding how hard to fight cases based on sexuality. That this might be a problematic tactic when assessing people who came from completely different countries and cultures to her own did not seem to have occurred to her.

There are perhaps three interlocking influences on officials, aside from their own personal beliefs. The first is government policy, whether official or unofficial. Civil servants are supposed to implement the policies of the government of the day, after all. Official government policy is, and has been since the 1990s, that asylum claims are bad. In 1991, Home Secretary Kenneth Baker said that the number of asylum claims being made at that time 'cannot be sustained year after year'.[5] Then, in February 2003, Tony Blair stated that he would like to reduce the number of asylum claims by half. 'In the end,' he said, 'the only way of dealing with this is stop the numbers coming in.'[6] In 2015, Theresa May said, 'I want us to work to reduce the asylum claims made in Britain.'[7] Blair got his way, as the chart below shows, but numbers actually rose on May's watch, despite her best endeavours.

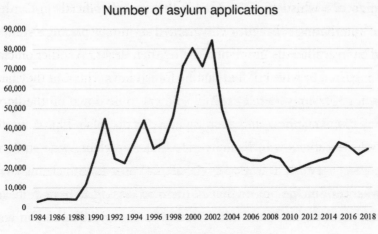

Number of asylum applications

Source: Migration Observatory.

The second influence is perceived public opinion, both indirectly through their political masters, who are particularly sensitive to public opinion, and because civil servants are themselves human beings who read newspapers, watch television and are part of the society in which we all live. In the early 2000s, for example, tabloids were inventing stories of asylum seekers eating swans and donkeys. 'SWAN BAKE: Asylum seekers steal the Queen's birds for barbecues' shouted the front page of *The Sun* on 4 July 2003. 'Asylum seekers eat our donkeys' added the *Daily Star*, not to be outdone, on 31 August of the same year. No doubt the journalists concerned thought these unsubstantiated headlines were a lark. Yet the media have since then constantly conflated asylum with crime, terrorism, illegality, fraud and worse.[8]

The third thing hovering over government officials is departmental culture. We have seen, in not just this chapter but throughout this whole book so far, that the Home Office has repeatedly been criticised by a range of external observers, including most recently

Wendy Williams in her 'Windrush Lessons Learned Review'. It has particularly been faulted for its defensive, inward-facing mentality and an institutional culture of disbelief. You might even say that they seem to be like Millwall football fans, singing their infamous chant: 'No one likes us, we don't care!'

Finally, distancing and even dehumanising refugees is a matter of self-preservation in this current climate. An academic study of the effects of asylum work on officials, lawyers, interpreters, charity workers and judges found that all these professionals pay a price for dealing day-in, day-out with such highly emotive accounts of fear, trauma, violence and persecution.[9] I have listened to clients describe horrific torture and seen their awful scars. I have heard detailed accounts of rape and violence. Clients have broken down in tears in front of me, both in court and outside, unable to continue. Others have described horrors dead-eyed and hollowed out. In this job, there is a high risk of 'vicarious trauma' and burn-out, leading to stress, depression and what the academics rather dispassionately call 'task inefficiency'.

Professionals thus quite understandably fall back on the emotional survival mechanisms of detachment and denial of responsibility, in order 'to protect themselves from the contagion of these emotions'. One Home Office official, who had spent years listening to and evaluating asylum seekers' accounts, told the academics, 'I don't think I've ever heard anything that's been harrowing, you know, that's distressed me in any way … I've never been personally bothered, I've never had a sleepless night about anything.' That level of detachment, disinterest and denial is genuinely astonishing, to me at least. It must surely be founded on a coping strategy of refusing to believe anything the refugees say. Indeed, another official explained their approach to getting the job done, telling the researchers, 'In your head, you have to go in thinking, "I don't really believe this story," because if you went in there believing that story, you couldn't really do your job.' The academics conducting the study found that it was common for officials (and judges) to refuse to engage with particularly traumatic incidents such as rape, and to avoid asking questions about them. Instead, decision-makers would focus on other, less unpalatable aspects of the case.

Other decision-makers showed signs of 'case hardening'; they were not just detached but actually started to regard the cases they encountered as routine and mundane. This led to an ever-escalating level of suffering for a story to break through these barriers and for the asylum seeker to win their case. Others avoided responsibility for their role by taking comfort in not being the final decision-maker, referring to the right of appeal to a judge and the low likelihood of an eventual forced removal, even if an appeal were to fail. One civil servant referred to the right of appeal as a 'nice comfort blanket' that cushions against the full weight of responsibility for making a decision.

Officials, lawyers and judges often take solace in being cogs in the larger machine of the justice system. The eventual outcomes are not considered to be the fault or responsibility of an individual professional, but rather the system as a whole. It is sometimes even argued that the machine is needed because there are fake refugees and they need to be identified and 'weeded out'. I have heard some say that this is required in order to do right by the genuine refugees, as if they benefit in some way by some claimants being refused. It is a false premise, though, and a transparently thin way of avoiding responsibility for deciding what may be life-or-death cases.

JUDGING LIFE-OR-DEATH CASES

None of this is to say that making decisions in asylum cases is easy. Some people coming to claim asylum probably do lie about what happened to them in the past. Some perhaps fabricate the whole story. Sometimes they are told what to say by a people smuggler. Other times they may pick up woefully misplaced ideas on the way to the UK, from within their community after arrival or at a notoriously gossipy detention centre, full of desperate people clutching at straws. Some might exaggerate or expand on what really happened to try to increase their chances of success and sometimes the events described just seem so unlikely that they might well sound made up. Sometimes asylum seekers say different things at different times, leading an observer to wonder which version is true, if any. I myself have been in a situation where a client has told me two different, seemingly inconsistent stories, and, when pressed, they asked me which I thought was better. I have also been told by a client, literally as I was about to step into court, that the documents he relied on were actually fakes.[10]

If you were genuinely in fear of your life and you found yourself in a mysterious country surrounded by strangers, is it possible you might lie, fake or exaggerate too, if you thought it might save you?

Rather unhelpfully for those trying to ascertain what really happened in the past, and then guess what might happen in the future, it is actually very hard for a person to accurately and reliably recall and describe the events in their life. Different experiences tend to blend together, the sequence becomes confused and it is hard or impossible to remember the specific day or date of a particular happening.

Lawyers and judges working in other areas of law know this very well. If you ask two genuine witnesses to a traffic accident what happened to whom, where and when, they will inevitably tell you different things. They are not lying; they just remember things differently, or different details seem more important to one than the other. As a fifteen-year-old work experience student at a local solicitors' firm in Northfield, Birmingham, I remember the principal asking a police witness what type of car was outside the shop at which a crime had allegedly taken place. I asked him afterwards why he was interested in the car, which seemed irrelevant. With the breezy, knowing air of a man dispensing questionable wisdom, he explained that no one remembers details like that, but the failure to answer the irrelevant question would then cast doubt on the rest of the witness's evidence. The effect of hostile questioning is much worse for victims of trauma, and genuine refugees are sometimes so damaged by the horrors they have experienced that they cannot string a comprehensible narrative together.

Asylum lawyers also know all of this well. We know that a client is unlikely to have perfect recall of the events about which they will be questioned, and we know that even if they can remember, they will be reluctant to disclose such horrible traumas, even to a sympathetic interviewer – which many are not. Good solicitors will spend many hours in multiple meetings with a client to try to piece together an account of what happened and when. The idea is that by answering questions, over time the client might, in a modern-day process of Socratic dialogue, eventually settle on what he or she considers, on reflection, to be a single version of the 'truth' of what happened. This will then be set out in black and white in a witness statement, at which point the ambiguity and uncertainty appears to the outside world to have fallen away. We lawyers know that this ends up producing an artificially certain, sanitised version of 'the truth', but we also know that failing to go through this process with a client is to consign that client to an inevitable refusal. The Home Office applies impossible standards in asylum cases, as the reports by Asylum Aid, Amnesty International and everyone else show, and the adversarial legal process does not allow any place for uncertainty.

Like those in the legal profession, psychologists are also very aware of the impact of trauma on memory. One of the main symptoms of post-traumatic stress disorder (PTSD) – indeed arguably one of its defining features – is an inability to recollect and describe key distressing events.[11] This is Psychology 101. Think about it for a moment: officials and judges expect genuine refugees to recount events accurately and consistently, and yet we also know that a truly traumatised individual will usually be unable to do just that. Returning to the traffic accident example, it is well known that the victim of an accident will often have no memory of the event itself. It is also, if you pause for a minute to think about it, really, really hard to tell a complete stranger about something that happened to you where you felt humiliated and vulnerable. Even if you can remember exactly what happened in detail, you might well be reluctant to tell an official about it in a formal interview room, through an interpreter, when you are meeting that person for the first time. On top of that, the official may not seem terribly friendly and you have good reason to be afraid of authority figures in your own country. Having sat in on, read the notes from and listened to the recordings of thousands of interview records, I can tell you that the tone of many asylum interviews is not what you might hope for in an ideal world.

Back in 2014, for example, I was increasingly horrified as I read through the notes of an interview that had taken place the year before. There had been no lawyer present. The questions were clearly intended to degrade, humiliate and intimidate and included the following:

How often did you have intercourse together?

Is that every day?

Did you put your penis into X's backside?

When X was penetrating you did you have an erection?

Did you ejaculate?

Did X ejaculate inside you?

Why did you use a condom?

How did you feel when having sex?

Did you have feelings for other boys?

Did you have physical relationships with other boys in [city]?

Did you love X?

When was his birthday?

Did you buy him presents?

Did he buy you presents?

How could you afford to buy him presents if you were studying?

In [city] did you have sex with other men?

What do you find attractive about men?

Tell me what you like about men that turns you on?

What is it about the way men walk that turns you on?

What is it about men's backsides that attracts you?[12]

I posted this and other extracts from the interview on my website and a journalist at *The Observer* got in touch. This was long before most journalists were actively looking for immigration stories and I had to send a photocopy of the interview notes before the editors would believe it was genuine. The following *Observer* story led to questions in Parliament and a fundamental review of the way the Home Office deals with asylum claims based on sexuality.[13]

The case was by no means an isolated one. In a study published in

2014, the UK Lesbian and Gay Immigration Group found that inappropriate questions had been asked in multiple cases. For instance, during one tribunal hearing, a Home Office official had asked a series of increasingly explicit questions 'of no probative value' that were bordering on the pornographic. The same study revealed that the questions asked in other cases included, 'Was it loving or rough sex?', 'What have you found is the most successful way of pulling men?', 'So you had intercourse with him and not just blow jobs?' and 'You have never had a relationship with a man. How do you know you are a lesbian?'[14] In another case of mine, at around the same time, I visited a client at a detention centre who was claiming asylum on the basis of his sexuality. His case was that he would be persecuted if his family and others found out that he was gay. However, the Home Office denied he was gay at all, citing a previous attempt at a sham marriage to a woman. The fact that his boyfriend was at court with us, and had brought with him a suitcase of printed-out, sometimes explicit social media messages and more, was insufficient to persuade the official to change the government position. Even several years later, when the same case was being re-heard after bouncing up and down the court system for years, another official took the same view. The same boyfriend was present again, and two suitcases were now available. Yet the judge was unimpressed and told us no further evidence was needed on this issue.

On the surface, at least, things have improved since 2014 – due largely to media pressure on this narrow issue of sexuality and asylum, rather than any innate desire at the Home Office to do better – but the success rate for asylum claims based on sexuality remains below the average success rate for asylum claims as a whole.

Other types of asylum claims are decided on the basis of absurd rather than perverse questions. Those claiming to be Christian converts, for example, face a religion-themed pub quiz about the books of the Bible, the names of apostles and the date of Pentecost.[15] In fact, sincere converts often have no idea about these things; converting to another religion is much more about emotion, sentiment, identity and overall message than it is about the finer details. One atheist had his claim rejected on the basis that he failed to identify Plato and Aristotle as humanist philosophers, which was taken by the official concerned to mean that his knowledge of humanism was 'rudimentary at best'. The organisation Humanism UK wrote to then Home Secretary Amber Rudd to point out that neither Plato nor Aristotle were actually humanists.[16] Likewise, those claiming to be political activists might be asked obscure questions on the details of policies in a party's last election manifesto, or the names of party officials. Imagine if supporters of former Labour leader Jeremy Corbyn were persecuted; if quizzed, how many would be able to explain the details of specific policies or personnel within the party? Similarly, many fervent Brexit supporters would likely be unable to describe exactly how Brexit will make Britain great again. Politics is often about general direction, sentiment and trust, but an asylum seeker's case will usually turn on obscure and seemingly insignificant details.

It is not just individuals but sometimes whole national groups of asylum seekers who find themselves collectively refused refuge. The worst recent example of this concerned Eritrea, a small country in the Horn of Africa that achieved independence from Ethiopia in 1993. All human rights organisations, and indeed the UK's own Foreign Office, recognised that by 2015 the Eritrean government was almost uniquely repressive. The authorities closed the borders to those attempting to leave, shot or imprisoned citizens who tried to escape and forced a huge percentage of the population to undertake hazardous and sometimes unending military service. The only real comparator is North Korea. The courts recognised that any Eritrean that did make it to the United Kingdom should almost automatically be considered a refugee.[17] And the Home Office agreed, granting asylum to nearly nine out of ten Eritrean asylum seekers.

The numbers of Eritrean refugees had not been huge, but nevertheless an increase in claims led someone at the Home Office to change the official approach in 2015. The premise for the change was a report by the Danish Immigration Service the previous year. The report had been controversial. Amnesty International condemned it as 'completely absurd', while Human Rights Watch said it was 'deeply flawed'. The expert upon whose testimony much of the report was based publicly disassociated himself from it. Two of the three writers of the report also openly criticised the summary section and conclusions drawn by the third (supervising) writer, which were based on their input and research. The Danes backtracked and ceased relying on the report, while here in the United Kingdom, the chief inspector of borders and immigration also criticised it.

None of this deterred the Home Office. Instead of granting asylum to Eritreans promptly on arrival, the department started to refuse almost all applications. This meant that most refused Eritreans then lodged appeals to take their cases to court. The number of appeals brought by Eritrean nationals against rejected claims rose from 224 in the year ending March 2015 to 1,760 in the year to March 2016. And a staggeringly high proportion of them eventually won their cases – the same figure, in fact, of nine out of ten, as had previously been granted by the Home Office – though not before waiting in limbo for many months. In the meantime, the Ministry of Justice had to pay both for the judges' salaries and the legal aid bills for those concerned, while the Home Office itself had to carry on supporting those pursuing an appeal and pay yet another set of civil servants to defend the appeals.

This was all for nothing. The Home Office reversed its position again in 2016 after losing a major court case. It was a colossal abuse of public money, as well as an appalling abuse of vulnerable refugees. In a system that functions well, genuine refugees will quickly be recognised as such and then given the maximum help to get themselves established in their new country. If they are going to be allowed to stay, then better to let them get on with it and give them the best possible chance of making a success of their new life. Instead, Eritreans destined to win their cases were refused, were kept waiting for months in squalid poverty, were put through the stress of court and were thoroughly alienated by the whole system – all before eventually being allowed to stay anyway.[18]

There is no real doubt that asylum decision-making is dysfunctional. It is possible that the 'right' people are being refused but, if so, the reasons given being so nonsensical, this is surely a matter of coincidence rather than competence. The big question is why the Home Office behaves in this way and has done so for decades, since the numbers of asylum claims started to rise in the 1990s.

SECURE BORDERS, INACCESSIBLE HAVEN

To make themselves see reasonable and compassionate, politicians like to distinguish between 'genuine' and 'bogus' – or deserving and undeserving – refugees. Genuine refugees are supposedly to be welcomed and given sanctuary, whereas the bogus ones are to be prevented from arriving in the first place, or otherwise promptly expelled if they do somehow sneak in. In reality, politicians do everything possible to exclude *all* refugees from entering the United

Kingdom, no matter how much they need protection. There were two main strands to the policy: deterrence and prevention.

The essence of the policy of deterrence is to make life as miserable as possible for the refugees who do reach the UK, in the hope that this will somehow deter others from following suit. The idea is to eliminate the 'pull' factors that attract asylum seekers to come to the UK in preference over other countries, as evidenced by the build-up of migrants and refugees at Calais and along the French side of the English Channel. Asylum seekers were stripped of the right to claim mainstream benefits or housing back in the 1990s, a food voucher system was briefly introduced in 1999, and even though this was scrapped after a campaign led by trade union leader Bill Morris, the meagre support available has been essentially frozen for years. The current level of support at the time of writing is £37.75 per migrant per week. The system of 'dispersing' asylum seekers around the country was also introduced in 1999 and continues to this day. Accommodation is provided by private contractors, is sometimes squalid and is located far away from established communities of compatriots.

Asylum seekers are also banned from working or studying or even undertaking voluntary work, and yet their cases are put on hold – sometimes for years. The benefits of the status granted to recognised refugees have also been repeatedly downgraded with, for example, the legal status granted to refugees being made less and less secure. Family reunion is prevented for children and is made as difficult as possible for adults, with government funding for DNA tests withdrawn in 2012. Almost overnight, the refusal rate for Somali family reunion applications shot from just 17 per cent to 80 per cent, with the refusal rates for Eritrean, Sudanese, Syrian and Iranian applications all trebling.[19] A system of accelerated 'fast track' asylum decision-making was introduced, with asylum seekers detained in the initial and sometimes even the appeal stages of their claims. A massive building programme for immigration detention centres was launched (see Chapter 11). Legislation was also introduced to criminalise asylum seekers who were thought to have destroyed their documents, and to encourage judges to reject claims based on ill-founded stereotypes of how a 'genuine' refugee might be expected to behave, a point to which I return at the end of this chapter.[20] Eventually, as discussed in Chapter 3, the whole hostile environment policy was developed, with the declared intention of making Britain a less welcoming destination for unauthorised migrants.

Perhaps the single most stark example of deterrence came with the refugee crisis that was sparked by the civil war in Syria. Baroness Anelay, who was minister of state for foreign and Commonwealth affairs in 2014, stated in Parliament, on behalf of the government, 'We do not support planned search and rescue operations in the Mediterranean. We believe that they create an unintended "pull factor", encouraging more migrants to attempt the dangerous sea crossing and thereby leading to more tragic and unnecessary deaths.'

This was the 'let them drown' policy. The UK soon relented and did end up assisting with search and rescue, sending boats to help in the operation, but the first instinct of the government had been to deter some refugees from setting out in boats by letting others of them drown.

If the purpose of deterrence was to dissuade refugees from coming to the UK, this was all an epic failure of evidence-based policy-making. It focused on the 'pull' factors supposedly attracting refugees to the United Kingdom but ignored the 'push' factors that cause them to leave their own war-torn countries in the first place. As poet Warsan Shire puts it, 'No one leaves home unless / home is the mouth of a shark / no one puts their children in a boat / unless the water is safer than the land.' Even aside from this fundamental flaw, there was never any evidence base to suggest that the supposed pull factors really influenced refugees in the first place. None of the available research suggests that refugees decide which country to come to on the basis of how they are treated when they arrive, or even what dangers they might face along the way.

In 'Deciding Where to go: Policies, People and Perceptions Shaping Destination Preferences', researchers Heaven Crawley and Jessica Hagen-Zanker write that 'destination preferences', as they put it, are rarely shaped by the deterrent or other migration policies of receiving countries. Rather, they found that decision-making is shaped by a wide range of factors including 'access to protection and family reunification, the availability/accuracy of information, the overall economic environment and social networks'. The Home Office already knew this, having commissioned a piece of research back in 2002 entitled 'Understanding the Decision-Making of Asylum Seekers', which reached similar findings.[21] The researchers found that there was 'very little evidence that the sample respondents had a detailed knowledge of: UK immigration or asylum procedures; entitlements to benefits in the UK; or the availability of work in the UK'.

It is true that some refugees, once they are on the move, seek prosperous countries in which to settle and rebuild their lives. It is possible to be both a genuine refugee and also an economic migrant at the same time. In fact, though, the majority of refugees stay close to the homes from which they have fled. There are around thirty million refugees in the world today and 80 per cent of them live in refugee camps in countries neighbouring their own.[22] There is little to do in these camps and some do not want to subsist only on handouts from the UN High Commission for Refugees. This takes us to the second strand in the attempt to reduce numbers: preventing physical entry. Deterrent policies are very unlikely to succeed, at least in their overt, declared aim of discouraging arrivals. Migrants and refugees will keep moving, whether driven by push or pull factors. As Bridget Anderson writes, 'No set of border controls has ever worked to contain fully people's desire and need to move. But when migrants and refugees do move, they now encounter unprecedented physical and bureaucratic barriers to entry.'[23]

The UK border has been, wherever possible, pushed abroad, so that asylum seekers have no opportunity even to reach British soil and claim asylum. Immigration 'liaison' officers were introduced at foreign airports from which asylum seekers might try to embark for the UK. They carried out racial sifting, picking out and preventing the boarding of ethnic minorities, such as Roma from Eastern Europe, who were deemed more likely to claim asylum on arrival.[24] The Le Touquet Treaty was signed in 2003 to enable British immigration officials to operate in France, with the UK agreeing to fund high levels of security around the Channel ports, to scan lorries and prevent clandestine arrivals. Miles and miles of five-metre-high security fencing and razor wire and thousands of security staff, including riot police armed with guns, batons, body armour and dogs, now prevent migrants from climbing aboard lorries and trains bound for Britain. Security cameras are everywhere. Heat sensors are used to detect live bodies, carbon dioxide sensors detect breathing and X-rays and heartbeat monitors are also utilised.

The Red Cross centre at Sangatte near Calais was shut down in 2003 and the informal camps that sprang up instead were cleared periodically thereafter. Also in 2003, Tony Blair pledged to halve the numbers of asylum seekers arriving in the UK and proposed 'regional protection zones' outside the European Union, where refugees would be held while their asylum claims were decided. The 'Dublin' system of removals within the European Union, named after the Dublin Convention that was the legal basis for the system, then came into effect, enabling the removal of asylum seekers from destination countries to their point of entry into the EU.

In contrast to the deterrent policies, the securitisation of the border has been effective at keeping people out. But the cost of that success in human lives has been heavy. The fences, scanners and dogs do not prevent people setting out on their journeys of hope, but, due to our geography as an island, they do undoubtedly make it harder to reach the UK. Some still try, and the level of security is such that extreme risks must now be taken by those who do. Journalists and charities who have met with the migrants camped on the French side of the Channel report that injuries from razor wire, moving lorries and brutal French police are commonplace. Some survive the journey to the United Kingdom, but others do not.

The body of Mohammed Ayaz was found in the car park of a branch of Homebase in Richmond in 2001, having fallen from a plane landing at Heathrow.[25] Jose Matada similarly died falling from the undercarriage of a flight from Angola onto a street in Mortlake in London in 2012.[26] Then, there was Carlito Vale, an orphan who stowed away in a plane's wheel well for an 8,000-mile journey in 2016. He was alive when he started to fall and died on impact.[27] A man thought to be an airport worker earning £2.25 per day in Nairobi, tentatively identified as Paul Manyasi, likewise stowed away, froze and then fell over 1,000 metres, creating a crater in a back garden in south London in 2019.[28] Masoud Niknam attempted to swim to the UK all the way from Dunkirk late in 2019 and died in the attempt.[29] Some now set out across one of the busiest shipping lanes in the world in inflatable dinghies. Mitra Mehrad, reported to have a PhD in psychology, died in the attempt, also in late 2019.[30]

As I was writing this book, tragic confirmation of the risks some are willing to take has been evidenced by the deaths by suffocation of thirty-nine migrants in the back of a sealed, refrigerated lorry. The incident echoed one at the very start of my career when fifty-eight migrants perished in similar circumstances in 2000. Yet even these tragedies are dwarfed by the number of deaths by drowning in the Mediterranean as refugees seek their escape from home. Deaths per year peaked at just over 5,000 in 2016, but even in 2019 well over 1,000 people died trying to cross that sea. At the time of writing, a total of 20,040 have drowned in the Mediterranean since 2014, a number which will have increased substantially by the time you read this.[31] The situation is so awful, with so many unidentified bodies washing up on the beaches and so many families not knowing what has happened to their loved ones, that two friends of mine founded a new charity, called Last Rights. They campaign for dignity in death and work to identify the dead, then inform their families. It is grim but important work.[32]

There is no attempt whatsoever in all of this to distinguish between a genuine refugee and a bogus one. All these deterrent and security measures affect *all* refugees, no matter how strong their claim to asylum. It is now basically impossible for a refugee to lawfully reach the United Kingdom to claim asylum. If a refugee wants to make it to Europe or the United Kingdom – perhaps because of historic links, the language, family members or perceived opportunities – then he or she must take high risks to do so.

The one exception to this is the refugee resettlement programme. This was launched by David Blunkett in 2002 as a counterbalance to the general approach of deter and prevent. Initially the numbers involved were very low, with just a few hundred being admitted each year under three different schemes. Blunkett argued that it was legitimate to prevent the irregular entry of asylum seekers; doing so reduced public concern, he said, as many such arrivals were bogus and, in any event, only the fittest and healthiest refugees with access to some resources were capable of making the hazardous journey to the UK. He argued that opening up safe and legal routes for asylum with his programme would reduce demand for the services of people smugglers and traffickers.[33] Implicitly, Blunkett suggested the UK could meet its moral and humanitarian obligations, not by allowing refugees irregular entry, but by resettling them from refugee camps.

Offering refugee resettlement is undoubtedly very welcome; safe routes to sanctuary are essential and it is unfair to expect only the neighbours of a refugee-producing country, often poor countries themselves, to host those refugees. There is also truth in the point that the most vulnerable refugees around the world will never make it to the United Kingdom. However, Blunkett's argument was founded on the assumption that only a limited number of refugees can or should ever be admitted – a premise that was to be made explicit by Theresa May late in 2015. After the circulation of images showing the dead body of toddler Alan Kurdi washed ashore on a Turkish beach, David Cameron was forced to expand the existing programme. To his considerable credit, he pledged to resettle 20,000 Syrian refugees over the coming five years. A few weeks later, when giving a speech setting out 'a new plan for asylum', then Home Secretary Theresa May explicitly proposed a compassion quota:

What I'm proposing is a deal: the fewer people there are who wrongly claim asylum in Britain, the more generous we can be in helping the most vulnerable people in the world's most danger- ous places. And my message to the immigration campaigners and human rights lawyers is this: you can play your part in making this happen – or you can try to frustrate it. But if you choose to frustrate it, you will have to live with the knowledge that you are depriving people in genuine need of the sanctuary our country can offer. There are people who need our help, and there are people who are abusing our goodwill – and I know whose side I'm on.[34]

This was consistent with the net migration target; if the target was to be met then it was logical that, if a certain number of refugees were to be allowed in, a certain number would have to be excluded too. I was not sure at the time, and I certainly do not know now, how human rights lawyers like me were supposed to make this happen. Perhaps we should have been out patrolling the coastline, shooting out the bottom of dinghies from those we assessed as wrongly claiming asylum? In any event, Theresa May did nothing to expand the number of resettlement places Cameron had announced once she became Prime Minister.

ROOT CAUSES

What really drives the deterrence when we know that it does not work? And what drives the security apparatus when we know that it does not and cannot discriminate between the genuine and the bogus?

One possibility is that the policies are intended only to reassure the public and assuage concern. This seems to have been the thinking in the early 2000s, when the Labour government legislated on immigration over and over again. Similar thinking also seems to have motivated David Cameron's increasing focus on immigration from 2010 onwards, at a time when he clearly felt his Conservative Party was under pressure for votes from the Nigel Farage-led UK Independence Party. The idea seems to have been that passing restrictive laws and constantly claiming to be 'cracking down' would reduce public anxiety about immigration.

There is no evidence to show that this really works, though. It seems just as likely that forever talking about immigration and passing new immigration laws actually heightens public concern, rather than suppressing it. As the authors of the British Future report 'How To Talk About Immigration' put it, the public 'are regularly told that there is a new crackdown – more evidence that it wasn't working before – and then nothing seems to change as a result'.[35] It does not help that the public are deeply sceptical of official and government information about immigration, meaning that claims of a crackdown usually fall on deaf ears. The more that politicians make ineffective, empty and therefore self-defeating promises, the more the public become sceptical, and even cynical as a result. There certainly seems to be no negative correlation between government law-making on immigration and public concern. Quite the opposite; if anything, the more politicians pontificate, the more anxious the public becomes.

It could be that this opposite is actually intended, and perhaps the policies are supposed to manufacture public concern for political gain. In the populist age of Donald Trump, this degree of cynicism is far from implausible. Cameron was no Trump, but he certainly used some of the same techniques to bolster his political position. As discussed in Chapter 2, there is evidence that Cameron increasingly focused on immigration from 2010 onwards, in the belief that immigration was an issue that favoured the Conservative Party. Many have argued that blaming migrants for difficulties in the employment market, shortages of housing and pressure on public services was a distraction from the real cause: the government policy of austerity.[36] Theresa May followed Cameron's example, although some might suspect she believed rather more in what she was doing than her always opportunistic predecessor. This blaming of refugees and migrants, though, can be carried out much more effectively by proper populists and outright racists, who are not constrained by the need to actually govern and to therefore implement their own policies. A mainstream politician trying to beat the populists at their own game is, in the end, always going to lose that ever-escalating arms race.

A more subtle possibility is that the policies are indeed political but are aimed not so much at the public as at other politicians and perhaps sections of the media. Every political party is home to a range of different political perspectives and one of the jobs of a leader is to try to keep that coalition together. For David Cameron, who came from the liberal wing of the Conservative Party, this meant keeping right-wingers such as the European Research Group inside his tent. Veteran Member of Parliament Ken Clarke once said of Cameron's strategy for managing this faction, 'If you want to go feeding crocodiles then you'd better not run out of buns.' Restrictive, harsh asylum policies can be seen as the buns to feed the right, supposedly balancing out the more socially liberal policies some right-wingers hated, such as gay marriage, prison reform or environmental policies. Again, there is some evidence to support this thesis. In 2012, David Laws, schools minister during the coalition government, drew on a similar metaphor. He noted that Cameron saw the hostile environment policy as 'red meat' to feed the right-wing of the Conservative Party, as well as being a way of countering the rise of UKIP.[37]

Finally, it is also possible there was no ulterior motive nor purpose behind all this at all. Perhaps it was just politicians doing what politicians do: a messy, uncoordinated, pragmatic combination of what they genuinely think is needed for the good of the country, with, at the very least, half an eye on how they think their political base – whether in the wider electorate or the political party selectorate – will respond. Blair, Blunkett and the Labour government of 1997 to 2010 may well have genuinely thought that there were too many refugees seeking sanctuary in the United Kingdom, that too many were ingenuine refugees and that legislating repeatedly would both solve this 'problem' and position the party better with the electorate. Cameron and May might likewise have thought it right to restrict immigration, as well as believing that doing so would work to their political advantage both within their party and for their party. Politics is a messy business and outcomes like the deter and prevent approach to asylum were no doubt a mix of intentions both noble – if arguably ignorant – and ignoble.

INTEGRATION AND INGRATITUDE

Public opinion seems to be particularly sensitive to increases in refugee arrivals compared to other forms of migration. When asked, people are less resistant to the idea of skilled migrants, students, those who speak English, those who stick to the rules and migrants from certain countries.[38] Migrants with these characteristics are perceived as being more capable of 'integrating' – a loaded word and one that for good or ill plays an important role in discourse about immigration. Race certainly plays a role here, and Rob Ford has written about the 'ethnic hierarchy' in attitudes to migration.[39] In one survey, 10 per cent of respondents said no Australians should be allowed to come and live in the United Kingdom, compared to 37 per cent of respondents saying likewise about Nigerians. This may in part be due to a perceived difference in income and skills, but it would be naive to suggest that skin colour is irrelevant. And refugees, rightly or wrongly, are identified as scoring poorly by all these measures, meaning that attitudes towards them are often particularly negative.[40]

Refugees are also unpopular because they are often perceived as being fakes and because some members of the public perceive them as a security risk. Some believe that those arriving as refugees are not, in fact, in danger in their own countries, but have instead travelled to the UK for quite different reasons. In global studies conducted in 2016 and 2017, the opinion research company Ipsos MORI found that well over half of respondents agree with the following statements: 'Most foreigners who want to get into my country as a refugee really aren't refugees. They just want to come here for economic reasons, or to take advantage of our welfare services' and 'There are terrorists pretending to be refugees who will enter my country to cause violence and destruction.' In contrast, less than half agreed with this statement: 'I'm confident that most refugees who come to my country will successfully integrate into their new society.'[41]

The public's differentiated approach was instinctively understood by Labour politicians like David Blunkett in the early 2000s. In 2003, he told *The Guardian* that new asylum legislation would encourage people to come to Britain to work legally, while being 'as tough as old boots' on those who abused the system. As Don Flynn argued in his far-sighted pamphlet based on these words, this came to typify government policy under Labour.[42] Some migration routes were expanded and promoted – those for skilled workers and international students for example – while others were relentlessly clamped down on. Asylum seekers were perceived as abusers of the immigration system. The fact that many of those seeking asylum came from countries where there was civil war and well-documented persecution of minorities – Bosnia, Kosovo, Sri Lanka, Somalia and, later, Zimbabwe, Afghanistan and Iraq – seemed to be irrelevant.

The narrative of the 'bogus asylum seeker' – the idea that asylum seekers from Afghanistan, Kosovo, Iraq and Zimbabwe, amongst other places, were liars who did not need or deserve our protection – was allowed to develop or perhaps even encouraged. This enabled politicians to feign concern for the genuine refugees, while simultaneously doing everything possible to deter and prevent their arrival. The majority of asylum claims in this climate were assumed to be fraudulent and that assertion was seemingly supported by their low success rate. But it was a self-fulfilling prophecy, a classic example of circular logic: the low rate of success was a result of the culture of disbelief, and the culture of disbelief was itself founded on that same low success rate. Cynicism directed at asylum seekers also ignored the reasons that at least some were being refused asylum. When claims failed, it was often for legal reasons rather than because the asylum seeker was thought to be lying. For example, it might be said that there was still a safe area in their country of origin, that they had travelled through a safe country to reach the UK or that the Refugee Convention did not apply to them.

But it is not all doom and gloom. The refusal rate has gradually fallen over time and many of the palpably perverse decisions I have highlighted are not recent ones. In the early 1980s, when the number of asylum claims was running at around 3,000 per year, the success rate was as high as 87 per cent.[43] A decade later, after a dramatic increase, there were around 30,000 asylum claims made in the United Kingdom per year and the success rate was just 4 per cent.[44] Yet, today, with the numbers having shot up in the early 2000s but then fallen back to between 20,000 to 30,000 over the past ten years, the Home Office grants status in 38 per cent of initial decisions. Once appeal outcomes are taken into account the total is around 55 per cent.[45]

This is a sign of a gradual and welcome change in culture at the Home Office. There is a lot more to be done, of course. The single biggest improvement would be for officials to discard the whole concept of the 'stock narrative' of being a refugee.[46] Politicians and officials expect refugees to behave in certain preordained or 'stock' ways. In truth, these expectations are all about how they would *like* refugees to behave, rather than about how they actually do. For example, it is commonplace to say that genuine refugees claim asylum in the first safe country they reach. There is no evidence base at all to support this assertion; many genuine refugees who would be persecuted if they returned to their home countries decide not to remain in refugee camps and instead try to build a better future for themselves and their families by moving on. They are still refugees as defined by the Refugee Convention.

It is also often assumed that a genuine refugee will take decisive action to flee in response to a specific trigger event that discloses a certain level of risk. For many real refugees, though, the decision to leave their home, job, family and friends is a very difficult one and so may well be reached gradually. The unfounded belief that a genuine refugee will claim asylum at the first opportunity on or after arrival seems to be widespread. But, like the decision to leave in the first place, a decision to claim asylum can also be a hard one to make. Many refugees know little or nothing about the asylum system and many are (arguably rightly) afraid of both the authorities and the process itself.

This wishful thinking about how a real refugee is supposed to behave is not just deeply ingrained at an unconscious cultural level with officials and judges, it is also embedded in rules and legislation. Politicians have actually passed laws based on these stock narratives, in effect describing how real refugees are expected to behave. Perhaps unsurprisingly, the general tenor is that real refugees should claim asylum somewhere else and not come to the UK at all.[47] Much of the training that has been given to civil servants in recent years to help them to decide sensitive claims (those based on sexuality or religion, for instance) has been about widening or adjusting the stock narrative. For example, in one recent interview for a claim made by a gay man I represented, the official repeatedly quizzed him about his emotional journey through the discovery of his sexuality. Officials have been (rightly) instructed in recent years not to quiz asylum seekers about sex, after all. The line of questioning was well-intentioned, but the official was clearly stumped when the man replied that he found his roommate sexually attractive, and the claim was refused. One stock narrative – that gay men have lots of sex and can be expected to talk about it – had been replaced by another: that gay men experience a gradual emotional journey of coming out. The whole idea of stock narratives needs to be comprehensively abandoned.

As we have seen previously, most of the asylum seekers who do manage to reach the United Kingdom are actually genuine refugees. But you would not know this from the pronouncements of politicians or from more general public attitudes. The rhetoric surrounding the relatively small numbers of Channel crossings is a case in point. Around 1,900 asylum seekers made this dangerous crossing in 2019 and most were reported to be Iranian nationals. Iran is ruled by a repressive regime that treats political dissidents and ethnic and religious minorities with brutality. 'We will send you back,' was the response of Prime Minister Boris Johnson. 'If you come illegally, you are an illegal migrant and, I'm afraid, the law will treat you as such.' None of this is true. Refugees are protected from prosecution for illegal entry by Article 31 of the Refugee Convention and by

Section 31 of the Immigration and Asylum Act 1999. The reality is that 63 per cent of Iranian asylum seekers are granted refuge in initial decisions by the Home Office, and many more win their appeals against refusal. Most are genuine refugees and only a tiny percentage are sent back either to France or to Iran.[48] And actually, with the UK's departure after Brexit from the Common European Asylum System, the set of laws that enables the UK to remove asylum seekers to other EU countries, future returns to France or other EU countries will become virtually impossible.[49]

There is one other example of a self-perpetuating myth to which I want to draw attention as a conclusion to this chapter. One of the major reasons that refugees are perceived negatively by the public – and probably therefore also by officials – is their supposed inability to 'integrate'. Where this is founded on simple racism, there is nothing to be done other than continue the hard slog of gradually shifting public attitudes towards race. But where such negativity is based on assumptions that the culture, religion, language, poverty and lack of skills of refugees makes adaptation into their new host society harder, these potentially self-fulfilling assumptions are not necessarily well-founded.

Studies have shown that Somali refugees in the United States and Canada end up far better integrated into the workforce, and with far better economic outcomes in terms of wages, than those in the United Kingdom.[50] There is something that the UK is doing, or perhaps not doing, that actually holds back refugees and prevents them from integrating. For plain reasons of geography, most refugees in the US and Canada are resettled there rather than being spontaneous arrivals. They therefore do not experience the deliberately inflicted indignities of the asylum process in their new country. The same is true of refugees arriving through resettlement schemes in the UK, who are welcomed with comprehensive and ongoing assistance in finding accommodation and employment and accessing local services like a doctor and a school. This support stands in stark contrast to those refugees who arrive irregularly without prior permission. The asylum procedure itself is incomprehensible, prolonged and degrading. It gets little better once refugee status is granted. Children cannot be joined by their parents even once they are recognised as refugees, forcing them into local authority care. The handover from Home Office support as an asylum seeker to local authority support as a recognised refugee is virtually non-existent. Housing and welfare support is simply withdrawn by the Home Office with twenty-eight days' notice; the refugee is expected to fend for him- or herself and, if without resources, work out how to access local authority assistance alone. Many are made homeless as a result.[51]

The main justification for these deliberately harsh policies is that they reduce the supposed pull factors that are said to make the United Kingdom an attractive destination for refugees. Politicians like to talk about these pull factors because they are something ministers themselves can control; legislating to cut off the right to work, reducing benefits and so on, makes it seem as if the politician has some concrete answer to, and control over, the perceived problem of refugee numbers. However, the research shows that country-specific pull factors have very little, if any, influence on refugees. The legislators are kidding both themselves and the public and are therefore setting unachievable expectations. The only real consequence is that refugees like my clients are so traumatised and exhausted by the process that it is no surprise they struggle to adapt to life in the United Kingdom afterwards. The deterrent policies the government has introduced since the late 1990s leave both them and their children deliberately and permanently disadvantaged.

If politicians were honest and open about the fact that most asylum seekers arriving in the UK are now genuine refugees, this might start to shift public attitudes. The majority will ultimately be allowed to stay in the UK anyway and it is time to start recognising that truth. Once they are allowed to remain, do we want them to be isolated, disadvantaged and perhaps even resentful because of their harsh and inhumane treatment on and after arrival? If we were less hostile and more respectful, it is likely that they would find it easier to integrate and build new lives for themselves when they are allowed to stay, which, in turn, might help to shift negative public opinion.

CHAPTER 7

ECONOMIC MIGRATION: POINTS MEAN PRIZES

Mohammed Imam plied his trade as a chef at a restaurant called Alishaan in Sompting on the south coast of England. He was from Bangladesh, so needed a visa to live and work in the UK. Having entered lawfully in 2010, in 2016 he applied to extend his visa for a further five years and his application was initially granted. But to his surprise – and his employer's chagrin – a year and a half later, the Home Office wrote to him out of the blue and cancelled the visa. The reason was that 'under SOC code 5434 in Appendix K of the Immigration Rules it is stated that the job must not be in either a fast food outlet, a standard fare outlet or an establishment which provides a take-away service'. Someone at the Home Office had evidently been googling restaurants, presumably on what lawyers call a 'fishing expedition' to try to catch out chefs. 'There is evidence available on the internet', the refusal went on, 'that your prospective employer does offer a take-away service.'

KAFKA WOULD BLUSH

The jargon in that cancellation letter alone tells you a lot about the complexity of the rules Mr Imam and his employer were trying to navigate. A 'SOC code' is a reference to the Standard Occupational

Classification, which is basically a list of all conceivable jobs and occupations, compiled and published every ten years by the Classification and Harmonisation Unit at the Office for National Statistics. This includes everything from '3239. Adviser, cessation, smoking' to '9244. Warden, patrol, crossing, school'. There are 28,749 entries on the list. The SOC code for chefs in particular includes several different roles, such as 'Chef, development', 'Chef, head', 'Chef, pastry', 'Chef de cuisine', 'Chef de partie', 'Chef-manager' and then just plain 'Chef'. A 'Chef de rang' has a different SOC code altogether, of course, being essentially a fancy name for a waiter.

Perhaps surprisingly, Appendix K of the Immigration Rules is not a reference to the protagonist of Franz Kafka's *The Castle*. That K finds himself summoned by bureaucratic error to an unfamiliar environment, where he struggles to gain access to the mysterious authorities governing a village, with copious, contradictory paperwork from an inaccessible, impenetrable castle. Although it was unfinished at the time of his death, Kafka had written to a friend that *The Castle* would end with K being informed by the authorities, while on his deathbed, that his 'legal claim to live in the village was not valid'. No, Appendix K is the official 'Shortage Occupation List' issued by our own beloved Home Office. This is the list of jobs for which employers do not need to advertise a role and which fall outside the general cap on the number of skilled workers who can be recruited from abroad. The list consists of certain SOC codes, often with additional provisos attached. For example, the entry for code 5434 at the time of Mr Imam's application stated:

> *Only* the following job in this occupation code:
> Skilled chef where:

- The pay is at least £29,570 per year after deductions for accommodation, meals etc; and
- The job requires five or more years relevant experience in a role of at least equivalent status to the one they are entering; and
- The job is not in either a fast food outlet, a standard fare outlet, or an establishment which provides a take-away service; and

The job is in one of the following roles:

- Executive chef – limited to one per establishment
- Head chef – limited to one per establishment
- Sous chef – limited to one for every four kitchen staff per establishment
- Specialist chef – limited to one per speciality per establishment

Unusually, Mr Imam's employer stood by him and challenged the decision in the courts. Good, experienced chefs are not easy to come by, after all. Curry houses were particularly hard hit by this otherwise obscure rule and in 2017 the Asian Catering Federation told the *Telegraph* that 50 per cent would be forced to close within ten years.[1] Mr Imam and the restaurant argued in court that the rule against foreign chefs working 'in an establishment which provides a take-away service' was perverse and outdated given the growth of delivery services such as Deliveroo. They noted that some Michelin-starred restaurants also offered a take-away service and Mr Imam's restaurant was primarily an eat-in establishment, making only around 10 per cent of its earnings from take-aways. The arguments were hardly unfounded, but the challenge failed both at the High Court and, eventually, in late 2019 at the Court of Appeal (and it is from that judgment I draw these facts).[2] Mr Imam and the restaurant were then left to pay not only for their own legal bills but also for the legal costs that the Home Office incurred in defending the claim. We lawyers do not come cheap and the cost of unsuccessful litigation against the Home Office would have come to tens of thousands of pounds.

There was a twist. By the time the Court of Appeal handed down its decision, the take-away rule, which was indeed perverse and outdated, had been scrapped. The Migration Advisory Committee of economists and academics, which offers guidance to the Home Office on labour market shortages, had advised that the rule should be abolished in May 2019. Home Secretary Priti Patel announced that she would accept this recommendation and, in a piece in the *Sun* newspaper in September 2019, styled her decision as the creation of a 'vindaloo visa', intended to 'save the nation's curry houses'. The change was implemented in new rules on 6 October 2019. Mr Imam's case was heard in the Court of Appeal on 8 October 2019 and was dismissed two weeks later. Yet, because the case concerned an application made in 2016, the fact that the rule had been scrapped three years later was of no avail to Mr Imam and his employers. In fact, changes to the status of migrant workers wrought by the Immigration Act 2014 meant that Mr Imam had been unlawfully resident all the time that he brought his legal case. And once a migrant becomes unlawfully resident, there is usually no way back.

Applying for a work visa in the UK can be a capricious lottery, as Mr Imam discovered to his cost. The rules are insanely complicated, the cost of applying is huge and while one hand of the Home Office actively seeks innovative ways in which to defeat applications, another hand simultaneously recommends that the same applications should succeed. Not only that, but Mr Imam was actually on one of the easier points-based routes to navigate.

ENDING IN TIERS

The five-tier points-based system was first announced in 2006 as the culmination of attempts to modernise and reform the immigration system. After decades of the United Kingdom being a 'zero immigration' country, Tony Blair's Labour government of 1997 to 2007 had introduced an active economic immigration policy for the first time since the immediate post-war years.[3] With incoming new ideologies of globalisation, modernisation and evidence-based policy-making, the idea that immigration might be economically desirable spread from the Treasury and Department for Trade and Industry, to the Cabinet Office, to the Home Office.[4] Certain migrants would be actively sought and recruited, it was decided.

The revolution began with the Innovator Scheme, which was launched as a pilot in 2000 to attract high-tech entrepreneurs. The Highly Skilled Migrant Programme followed in 2001 and, separately, work permit criteria were loosened. The number of permits issued every year more than doubled, from around 63,000 in 1997 to over 135,000 by 2005. By then the Highly Skilled Migrant Programme was attracting over 17,000 entrants annually. What had become a messy hodgepodge of different routes into the UK was eventually deemed to lack modernity and plans for an amalgamated system were drawn up. The purpose of the resulting points-based system would be 'to admit people selectively in order to maximise the economic benefit of migration to the UK'. The consultation paper heralding its introduction stated that the new system should be simpler and easier to understand than the old routes it replaced. The key tests of success would be whether it was 'operable, robust, objective, flexible, cost effective, transparent, usable'.[5]

Each tier includes several different immigration categories and some of those include different sub-categories. In reality, though, none of the sixteen groupings operate on a meaningful points-scoring system, allowing for different combinations of attributes to add up in order to secure a visa. The only genuine points-based route, the successor to the previous Highly Skilled Migrant Programme (which awarded different points for different attributes or qualifications), was scrapped by Theresa May at the end of 2010. Even before that, calling the system 'points-based' was always more about branding than reality. Apparently, members of the public in focus groups liked the sound of an 'Australian-style points-based system' because it evoked images of refugees in boats being turned around at gunpoint by the Australian navy.[6] The fact that the actual Australian points-based system had nothing to do with refugees and was actually a way of *increasing* economic immigration was irrelevant. The Conservative Party then revived use of the phrase during the 2019 general election campaign, despite the fact the UK system was literally already called the 'points-based system'.

Turning to the individual tiers of the system, Tier One is applicable to unsponsored migrants with lots of money. The categories within this tier include investors, global talent and, until 2018, entrepreneurs. In the early years of the scheme Tier One also included the 'post-study work' visa, which allowed graduates of UK universities to remain in the UK to work for up to two years after graduation, and also permitted them to switch into other work routes at the end of that period if they qualified. This particular route was abolished by Theresa May in 2012. Currently, investors are required to put in a minimum of £2 million of their own money in certain, rigorously specified ways. This will then put them on a five-year route to settlement. If they increase the level of investment to £5 million, they need only wait for three years. And if they invest £10 million, the wait is reduced to a mere two years. This is the preferred route of Russian oligarchs and the Chinese elite. The number of applicants who are accepted through this uncapped method are relatively small, with less than 400 visas being issued to the main applicants (not including family members) in the year ended September 2019.[7]

Tier One's global talent route, until January 2020 known as exceptional talent, is designed for outstanding individuals who are endorsed by leading industry, science and arts bodies. Just under 700 visas were issued in the year ending September 2019. Bizarrely, the number was capped until 2020, and although the notional cap was increased from 1,000 to 2,000 in 2019 and then scrapped in early 2020, there was no sign that there were anywhere near as many as 1,000 exceptionally talented individuals who wished to relocate to the UK under such a scheme in the first place.

The other category within Tier One is for entrepreneurs, who needed to be able to invest at least £200,000 in a new or existing business in the United Kingdom, or £50,000 if the applicant was a graduate of a UK university. There were around 2,000 visas issued under these categories in their last year in operation and it is thought much of the money went into the struggling care home sector. The visa was replaced with two new routes outside the points-based system in 2019: the start-up and innovator routes. However, the new requirement that applicants must have buy-in from a business incubator or venture capital firm has made it all but impossible to secure visas in this way. In the first six months of the new route, just fourteen applications had been made and only twelve of those were approved. In effect, the route was shut down by the reforms. Whether this effect was intended or accidental is unclear, but press releases and ministers were simultaneously touting Britain as being open for business.

Tier Two is for skilled workers who have been sponsored by a specific employer. There are four different categories within the tier: general applications, intra-company transfers within multinational companies, sportspeople and ministers of religion. Relatively few visas are granted in the second two categories, although the few sportspeople issued with visas were often household names like Sergei Aurier, Didier Drogba and Luis Suarez. The main Tier Two General route replaced the old work permit system and is similar but more complex for employers, who now need to apply for a sponsor licence in order to get permission from the Home Office to employ foreign workers. A hefty fee is payable for this licence and the employer must agree to certain conditions, including unannounced Home Office site inspections. Since 2017 the employer must also pay the immigration skills charge, which works out as an additional £5,000 for a large firm paying for a five-year visa.

The minimum salary level for a worker recruited under Tier Two is £30,000, but a higher salary is demanded for some roles. To recruit a skilled worker an employer needs to show that they genuinely attempted to recruit for the position from the UK or European Union, but that no suitable applicant applied. Lawyers and officials call this the resident labour market test. Adverts for roles must be placed on certain websites and held open for at least twenty-eight days. If a person does apply but is not recruited, there should be clear reasons as to why.

In 2010, Theresa May imposed a cap of 20,700 on the number of visas that could be issued under the general Tier Two route every year. Some have pointed out that limiting the number of skilled migrants entering the UK to fill vacancies that cannot be filled by home-grown workers is not necessarily sensible. Set at a fairly generous level, it was only in late 2017 that the number of workers recruited started to bump up against that ceiling. The cap operates on a monthly basis and when it is reached the Home Office applies a complex formula to decide who will and will not be offered a visa, taking into account whether a job is a shortage occupation role, as well as the salary and the skill level. In early 2018, this meant that only those being offered a salary of £50,000 might actually get a visa; far in excess of the salary level for many vital roles in the National Health Service, for example. The idiocy of preventing desperately needed doctors and nurses being recruited eventually led to those professions being exempted from the cap in June 2018, freeing up more spaces within the cap for other skilled workers. In the meantime, it is thought over 2,000 doctors and nurses had been refused visas. Nevertheless, because of the exceptions to the cap discussed below, the number of main applicants issued with a Tier Two general visa in the year ended September 2019 was just over 33,600.

The not-so-simple rules I have sketched out here are riddled with exceptions, making the whole system even more complex than it first appears. For example, the resident labour market test does not apply if the skilled worker is earning in excess of £159,600, if the job is listed in the shortage occupation list (the list of jobs Mr Imam relied on) or if the person is changing from a Tier Four student visa, having completed a bachelor's or master's degree in the UK. You will also be exempt from the cap if you are applying for the extension of an existing

Tier Two visa. In most cases, a minimum salary level of £30,000 is required, but this is just a minimum and a higher salary applies for some jobs listed in Appendix J of the Immigration Rules. Appendix J is 212 pages long and consists of seven extremely long tables setting out different levels of job, from PhD level downwards. Each entry includes a SOC code, job description, examples of typical tasks and two minimum salary levels, one for experienced workers and one for 'new entrants' who had previously been degree-level students in the UK.

Tier Three of the points-based system was already dead on arrival in 2008. It was intended for 'low-skilled' workers in specific industries, such as agriculture and food processing. Programmes like the venerable Seasonal Agricultural Workers' Scheme, which allowed for the temporary and seasonal recruitment of farm workers from abroad, and more recent sector-based schemes in food processing and other low-paid and difficult but important jobs, would have slotted nicely into Tier Three. But the influx of workers from other European Union countries from 2004 onwards meant there was no economic or political demand at the time. The politics of immigration fundamentally changed and the case for high-skilled migration had, if anything, been made too successfully. The vital contribution of 'low-skilled' workers was minimised and dismissed right across the political spectrum following EU expansion, and the new low-paid EU migrants were massively taken for granted. While it is true that a high level of education is not needed for these types of job, labelling them disdainfully as low-skilled underplays how dirty, dangerous and demeaning yet also critical their roles are. The redesignation of these labourers from 'low-skilled workers' to 'key workers' during the coronavirus crisis was both welcome and overdue, but it would be optimistic to think this change of attitude is likely to last.

Tier Four is designed for foreign students attending private schools and colleges or universities. Why students are included at all within a system that is seemingly aimed at workers has always been unclear. Like employers recruiting workers under Tier Two, though, schools, colleges and universities must apply for a sponsorship licence from the Home Office in order for foreign students to take their courses. These licences have become essential to business for many, if not most, private schools, colleges and publicly funded universities. Indeed, 262,000 such students entered the UK in the year ended September 2019.

Tier Five is an odd ragbag collection of other miscellaneous short-term routes into the UK. It includes temporary permits for those working in the creative and sporting industries, unpaid voluntary charity workers and religious workers, schemes for government-authorised exchanges and entry under international agreements, and a 'youth mobility scheme', which is a replacement for the old working holidaymaker scheme. Notably, none of these categories include a route to settlement. A total of around 42,000 main applicants (before dependent family members are counted) were issued with visas under this collection of routes in the year ended September 2019.

The other defining features of the points-based system are: firstly, a much greater role for employers and educational institutions as sponsors than had previously been the case; and, secondly, the use of external advice to adjust the criteria for admission. The five-year strategy paper in 2005 referred to 'an independent body to advise us on labour market needs', which would be employer-led. In 2007, the Migration Advisory Committee convened its first meeting. The MAC, as it became known, proved to be an increasingly important feature of the new system for migration, although from the ever-growing number of its recommendations that have been ignored by the government you might be forgiven for thinking otherwise. Arguably, the MAC has often been used as a fig leaf for pre-determined government decisions. If so, that function has proved to be very helpful. Ministers and civil servants alike have found it useful to appear to outsource decision-making to an independent body, freeing them of apparent responsibility.

For the sake of completeness, I should add that a number of further work and study routes have persisted outside this points-based system. The UK Ancestry visa, for instance, a hangover from an earlier age, has remained in place, enabling Commonwealth citizens who can prove that at least one grandparent was born in the territory of the United Kingdom to enter on a five-year work visa. By its nature, it mainly benefits those of white ethnicity. A visa has also been retained for representatives of an overseas business setting up a UK office. Domestic workers in domestic and diplomatic households likewise continue to be admitted, although on conditions that prevent changes of employer and thereby encourage employer abuse of the system. A student visitor visa also remains for those entering for six months or less.

FLAWED FROM THE START

Over a decade after its introduction, it is clear that the points-based system has failed in every way. A House of Commons library report in 2018 stated without controversy that the system 'has come to be widely regarded by individual applicants, sponsors, immigration lawyers and the judiciary as unduly complex, burdensome, costly and ill-suited to the needs of its users'.[8]

At the time the points-based system was launched, one of its primary selling points was that it would contain objective criteria, removing the need for subjective judgement calls by civil servants who had no real-world experience of business needs and processes. This matched with the overall ideology of evidence-based policy-making that was central to the New Labour governance project. This quest for objectivity proved to be one of the main drivers of the length and complexity of the new rules. Civil servants ended up trying to set out exact documentary requirements for every conceivable real-world situation that might arise. And there are a *lot* of these.

For example, for every immigration category, it would be necessary to prove possession of a fixed amount of money in a bank account, and to achieve this, an applicant would need to submit bank statements. Civil servants were anxious to ensure that these documents could not be forged, and yet were also faced with prescribing the exact requirements for what would and would not be considered a bank statement. Copies would not be accepted because they were thought easier to forge, so the original versions would need to be sent in for inspection. A formal bank letterhead would be needed with the bank's name and logo. The statements would need to show the applicant's name (or the name of the parent of guardian for child applicants), the account number, the date of the statement and any transactions during the statement period. This sounds sensible enough and would be simple for most people in the UK. Most standard bank statements in the UK meet these requirements. But what about those with a building society passbook instead of bank statements, those who had opted out of paper bank statements, or those from outside the UK, where bank statements do not adopt this format? Separate detailed rules were set for each of these scenarios as well. Each of these sets of requirements makes the rules longer and longer, with the result that the rules are as a whole more complex and harder to use for everyone.

The sheer weight of words involved in the points-based system is astounding. There is a whole section of the Immigration Rules devoted to the system, which is itself seventy-eight pages long. But this part of the rules also cross-refers to, by my count, a further twelve appendices, and the rules include another seventeen separate appendices on top of those. The category under which foreign businesspeople entered the UK before 2006 was just over 2,000 words long. Its replacement now consists of nearly 12,000 words, which is an increase of 600 per cent.[9] Admittedly, some of this verbiage had to be added in 2012, after the Supreme Court ruled that the government must include any requirement that might lead to the refusal of a visa application in the main rules. Until then, much of the detail of the scheme had been hidden away in policy documents that could be changed at will without having to go through a parliamentary scrutiny process.[10]

Some of the appendices are quite short, like the lists of approved, government-authorised exchange schemes. Others are hundreds of pages long. There are additional, separate documents setting out the rules for sponsoring employers and educational institutions, for example, and further guidance documents for each of the multiple immigration categories expanded on previously. To make it worse, the words change regularly. A lawyer working in this field needs to know all this material, at least in outline, in order to provide the best assistance possible. It has become pretty much impossible for an employer, school, college or university to wade through the morass alone. So, the system is far from simple, accessible, transparent or usable, as it was first intended.

This peculiar way of implementing objective criteria, focusing on form only and not on substance, has caused the system to become extremely inflexible in individual cases. Most people think of an 'illegal immigrant' as someone who smuggles themselves into the country in the back of a lorry or deliberately goes to ground when their visa expires. However, an increasing number of highly skilled workers, students, academics and others have found themselves on the wrong side of the law simply because the rules have become so obscure and inflexible. Such people often wanted to make lawful applications on time, but it has become all too easy to make a mistake and be forced to leave the country as a result.

Continuing with the earlier theme of the voluminous rules on bank statements, for example, those who had electronic bank statements – which would be easy to forge – were told that these needed to be accompanied by a supporting letter from the bank or building society, on company headed paper, confirming that the statement provided is authentic, or otherwise printing statements bearing the official stamp of the bank or building society on every page. It is easy enough to cook up a rule like this in a building in Whitehall, but no one talked to the banks or building societies first. Many simply refuse to provide these letters or stamps, leaving some applicants having to tour different branches in the hope they will find a sympathetic employee. Where a series of bank statements was demanded, an accidental missing statement was fatal to an application. Civil servants would not pick up the phone to the bank and ask for a copy to be sent in themselves; they would simply refuse the application and render the applicant illegal.

As a further example, the financial rules in several categories included a requirement to hold a specified amount of money continuously in a bank account for a specified period of time. Allowing your bank balance to dip even one penny below this amount for one day, for example because of an unexpected charge or direct debit, would lead to a visa refusal. Those who tried to challenge such decisions in court often failed. 'It's the law,' said the judges.

In 2011, the National Audit Office found that half of all points-based system refusals were due to not providing the right information or evidence.[11] In some of these cases, the applicants may well not have had the evidence. If so, why would they knowingly have paid a huge fee to make a doomed application in the first place, though? It was obvious to everyone outside the Home Office, and perhaps it was, in truth, obvious even to those within, that the new system was anything but simple, clear and transparent for those actually applying under it. In an attempt to mitigate the worst excesses of its new 'objective' approach, in 2009 the Home Office belatedly introduced what it called an 'evidential flexibility policy'. This allowed officials some added flexibility around some of the more painstaking requirements but was initially secret, known only to officials and not to applicants; and because it was secret, if it was not followed by an official then an applicant could not complain, as they would not know about it to begin with – and neither would their lawyer. The secret policy was eventually leaked and published, leading to a string of legal cases about whether the Home Office had properly applied it in individual cases, whether applicants could rely on the principle of fairness and so on.

All this rather than addressing the fundamental, underlying problem: the rules are utterly incomprehensible to normal people.

DEFINING AND PREVENTING ABUSE

The way in which the objective criteria have been implemented has also opened the system to unintended consequences, and even to

outright abuse. As it turned out, civil servants were no better at designing objective criteria than they had been at making subjective
judgement calls. For example, the predecessor to Tier One of the
points-based system, the Highly Skilled Migrant Programme, had
aimed to attract highly skilled migrants – obviously – with the intention that they would make a valuable contribution to the economy of
the United Kingdom. Unlike conventional work permits, their visas
would not be tied to a particular employer. Instead, they would be
free to find whatever employment or self-employment they could.
Civil servants at the Home Office, however, trained as they were in a
departmental culture of keeping migrants out, became increasingly
suspicious that their rules were allowing in more than just the brightest and the best. Indeed, a review in 2006 found there was evidence
that some migrants were using forged documents to show how they
supposedly met the set criteria and, for various reasons, some entrants were ending up in relatively poorly paid employment, as taxi
drivers or in fast food chains.

Changes were made and a new points assessment was introduced
requiring, amongst other things, a migrant to achieve a minimum level
of earnings before qualifying for settlement. The reforms applied even
to those who had already entered, in effect retrospectively changing
the rules of the game after these people had given up their homes
and jobs to move to the UK. Those caught out like this succeeded
with a group challenge to the new rules in court, but the regulations
remained in place for new applicants.[12] The reforms seemed to work.
When the Migration Advisory Committee reviewed Tier One of the
points-based system in a report published in 2009, they found of
the highly skilled migrants admitted under that latter system that 'a
high proportion are in employment and that employment is strongly

skewed towards more skilled occupational groups'.[13] Furthermore, the report found that many employers 'regard this route as crucial to their economic success and international competitiveness'. This was insufficient to save the route. In Parliament, Theresa May chose to emphasise the perceived failures rather than the successes: 'At least 30 per cent of Tier One migrants work in low-skilled occupations such as stacking shelves, driving taxis or working as security guards, and some do not have a job at all.'[14] The scheme, by then called 'Tier One General', was closed by Theresa May in December 2010.

As a further step towards ensuring that only the intended bene-ficiaries of the points-based system would receive visas, the Home Office also gradually reintroduced subjective discretionary judg-ments on whether an applicant was 'genuine'. This term was never defined, but students had to show they were 'genuine' students from 2012 onwards and entrepreneurs had to show they were 'genuine' entrepreneurs from early 2013 onwards, after a sudden increase in the number of applicants caused officials to panic. What is a genuine student, you might ask, and how would a civil servant answer that question? Particularly before the student begins his or her course. And how would one tell a 'genuine' entrepreneur from a fake one? There is no *Dragons' Den*-style panel of established entrepreneurs to judge applications, after all. No, it was for civil servants to do that, almost all of whom, pretty much by definition, have experience only of salaried employment in the public sector.

One way of looking at these changes is as a welcome reintroduc-tion of some common sense into the process, enabling officials to refuse applications that might meet the technical requirements of the rules but which do not satisfy their intention or spirit in some way. Another way of seeing the new genuineness tests, though, is that they increase the potential for different officials to take different approaches, for different subcultures to grow up at different offices and for unconscious race, gender, age, disability and other biases to creep into the decision-making process. Either way, it marked a return to the days when even applicants who have all of the right paperwork might not know whether their application would succeed. The introduction of genuineness tests was an admission of defeat. The attempt to create an objective system had failed. We are left with the worst of all possible worlds: all of the complexity that was introduced in an attempt to create objective criteria, alongside subjective judgement calls made by inexperienced junior officials re-inserted anyway.

Mr Imam, with whom we began this chapter, was by no means the only skilled migrant to have come to grief in the minefield that is these ever-changing rules. The pages of the law reports are replete with examples of other black and Asian migrants similarly shipwrecked. Take the highly skilled migrants who found that the rules on settlement had been retrospectively changed, making it impossible for some of them to qualify, but only after they had given up their old jobs, homes and lives and moved to the UK. Most of those who brought the successful legal case against this obvious injustice were black or Asian.[15] Or the mainly black and Asian migrants accused by the Home Office (on the basis of dodgy evidence) of cheating in their English language tests, without being given any right of reply. With no ability to appeal, many were detained and bundled out of the country.[16] Or those alleged to have misled the Home Office about their past income and tax returns, most of whom were once again black and Asian.[17]

And these are just the ones who stood and fought. Many, many more no longer bring legal challenges, since the right of appeal against the refusal of work visas was abolished with the Immigration

Act 2014. Instead they have to rely on a more complex and much more expensive procedure called judicial review. Meanwhile, those migrants who are non-racialised and middle-class find their cases instead reported on the pages of the newspapers rather than in the law reports. These examples are euphemistically described as being 'media-friendly' and the Home Office press response team quickly reverses their decisions. This policy of deliberately mining the rules with obscure obstacles hidden below the surface, then selectively rescuing only those deemed to be 'media-friendly', is both transparently racist and unfair. Nevertheless, it has become standard operating procedure at the modern Home Office.

NO CUDDLY TOY

There are several underlying reasons that the points-based system failed. To begin with, the Home Office interpretation of the idea of 'objective criteria' was a peculiar and unnecessary one. The length and complexity of the rules flowed from this. Junior officials were expected to act like robots, merely checking whether the documents submitted by an applicant met precise predefined criteria and, if so, issuing a visa.

In a way, the Home Office could be accused of being too far ahead of its time. Today, technology entrepreneurs are using artificial intelligence to recognise everyday objects, utilising vast sets of data and complex detection and perception technology. Self-driving cars require computers to interpret, classify and predict the behaviour of a bewildering array of real-life objects. The Home Office tried something similar with no prior experience, no artificial intelligence, no data and no computers all the way back in 2006. Unsurprisingly, the project failed. When subjective assessments by officials were reintroduced, it was not a subjective assessment of the meaning and reliability of a given document, which should have been built in from the start. It was instead a potentially biased evaluation of whether the migrant qualified under the spirit and intention of the rules. This was the very antithesis of an objective criterion.

It did not help that senior civil servants seem to have had in mind a 'model migrant' for whom they were writing the admission rules. One suspects that this model migrant looked a bit like success-era Steve Jobs or Richard Branson, the entrepreneurs with whom civil servants might have been familiar. Officials perhaps overlooked the fact that neither were educated to degree level and that both had their share of business failures, as well as successes. Both are also white. As Wendy Williams noted in her 'Windrush Lessons Learned Review', there are few minority ethnic senior officials at the Home Office.[18] The migrants who applied for visas literally did not look like the kind of entrepreneurs some civil servants held in their minds. Economists deal with averages, patterns and generalities. On average, migrants make a positive contribution to the public purse; in general, skilled migrants improve productivity; and overall, migration promotes economic growth. An economist might identify that the characteristics of those most likely to succeed in the labour market include educational attainment, language ability and experience, but they would also be very well aware that there are plenty of people in possession of those characteristics who do not outperform their less privileged peers.

In contrast, officials at the Home Office are trained in a culture of dealing with individuals, and education and competency in economics or the social sciences does not seem to be widespread. The complex messages from research are often only partially digested. A migrant investing in a care home or a fast food franchise or finding work as an analyst or a middle-manager, for example, was not the paradigm civil servants had in mind. Many of these migrants did not seem to fit the preconceived 'brightest and best' model, and it was therefore considered that there must be failures in the design of the rules. As a result, the criteria were adjusted and tightened. What civil servants were really looking for, it seemed, were those elusive migrants who would immediately start a pioneering, world-beating, instantly successful high-tech business, as ministers seemed to have promised in the press releases.

But designing rules to filter out all but the most successful migrants is impossible. It is basically an exercise in crystal ball gazing. There are many reasons why a migrant might 'succeed' or 'fail' in the labour market, including race discrimination, gender, mental or physical health, caring for a young or ageing relative, changing life priorities and more, all of which might be more important than educational attainment or prior experience, but none of which are taken into account by the objective criteria of the points-based system. Rather than being known as the Highly *Successful* Migrant Programme, it was called the Highly *Skilled* Migrant Programme for a reason.

Civil servants were trying to predict migrant life outcomes to a high degree of certainty based on limited inputs and then evaluating this over a snapshot time frame of just a few years. This perhaps explains the difference between the 2006 evaluation of the Highly Skilled Migrant Programme by the Home Office and evaluation of its almost identical successor, the Tier One General visa, by the Migration Advisory Committee in 2009. It seems plausible that the scheme did not, in truth, change a great deal over those three years. Rather, officials in 2006 felt that there were too many migrants being admitted who did not match the right profile, whereas experts in 2009 assessed that the overall effect was positive and as intended. The outcomes were the same, but perceptions of success differed depending on perspective.

THE RISE AND FALL OF ECONOMIC IMMIGRATION POLICY

Ultimately, the failure of the points-based system was political. Initially, despite its flaws, it did what it was supposed to and allowed and encouraged skilled migration. The issues with the complexity of the system could perhaps have been ironed out over time. The real problems came when the government of the day decided quietly to change the purpose of the system from encouraging to discouraging migration. The incoming Conservative-led government in 2010 was bound by its own net migration target, which required lower immigration and higher emigration. As the self-styled party of free trade and enterprise, it was difficult for the Conservatives to challenge the self-evident truth that skilled migration was economically valuable and the new orthodoxy that it was therefore to be encouraged. The response was to hollow out the contents but retain the shell. Complexity was transformed from a bug in the system to a fully-fledged feature. Visits to employers increasingly became excuses to terminate sponsor licences rather than assisting compliance with the onerous terms. Routes within the points-based system were actually or effectively closed. Numerical caps were introduced to others. Subjective screening was re-introduced, and criteria were toughened. The language of encouraging skilled and entrepreneurial migration was retained – but only the language, not the intent.

The whole edifice of the points-based system was founded on economic arguments that proved to be rhetorically durable yet also intangible and, to many people, irrelevant. The economic benefits were effectively invisible because it was impossible to imagine an alternative, less prosperous universe without them. Early New Labour research papers at the turn of the millennium discussed not only fiscal and economic effects and benefits but also social and cultural ones. This subtlety was lost in the political messaging machine, where immigration was promoted and sold in brutally utilitarian terms. Migrants were discussed as if they were a natural resource to be managed, mined and exploited.

David Blunkett was central to the change in thinking at the Home Office and it was he who, as Home Secretary from 2001 to 2004, popularised the term 'managed migration'. By 2005 and 2006, government proposals on immigration routinely bore the strapline 'Making migration work for Britain'. It was uncomfortably close to 'Making migrants work for Britain'. In his foreword to the 2005 five-year strategy paper on immigration, Tony Blair wrote that the government must 'ensure Britain continues to benefit from people from abroad who work hard and add to our prosperity'. The consultation paper, issued in 2005, included a section entitled 'Benefits, Costs and Impacts of Migration', which contained only two subsections: 'Economic Benefits' and 'Costs and Impacts'. In the final White Paper, which set out the detail of the proposed new system, the Home Secretary of the day, Charles Clarke, wrote that the UK needed 'a world class migration system to attract the brightest and the best from across the world' so that 'only those who legitimately apply and have the necessary skills can come to this country'.[19] Others should stay away, he did not need to add.

There is nothing wrong in making an economic case for immigration, but there are potential dangers if one is not careful. And Labour politicians were not careful. They were reckless. By making the case all about economics, it was implied that those who are not perceived as economically beneficial, like refugees or family members, were a burden. Even the skilled workers, seen as desirable during the good times, were left vulnerable when hard times hit in 2008. The entire case for immigration seemed to vanish with the global financial crisis. As Maya Goodfellow argues, 'Eventually New Labour's claims that immigration was good for the economy would look like a lie when wages began to stagnate and right-wing politicians laid the blame at the door of the newcomers.'[20]

Perhaps worst of all, a significant segment of public opinion was never open to purely economic arguments, yet the Labour government went ahead regardless. Economics are complex, ephemeral and indirect. When members of the public felt the pinch, they did not feel any personal benefit from immigration, but they could easily imagine a personal cost. Others would rather have lower economic growth but also lower immigration. While surveys show that the public can and do distinguish between high- and low-skilled migrants when questions are put to them, there is little evidence that these niceties come into play when 'immigration' is discussed as a supposedly simple, generic, broad issue – as it is, for example, during an election campaign. There are plenty of commonplace myths regarding economics and immigration that feed this narrative, such as the 'lump of labour fallacy' – the idea that an economy includes a finite number of jobs – or that immigration suppresses wages. That these enduring myths are false is irrelevant; they are widely believed by the public and by many in the media and the political classes. By promoting increased immigration, taking ownership of immigration as an issue but making a purely economic case for increased immigration levels,

Labour ensured that its record was always going to be vulnerable to later attack.

The points-based system was effectively the personification of New Labour's approach to immigration, once it was filtered through the implementation of civil servants at the Home Office. It was New Labour's approach that was fundamentally flawed; there is undoubtedly an economic case for immigration, but it was vastly oversold with all the talk of 'the brightest and the best'. In 2003, Don Flynn was the policy officer at the Joint Council for the Welfare of Immigrants. In a prescient pamphlet entitled '"Tough as old boots?" Asylum, immigration and the paradox of New Labour policy', Flynn argued that apparently contradictory liberal economic immigration policies and illiberal asylum policies were actually entirely consistent. Both were guided by a belief, he said, that 'the movement of people across the globe should be guided at every point by the economic objectives of growth and modernisation'. He also predicted that the approach would not age well:

The point being made here is that the hitching of immigration policy to the interests and functioning of the global economy is, in itself, most unlikely to enable the construction of a calm and stable point from which to manage migration. It is more likely that we will see instead the conditions of the 1990s and the early new century being reproduced indefinitely into the future, with constant campaigns to address the latest crisis in the system of control, resulting in more administrative changes, fresh primary legislation every second or third year, and the ratcheting up of public apprehension as politicians and groupings use the issue to jostle for power and preferment. Over time the sense of crisis itself will become a permanent feature of the system producing demoralisation amongst those expected to administer it and a loss of faith in its effectiveness and legitimacy amongst the wider public.

He was right. Labour's economic immigration policy undoubtedly did enhance economic growth, but it was also too ambitious in scope and its public appeal was doomed by the narrow, utilitarian justification relied on by its proponents. Economic migrants were mere tools. In other spheres of immigration policy, refugees were to be kept out at all costs and were dissuaded from coming to the UK with harsh treatment on and after arrival. Family migrants, for their part, were said to be failing to integrate. With leading politicians making these arguments themselves, it is little surprise that hostility towards immigration more generally and towards migrants themselves grew rapidly during this period.

CHAPTER 8

STUDENTS:
AWESOME OR BOGUS?

Priyanka Ann Joshi was a model student. She first arrived in the United Kingdom from India, her home country, in 2005. Joshi studied hard and obtained both a bachelor's degree and a master's degree. In June 2014, she applied for further permission to stay in the country to study for a PhD. Everything seemed to be in order. Unknown to Ms Joshi, though, the sponsor licence of the college to which she had applied was revoked by the Home Office a few weeks after she had submitted her application. This meant that her request for permission to stay would inevitably be rejected. It took the Home Office a long time to tell her what the problem was, but she eventually found out in January 2015. She was then given sixty days to either make a new application or leave the country.

Unfortunately, that was nowhere near enough time to actually find another institution at which to study. As the end of the period approached, she put in a holding application explaining the difficulty and asking for more time. A decision was made on 6 May 2015 to reject this request – and yet no one told Ms Joshi. Instead, the refusal sat on her file at the Home Office. Ms Joshi only found out four weeks later, at 6.15 a.m. on 11 June 2015, when a team of immigration enforcement officers arrived at her house, woke her and her husband, bundled them both into a van and detained them. Ms Joshi later complained that the immigration officers were 'extremely rude' and had wrongly accused her of lying when she said she was still waiting for a decision from the Home Office.

Ms Joshi and her husband were eventually released two weeks later. Neither had broken any law or overstayed their visa, yet they had been detained for no obvious reason in extremely distressing circumstances. It seemed that the enforcement team at the Home Office wrongly thought that the refusal had been served; that one month was long enough for a migrant to leave; and that a dawn raid with no prior warning was an appropriate way of ensuring that Ms Joshi left the country, after almost ten years of lawful residence and studies. Ms Joshi brought a legal case against the Home Office, which ultimately failed. While the judge expressed 'considerable sympathy' for Ms Joshi and her husband, and said it was not clear that it really had been 'necessary' for them to be detained before they were even informed of the negative decision, he still found that the Home Office had not actually acted illegally, as such.[1]

ATTRACTING INTERNATIONAL STUDENTS

Ms Joshi had entered the UK at a time when foreign students were being actively sought by the British government. They were seen as an unalloyed good. The high fees they pay to study injected much-needed funding into the further and higher education sectors, cross-subsidising academic research and the education of home-grown students. While living in the UK, they also spent money in the local economy on accommodation, food, entertainment and more. The vast majority leave at the end of their studies, as we will see in a moment, but those who remain are by definition highly skilled and economically beneficial. Educating foreign elites in the United

Kingdom also potentially increases British 'soft power' and influence abroad in the long term: think of Bill Clinton or Benazir Bhutto, both of whom attended British universities before becoming premiers of their respective countries. Finally, the public have historically been relaxed about the entry of foreign students, at least when responding to opinion polls.

In 1999 Tony Blair launched an official Prime Minister's Initiative to increase the numbers of foreign students by 50,000 over six years. It was accompanied by a major marketing campaign, revisions to the student visa routes and a relaxation of the rules on students working. In the end, the target was exceeded by 43,000, which, on the face of it, looked like a high level of success. The British government was not acting in a vacuum, though; more and more students were studying abroad over this period anyway, and other countries, such as the United States, Australia and Canada, were also targeting the same, relatively small number of internationally mobile students. In reality, the British share of this market for international students actually fell over the period. A new initiative was duly launched in 2006 to recruit an additional 100,000 students from a more diverse range of countries.

Problems with private colleges first started to emerge in 2004. These colleges were unregulated, meaning anyone at all was able to set themselves up in any premises in the country, fire up a website and offer any course they had invented themselves. Some were providing very poor-quality or even non-existent teaching, offering false attendance records and allowing their students to work full-time alongside their 'studies', in breach of their visas. Some of the students applying to these colleges may have known, or arguably should have known, what they were getting themselves into.

But it is impossible to tell from a website and prospectus what you are really going to get when you arrive, and considerable fees had to be paid up front. Legitimate students might well find that they had been duped and their money wasted. Some had spent a substantial amount of their family's money or had borrowed the funds needed. One Nepalese student was defrauded of £9,500 by a corrupt college and, despite assisting the police with their enquiries, she was still forced to leave the United Kingdom before being able to commence an alternative course.[2] A student in this position faced either leaving the UK empty-handed or trying to make the best of a bad job and at least getting some work experience and picking up some language skills while they could. With students restricted to working no more than twenty hours per week and plenty of genuine students on high-level courses at top institutions breaking the rules, it was sorely tempting for others to follow this example and violate the given student visa laws.[3] In order to fix the problem, from January 2005, international students were only permitted to study at a list of accredited institutions. As the list was being drawn up, the Home Office visited 1,200 private colleges. Twenty-five per cent were found to be ingenuine and were removed from the list.

Student visas were absorbed into the points-based system in 2009. The number of students entering the UK rose sharply but, to the chagrin of educational institutions, so too did the level of administration associated with them. Any school, college or university that wanted to teach international students now needed to apply for, gain and keep a precious sponsor licence. Loss of a sponsor licence would be financially catastrophic for any university and many colleges.[4] The new system meant that a digital 'confirmation of acceptance for studies' had to be issued to every student, and detailed attendance and other records needed to be kept. Students were prevented from switching courses even within the same institution. Significantly, the licence also imposed general duties to 'support immigration control' and to co-operate with the Home Office.[5] This was not restricted only to the international students for which each individual institution was directly responsible.

DETERRING INTERNATIONAL STUDENTS

A serious, high-profile crisis hit the Home Office in 2009, when it emerged that eight Pakistani nationals arrested in the UK under terrorism laws had first entered the country on student visas facilitated by a fake college. A subsequent Home Affairs Committee report was highly critical of Home Office oversight of student visas, and the language of 'bogus students' and 'bogus colleges' became commonplace.[6] When David Cameron and Theresa May entered government in 2010 promising to reduce immigration, international students seemed an obvious target. May soon announced a range of measures intended to combat the perceived abuse of student visas by closing colleges, tightening visa requirements, restricting the right to work during and after the completion of courses and restricting the entry of the dependents of students.[7]

The idea now seemed to be to deter foreign students from coming to the UK rather than encouraging them. Twelve years after Blair's first initiative to increase international student numbers by 43,000 per year, in 2011 Cameron announced an intention to reduce student visa numbers by 80,000 per year.[8] The reforms met with some success, if it can be called that. Having increased gradually year-on-year since at least 1999 to 2011, the numbers of non-EU university students entering the UK started to fall slightly.[9] This came at a time when the total number of students studying abroad was increasing globally. The share of this market coming to the UK to study started to fall. The UK was in danger of losing its second place in the international rankings to Australia, which was successfully increasing its share. In particular, the number of Indian students deciding to come to the UK to study fell by more than 10 per cent.[10]

In spite of these measures, yet another scandal emerged in 2014 when the BBC's *Panorama* uncovered evidence of organised cheating by a handful of students at two different test centres for English language certificates. The Home Office had signed a huge commercial contract with an American company called English Language Testing (ETS), which would provide these tests remotely with minimal oversight by officials or by ETS itself. The test centre would play a recording provided by ETS, document the student's responses and send the recording off to ETS to be marked. However, the BBC journalists caught two test centres offering a 'service' to students, through which someone else could take the test for them.

ETS had previously detected some cheating back in 2012 and had informed the Home Office. Action was quietly taken against the 446 individuals concerned, but no wider review was undertaken. This time, though, with the cheating exposed in the media, the Home Office response was rapid and robust. Too robust. Having regularly touted their crackdown on bogus colleges and students, May and Cameron looked like they had lost control. A hasty review by ETS of its own exam recordings led it to accuse a staggering 97 per cent of its own students of cheating. The review was based on computerised voice recognition software that ETS had been developing but had not yet considered suitable for deployment. It seems to have been the scale of the review necessary and the short timescale demanded by ministers that led ETS to deploy the software now, rather than faith in its accuracy. Officials at the Home Office, untrained in linguistics or the technology and techniques deployed by ETS, simply accepted what they were told. The evidence produced by ETS to the Home

Office consisted merely of a list of people said to be cheats. ETS refused to hand over any recordings either to the Home Office or to the individuals concerned. Everyone just had to accept that ETS was right, whether ETS was actually right or not.[11]

It is certain that some students did cheat. It seems inherently unlikely that as many as 97 per cent did. Nevertheless, between 2014 and 2016, the Home Office took action against over 50,000 foreign students. Nearly 3,000 students were removed or refused re-entry to the UK. More than 12,000 appeals were heard by the courts, with 40 per cent of those who appealed winning their case. Over 11,000 students left the UK voluntarily. A subsequent inquiry report from the House of Commons Public Accounts Committee found that the Home Office had been 'quick to act on imperfect evidence, but slow in responding to indications that innocent people may have been caught up in its actions'.[12] The Home Office is nothing if not consistent, and it would seem that officials always assume the worst of immigrants. It is standard operating procedure to refuse, detain and remove migrants before they are allowed the opportunity to explain or challenge the assumption that they are dishonest.

On any rational level, it was hard to understand why Theresa May and David Cameron were so determined to drive down the numbers of international students. Mainstream opinion across the political spectrum was that such migrants should be encouraged to come to the UK. Preventing and, if necessary, punishing proven outright cheating is understandable, but the approach of the government went far beyond that. Responses to signs of wrongdoing were sweeping and indiscriminate rather than considered and proportionate. Wider reforms to the student visa route were not just about preventing fraud; they were clearly intended to apply a much more selective approach to student admission. Those students who did not meet preconceived ideas of who might be 'the brightest and the best' were to be kept out. These were the students studying at below degree level at private colleges, for example, or those at degree level but studying at universities that ministers seemed to regard as second-rate or even those taking external degrees from reputable universities. Like those lucky few to be admitted to degree-level courses at top universities, these migrants still injected money into educational institutions, cross-subsidised domestic students, pumped spending into local economies outside of London and, if they qualified to stay at the end of their studies, brought new skills, productivity and drive to the British economy. Yet, for some reason, they were no longer to be allowed in.

OPPORTUNITY OR THREAT?

There were two potential explanations for why international students were so unpopular at the top of government during the Cameron years. One was political: as ever, it all came back to the net migration target. As we have already seen, net migration measures the number of migrants in and out of the country, and a 'migrant' is defined in international statistical standards as a person moving from one country to another for a period exceeding one year. Most students therefore met the definition of 'migrant' and they were duly counted in the net migration target. With the government missing the target year after year, there was pressure to reduce immigration in any way, and indeed in every way, possible. Whether reducing immigration would be beneficial or harmful became irrelevant when viewed through this political lens. Reducing the number of international students coming to the UK can be seen as a simple matter of short-term political expediency.

There is a second way of interpreting the hostility that Cameron and particularly May seemed to feel towards international students, though: fear of change. Both were conservatives as well as Conservatives, after all. It is clearly true that reducing the numbers of students arriving would have an immediate impact on the net migration figures. However, net migration by definition measures both incoming and outgoing migrants. If students left the UK at the end of their studies, they would also show up as an outgoing migrant in the second part of the net migration equation several years later; in the longer term, this would help with meeting the target. But this assumes that the students would leave at the end of their studies, and both Cameron and May seemed concerned that they were staying. International students come from a diverse range of countries, with China, India, Hong Kong, Malaysia and Nigeria all amongst the top countries of origin. If such students made the United Kingdom their home, the ethnic composition of the population would change over time.

As we have seen, international students were welcomed with open arms during the Blair era and it was seen as positive if they chose to make their homes in the UK permanently: the evidence suggested that on average this would be good for the economy. In contrast, Theresa May devoted a whole segment of her speech at the Conservative Party conference in 2015 to international students and claimed, 'Too many of them are not returning home as soon as their visa runs out.' Showing her disdain for the university sector as a whole, she continued, 'I don't care what the university lobbyists say: the rules must be enforced.'[13] Elsewhere, Cameron and May had both already argued that it was important to 'break that link between temporary visas and permanent settlement'.[14]

The data at the time seemed to support May's claim that students were overstaying their visas: statistics from the Office for National

Statistics suggested that on average around 100,000 international students were remaining in the UK beyond the end of their visa every year.[15] However, these estimates were based on the notoriously inaccurate International Passenger Survey, the unreliability of which we considered back in Chapter 2. When in 2017 the Home Office used hard data from exit checks to assess what was really happening to students, it found that only around 4,000 remained in the UK at the end of their visas, meaning 97.4 per cent of international students left before their visa expired.[16] As a result, the Office for National Statistics had to dramatically revise its previous figures; it looked as if the entire crusade against foreign students had been founded on a massive misconception.

Either to settle the question once and for all or to kick it into the political long grass, the Migration Advisory Committee was commissioned to report on the impact of international students. Published in 2018, the report reviewed all the available evidence and confirmed the reasons Tony Blair had launched the drive to recruit foreign students in the first place. Evidence from Universities UK suggested that international students were worth £10.8 billion in export value and supported over 200,000 jobs in towns and cities across the UK. As much as 23 per cent of teaching income and 13 per cent of all university income came from international student fees.[17] The experts recommended that no cap on numbers should be imposed, that no tightening of visa rules was needed and that it 'would be better to loosen visa requirements and regulations as much as possible'. Although it was not feasible to remove students from the net migration figures because of the internationally accepted definition of 'migrant', the committee found that, if there was a problem with including students in those figures, 'we think it more likely comes from the existence of the target itself than the inclusion of students in that target'. Theresa May's reforms had created 'an image problem' that was harming the UK's reputation and the country's ability to recruit genuine students.[18]

Cameron and May were driven by more than merely a technocratic measure of numbers in and out; they wanted to reduce the speed at which the ethnicity of the population was changing. There were plenty of other policies aimed at breaking the link between migration and settlement in other areas of immigration policy: ending automatic grants of settlement to refugees after five years, tightening the family rules as we saw in Chapter 5, extending the probationary period for spouses from two to five years and the obstacles erected to naturalisation as a British citizen, which we will look at in Chapter 12, were all intended to achieve the same purpose: preventing migrants from settling permanently in the United Kingdom. Whereas previous governments had seen students as a natural resource to be exploited, the Cameron and May governments perceived them as a cultural and ethnic threat to be contained.

CHAPTER 9

FREE MOVEMENT: AUF WIEDERSEHEN, PET

F ree movement is generally something British citizens foist on other countries. In the imperial era, for instance, the British went where they liked whether the inhabitants of that country liked it or not. After the Second World War, we continued to move abroad in droves. Net migration to the United Kingdom, calculated by taking the number of immigrants and subtracting the number of emigrants, was actually negative until the 1990s. Britain was losing population through migration, not gaining it. Destinations of choice included Australia and New Zealand, but also other European countries, and that became a whole lot easier once the United Kingdom joined what was then the European Economic Community in 1973. The idea that citizens should be allowed to move between member countries was one of the founding principles of what eventually became the European Union. The British embraced the opportunity. From 1983 onwards, television audiences delighted in watching the international antics of previously out-of-work labourers in *Auf Wiedersehen, Pet*, first in Germany and later in Spain. By the time of the Brexit referendum there were around 1.3 million Brits living in other European Union countries.[1]

It is one thing for Brits to move abroad, but it is quite another for citizens of other countries to move here. British citizens living overseas are routinely referred to in the UK press as 'expats', invoking images of imperial dominance, tea on the veranda, and gin and tonic on ice. In comparison, anyone migrating into the UK is invariably referred to as an 'immigrant'. This word provokes quite a different reaction, and immigration was to be the decisive issue in the referendum vote for the UK to leave the EU in 2016. But it is only in the past twenty-five years that Europeans have really come to be seen as immigrants in UK public discourse at all.

EUROMYTHS AND BENEFIT TOURISM

Immigration was simply not an issue in the debate on UK membership of the European Economic Community, later to become the EU. The most vocal Eurosceptics in the 1960s and '70s were on the left of the political spectrum, with Hugh Gaitskell suggesting in 1962 that joining the Common Market would end 'a thousand years of history' and Tony Benn and Michael Foot leading the campaign to leave in the referendum of 1975. In contrast, Margaret Thatcher, as Leader of the Opposition, was an ardent pro-European campaigner in the 1975 referendum. She was highly sceptical of even the idea of a referendum at all, calling it 'a device of dictators and demagogues' and refusing to say whether she would respect a vote to leave if she were to be elected Prime Minister.[2]

Thatcher went on to sign the Single European Act in 1986, establishing the new Single Market. But by 1988 she was sounding a more sceptical tone. In a major speech that year in Bruges, she said she had not 'successfully rolled back the frontiers of the state in Britain, only to see them reimposed at a European level, with a European superstate exercising a new dominance from Brussels'. She also railed against the abolition of internal borders within Europe, arguing that

such borders 'protect our citizens from crime and stop the movement of drugs, of terrorists and of illegal immigrants'. No mention
was made of stopping Europeans crossing borders, though.[3] She
strongly opposed the idea of a single currency. In fact, it was her
stridency on this issue that triggered Geoffrey Howe's resignation in
late 1990 and thereby Thatcher's own downfall. The so-called 'Maastricht rebels', who dogged John Major's government in the early 1990s
by repeatedly voting against the legislation enacting the Maastricht
Treaty, followed Thatcher's Bruges template, making their stand on
the issue of loss of sovereignty. All of these elements involved some
traces of high principle mixed with copious quantities of xenophobia. The xenophobia was aimed at Germans specifically or at foreign
governments and foreign bureaucrats, though not at foreign citizens
moving to the United Kingdom. Ultimately, though, these arguments
had limited appeal with the public and were one of the reasons the
Conservative Party lost the 1997 general election so comprehensively.

But there were two people in the early 1990s who showed how
to build a broader base of anti-European support. Between them,
they invented, or at least perfected, what were to become the big
guns in the arsenal of the Eurosceptics in time for the most recent
referendum.

The first, Peter Lilley, was one of the founding members of the
Thatcherite 'No Turning Back' group of Conservative MPs in 1985.
His political career began as parliamentary private secretary to Nigel
Lawson, Thatcher's then Chancellor. After Nicholas Ridley was forced
to resign from Cabinet in 1990, having compared the European Community to Hitler, Lilley was suddenly brought into Cabinet to replace
him as Secretary of State for Trade and Industry and keep the right of
the party happy. He campaigned for John Major in the Conservative
leadership battle after Thatcher's fall and was subsequently kept on

by Major in Lilley's previous job. Nevertheless, he had close links to a group of backbench MPs who rebelled repeatedly against Major's attempts to pass legislation enacting the Maastricht Treaty in 1993 and was one of the three Cabinet 'bastards' of whom Major famously complained. Concerns about Europe were generally expressed in terms of loss of sovereignty at the time; Lilley's contribution was to make it about immigration as well.

At the Conservative Party conference in October 1994, Lilley, by then the Secretary of State for Social Security, stood up and launched into an extraordinary xenophobic tirade against a new bogeyman of his own invention:

> People travelling round Europe pretending to look for work … Not so much a Cook's Tour as a Crook's Tour … Just imagine the advice you might find in a European phrasebook for Benefit Tourists…
>
> *Wo ist das Hotel?* … Where is the Housing Department?
> *Où est le bureau de change?* … Where do I cash my benefit cheque?
> *Mio bambino è in Italia* … Send child benefit to my family in Italy.
> *Je suis un citoyen de l'Europe* … Give me my benefits or I'll take you to the European Court.
>
> But next year's edition will have just one phrase – Où est la société de something for nothing? Sorry, Jacques, Britain's branch is closed.[4]

Lilley was hardly the first politician to claim that immigrants were scroungers. He was the first major politician explicitly to say that Europeans coming to the UK were scroungers, to blame EU law and to apply classic xenophobic tropes to European citizens. He was not to be the last: David Cameron drew heavily on these arguments before and during his doomed attempt to renegotiate the terms of UK membership of the EU, as we shall see.

Moving on to the second man, as the *Telegraph*'s European correspondent between 1989 and 1994, Boris Johnson pioneered the so-called Euromyth. His articles lampooned officials and institutions, complaining incessantly of absurd regulations and excessive waste. Johnson drew from the same poisoned well, even then increasingly outmoded and unfashionable, as the explicitly anti-German sentiments of previous years. But his work seemed more acceptable because it was generically anti-European rather than explicitly racist. The stories were based on half-truths, perverse exaggerations and unrecognisable caricatures. One journalist who knew him at that time, Jean Quatremer, later wrote, 'Johnson was the incarnation of the gutter-press dictum: never let the facts get in the way of a good story.'[5] Other correspondents came under pressure from their editors to cook up similar stories, and a growing number obliged. This new form of populist anti-Europeanism made it seem that the foretold loss of sovereignty had come to pass. The cleverly written stories suggested that there was, or at least there was about to be, an annoying impact on real people's lives. Johnson imagined in one story that prawn cocktail crisps were to be banned and wrote another on a fictitious new standard 'Euro condom' size. Other journalists followed suit with tales of 'Bombay mix' snacks being renamed 'Mumbai mix' to satisfy politically correct 'EU twits'; of bans on barmaid cleavage; of British biscuits being outlawed and so on.[6] A detailed reading of such articles invariably revealed a will-o'-the-wisp, always dancing just out of reach. Fact-checking and myth-busting are like bringing a clipboard to a gun fight, though, and if anything only serve to reinforce the lies. The high principle and low xenophobia of the Eurosceptics were poor ammunition compared to the witty and explosive munitions Johnson and his journalistic heirs were able to provide for the cause.

Johnson's Euromyths and Lilley's benefit tourists were to prove powerful weapons, but they would probably have remained niche xenophobic jokes had it not been for the influx of European citizens from Eastern Europe and the Balkans that followed the expansion of the EU in 2004. This fundamentally changed the context of how the union was perceived and discussed in the UK. Suddenly, European citizens were seen as immigrants too. And there were a lot of them.

THE POLITICISATION OF EU FREE MOVEMENT

The United Kingdom had long advocated expansion of the European Union. This was essentially a foreign policy objective, intended to dilute the influence of the integrationist and social democratic French–German alliance within the EU. Margaret Thatcher's and John Major's governments had both been in favour and Tony Blair's was equally as enthusiastic.[7] EU Association Agreement negotiations for a sort of pre-membership status began as early as 1990, and under these treaties self-employed citizens from the Eastern European and Balkan states were allowed access to the EU from 1995. Formal EU membership applications followed in 1996; years of negotiations were finally concluded in late 2002; the Accession Treaties were signed in 2003; and membership finally began on 1 May 2004.

Expansion of the EU's borders meant extending free movement rights to millions of new European citizens. In order to ease any social and economic shock, the laws governing EU expansion allowed existing members to limit these rights for up to seven years. There was initially cross-party support to welcome new workers to the United Kingdom, and in 2002, Tony Blair announced that controls would not be imposed. This was uncontroversial at the time. However, as other countries announced they would impose restrictions, it gradually became clear that every other country except Ireland was going to impose controls of some sort. The Conservative Party was increasingly willing to use immigration as a 'wedge issue' to distinguish itself from Labour, and under new leader Michael Howard, their position started to harden from 2003 onwards.[8] At the last minute, Blair's government decided to introduce a mandatory monitoring scheme called the Worker Registration Scheme, but not to restrict new arrivals. By the time 1 May 2004 arrived, the official Conservative Party position was that controls should have been imposed.[9]

The official Home Office estimate for the number of new EU arrivals on UK shores in that first year was between 5,000 and 13,000.[10] The actual number turned out to be more like 300,000. The estimate, made in 2003, had been based on the assumption that other countries would not impose controls, and the researchers behind it tried to predict future behaviour based on past migratory patterns. Most migrants from Eastern Europe and the Balkans had historically headed for Germany, for instance, not the United Kingdom. The failure to predict the scale of migration from Eastern Europe and the Balkans would come to haunt the Labour government.

As in previous years, when hypothetical migrants had the temerity to become actual migrants, support quickly waned. The right-wing press went ballistic and the Conservative Party jumped with glee upon an issue that combined favourable political positioning with easy goal-scoring against Labour's competence. Meanwhile, a series of other unrelated immigration stories, particularly the 2005 deportation scandal discussed in Chapter 10, fed into a wider narrative that Labour was mismanaging migration and letting too many people into the country. When Bulgaria and Romania also joined the EU three years later, on 1 January 2007, controls were imposed on their citizens. And when Gordon Brown took over as Prime Minister later that year, the tone on immigration started to change. Within months, Brown had pledged to create 'British jobs for British workers', echoing the long-defunct language of the National Front from the 1970s.

Despite all this, immigration from the EU was initially of little interest to the incoming Conservative-led coalition government of 2010. Apart from anything, Cameron had said he did not want his party to 'bang on about Europe' the whole time. Read Cameron's early comments on net migration carefully and you will see that he said it was non-EU immigration he wanted to cut.[11] Efforts to hit the net migration target focused on asylum, family cases, economic immigration and foreign criminals. But the rise of UKIP changed all that.

In 2009, the small anti-EU party adjusted its electoral strategy, consciously shifting its target electorate from middle-class Conservative voters to working-class Labour voters. Immigration was the key issue used to achieve this, and it worked, with UKIP's position in opinion polls shooting up.[12] In the local elections in 2013, UKIP increased its number of local councillors from four to 147 and its vote share increased to 23 per cent in the wards in which it stood. Then, in 2014, UKIP effectively 'won' the European parliamentary elections by coming in as the biggest party in the UK and gaining twenty-four MEPs. Two Conservative MPs, Douglas Carswell and the aptly named Mark Reckless, defected to UKIP later that year. UKIP had put immigration from the EU at the front and centre of its campaigns, with its political messaging presenting EU citizens as a source of crime and a pressure on housing, benefits, schools and the National Health Service.

Cameron responded. At the start of 2013, he made his famous Bloomberg speech, committing to a referendum on UK membership of the EU. Immigration was not mentioned in that speech, which was presented as a high-level and principled critique of the direction of travel of the European Union.[13] Just days earlier, though, Cameron had told the BBC's Andrew Marr that it should be 'harder for people to come and live in Britain and claim benefits'. The *Telegraph* splashed this as: 'David Cameron: we will keep out EU benefit tourists'.[14] It came straight from the Peter Lilley playbook.

On 1 January 2014, UK controls on the entry of Bulgarian and Romanian workers expired. Dire warnings were made by Eurosceptics and UKIP, with Nigel Farage predicting 5,000 Bulgarians and Romanians would arrive 'each week, every week' for years to come. 'Benefits Britain here we come! Fears as migrant flood begins', ran the headline in the *Daily Express* on the fateful day of expiry itself.[15] In reality, there was no surge in entries at all, though this did not matter. Later that year, Cameron talked of 'addressing the magnetic pull of Britain's benefits system'.[16] The Conservative Party manifesto for the 2015 general election declared, 'We will insist that EU migrants who want to claim tax credits and child benefit must live here and contribute to our country for a minimum of four years.' And later that year, in a speech announcing the formal start of negotiations with the EU, Cameron added a fourth challenge to the earlier Bloomberg three: immigration within the EU. 'Countries need greater controls to manage the pressures of people coming in,' he said. 'We do need some additional measures to address wider abuses of the right to free movement within Europe and to reduce the very high flow of people coming to Britain from all across Europe.'[17] The central plank of Cameron's renegotiation effort in 2015 and 2016 was a curb on the rights of EU citizens to claim benefits in Britain. 'We'll halt EU dole tourists', ran a headline in *The Sun* in early 2016. 'The Prime Minister's very strong on this one,' Work and Pensions Secretary Iain Duncan Smith told the paper. 'People shouldn't use the free movement rules just to travel around looking for the best benefit that they can get.'[18]

Having identified this supposed problem, the government now needed to show that it was doing something about it. Ministers and civil servants rooted around for ways to limit and restrict 'free' movement and came up with a number of different schemes.

SOMETHING MUST BE DONE

In Peter Lilley's time, the new myth of the European benefit tourist was used to justify the introduction of the 'habitual residence test' before welfare benefits could be claimed. Lilley claimed that the test would deny benefits only to those who were 'strangers to this country'. But that was not how it worked out. EU law meant that any test had to be applied equally to EU and British citizens. Thus, over 20 per cent of those refused benefits under the test were British citizens returning from abroad, often after a relatively short stay or period of work in a European country.[19] This new test denied benefits to any person not resident in the UK for the preceding six months. Been travelling on a gap year and just returned home to look for work? Been abroad caring for an elderly relative? Been living overseas with a spouse or partner and need to return home because the relationship broke down? Been working abroad, *Auf Wiedersehen, Pet*-style, because work was hard to find at home? All of these scenarios ended with ineligibility for welfare benefits on return to the UK. As well as finding someone other than single mothers to blame for Britain's supposed ills, Lilley had also implied that benefits in the United Kingdom were so generous that citizens of other countries wanted to move here to claim them. It was starting to look as if the blame cast at immigrants was in fact cover for attacking the welfare entitlements of the British. The parallels with Cameron-era austerity are obvious.

Following the model established by Lilley, the Cameron government introduced a series of new regulations intended to limit and restrict EU law rights. It is possible that some ministers believed in the migrant bogeyman of their own invention, but the primary purpose of the reforms was political. Election adviser Lynton Crosby was reported by the *Mail on Sunday* to have given orders that the Conservatives 'must produce "a new policy to curb immigrants and benefits" every week'.[20] Presumably a policy to curb immigrants' access to benefits was even better.

A total of seven amendments were made to the key regulations in the ten years from 2000 to 2010, and most of these were unusually concise in nature. In contrast, there were nine sets of amendments in the five years from 2011 to 2016, and some of those were very wordy indeed. There were three separate sets of amendments made in 2014 alone. In common with other immigration laws, the previously easy-to-use rules quickly became complex and obscure. To be fair, some of the changes were mandated by judgments from the Court of Justice of the European Union and reflected genuine changes or clarifications in EU law. However, the majority were attempts to restrict access to benefits or residence rights. The definition of 'jobseeker' was repeatedly tightened, for example, as was the definition of 'self-sufficient'. Rights of appeal were restricted, so many of those relying on EU law were unable to challenge even incorrect refusals. New restrictions were placed on the entry of family members of British citizens returning to the UK from other EU countries. New powers to investigate suspected fraud or the alleged abuse of rights were inserted, despite an absence of evidence that this was a genuine problem or any evidence that existing powers were insufficient in some way.

In parallel with these measures, the government also sought new, more obstructive interpretations of existing law. There had always been a requirement under EU law for students or self-sufficient people to possess 'comprehensive sickness insurance', in order to benefit from free movement rights in countries other than their own for example. This made sense in most European countries, where health services are based on the insurance principle (i.e. you pay up front and the insurance company will pay out later). In the United Kingdom, however, the National Health Service is free at the point of delivery and there is no direct insurance element to it. One of the fundamental principles of the EU is reciprocity, and just like British citizens travelling to EU countries were entitled to free healthcare, so too were EU citizens travelling to the UK.

Since joining the EEC in 1973, the United Kingdom had never expected students and the self-sufficient to buy health insurance; the access to the NHS to which they were entitled was considered enough. In 2011, though, some bright spark at the Home Office decided to change that policy. No new law or regulation was introduced, but it was decided, as a matter of policy, that students and the self-sufficient would no longer be considered as properly and lawfully resident in the UK unless they had private health insurance or a European health insurance card. This must have seemed a wheeze at the time, as the resulting lack of residency for so many was also used to refuse welfare benefits to an increasing number of European citizens. In an important precedent case, the UK courts sided with the Home Office and denied benefits to a woman caught out by the new approach.[21]

The new interpretation had opened a can of worms, though. Hundreds of thousands of EU citizens were living in the UK without claiming benefits but also without private health insurance. After the shock Brexit referendum result, many started applying for formal residence documents and the Home Office turned them down because of this new mandatory insurance policy, causing growing anger and even panic. It had been easy to announce the new approach, but it somehow proved impossible to climb down from it again. A flood of articles from journalists across the political spectrum condemned its brutality and the reputation of the Home Office plumbed new depths.

New bureaucratic obstacles were also erected in the paths of EU citizens seeking to make use of their free movement rights. From early 2014, whether or not an EU citizen was considered a genuine worker had started to be measured against the 'Minimum Earnings Threshold', otherwise known as the level from which National Insurance contributions have to be paid.[22] Yet, there was no legal basis for this in EU law and it particularly discriminated against part-time workers. Perhaps the most infamous hurdle was a new form, to be used to apply for proof of permanent residence, that was eighty-five pages long. This was introduced early in 2015 and it was more than double the length of the previous version. The form proved to be highly controversial after the Brexit referendum, when large numbers of EU citizens started to seek some security in the shape of residence documents and found that they were faced with such absurdly long paperwork. Worse still was to come when, in 2017, use of the previously optional form was made mandatory for the first time. The government also fought (and lost) a series of legal cases to prevent EU workers who went on maternity leave from being able to rely on their EU right of residence.[23] In her study *Unity in Adversity: EU Citizenship, Social Justice and the Cautionary Tale of the EU*, Charlotte O'Brien details myriad ways in which 'street level bureaucrats' at the Home Office, at the Department for Work and Pensions and in local authorities created and followed processes seemingly designed to make it as difficult as possible for EU citizens to rely on their EU law rights.[24]

Finally, the Home Office led an active crackdown on EU citizens who were perceived to be undesirable because of their lifestyle or poverty. Less and less serious criminal offences were used to justify deportation. Local authorities, homelessness charities and community groups were recruited to report the location of suspected homeless EU migrants, who were then visited by Home Office enforcement vans, detained and deported.[25] The number of EU citizens in immigration detention shot up, rising twentyfold from just over 1,000 per year in 2010 to over 20,000 in 2019.[26]

PAYING THE PRICE

There was never any proof that EU citizens came to the UK to claim benefits as Peter Lilley claimed. Not in 1994. Not in 2015. As Daniel Korski, Cameron's close adviser, later admitted, the whole notion of benefit tourism was a myth:

> To be honest, we failed to find any evidence of communities under pressure that would satisfy the European Commission. At one point we even asked the help of Andrew Green at MigrationWatch, an organisation that has been critical of migration. But all he could provide was an article in the *Daily Telegraph* about a hospital maternity ward in Corby. There was no hard evidence.[27]

On the contrary, all the evidence on immigration suggests that people move to another country for work, not indolence. It is incontrovertible that, collectively, EU citizens as a group pay more in taxes than they claim in benefits.[28] Lilley may or may not have known that in 1994 but Cameron must surely have known it by 2015. Cameron used EU citizens as political punchbags to keep the right of his own party on board and to position his party as a whole against Labour.

And it worked on those terms. The Conservative Party stayed united even in coalition with the Liberal Democrats and went on to win the 2015 election. But it all came crashing down on Cameron the next year when the referendum result was announced on 24 June 2016.

Cameron's problem in the referendum was that, after years of marching the public to the top of the Eurosceptic hill, he then needed them to march back down again. In his Bloomberg speech in 2013, Cameron had said that the choice would be 'between leaving or being part of a new settlement'. And in his Chatham House speech in 2015, in which he had set out his key requirements for the renegotiation of the UK's EU membership, he went as far as to say that if his demands were not met, 'then we will have to think again about whether this European Union is right for us'. With the growth of immigration as a domestic political issue, the ability to impose some sort of limit on free movement would become a major focus of renegotiation.

The self-imposed short time frame of just one year for the negotiations, combined with Cameron's distance from other European leaders, meant that serious and ambitious reform would be impossible, though. The renegotiation and referendum project had been envisaged and sold as a project of changing the direction of the European Union. Once it began in earnest, it soon degenerated into a desperate search for a means to limit the numbers of EU citizens moving to the United Kingdom. The imposition of quotas or an 'emergency brake' permitting the suspension of free movement rules were floated as ideas but were fundamentally incompatible with the principles and treaties of the European Union. By the end of 2014, Cameron and his negotiators had settled on limits to welfare benefits for EU citizens migrating to the UK as the best they could hope for.[29] Rather than direct limits being imposed, the supposed incentives (or 'pull' factors) for moving to the UK would be addressed.

This small win proved to be Cameron's trophy achievement in the pre-referendum renegotiations. An emergency brake was agreed, limiting the access of EU workers to non-contributory in-work benefits for seven years. It was, however, woefully insufficient to win the referendum. Korski later wrote: 'Like many of our victories in the EU, it was too complex to explain to ordinary voters.'[30] The Remain camp did not even try. Having argued for years that the EU was mismanaged, failing and bad for Britain in its current form, Cameron in effect jettisoned his own deal and barely mentioned it during the campaign. He was arguing to remain in an essentially unreformed EU that he had previously argued Britain should leave. After years of the government denigrating EU jobseekers and low-paid workers, the public had come to believe that benefits tourism was a genuine problem. The same public did not believe that Cameron's renegotiation would do anything to solve the problem. It was a classic case of being hoist by one's own petard.

So, the changes to the benefits rules had no discernible impact on the imaginary problem of benefit tourism and, in political terms, they failed spectacularly. They were not without consequence for some EU citizens, though.

The measures had a real impact on a small number of Europeans, depriving them of welfare benefits when they were working part-time, were low-paid, between jobs, sick or pregnant. This could be taken to show that benefits tourism was real, albeit very limited in scope. The problem is, there was no evidence that these people had come to the UK specifically to claim benefits or that they had in any way been attracted to the country by its welfare regime. Those affected had come to work, some had fallen on hard times and some had been resident for many years, as academic and EU law expert Charlotte O'Brien found in her research.[31] Mariella was Belgian, had been resident in the UK for over fifty-five years and had worked for most of those. However, she found herself denied housing benefit at the age of eighty-five. Elsa had lived in the UK for over fourteen years, had a long but complex work history and had two school-age children born in the UK, but she was refused homelessness assistance. Irina had worked in the UK for over six years including two short breaks but was refused income support when she needed it. All these decisions were eventually overturned on appeal because they were wrong and inconsistent with EU law, but Mariella, Elsa, Irina and others like them were put through needless poverty and awful stress because of the initial wrong decisions. All the reforms achieved was to remove the safety net for genuine residents and workers. And all for nothing: the changes had no discernible effect on net migration.

Brexit was the outcome of Cameron's spectacular miscalculations. As a result of Brexit and the decisions taken by Cameron's successors, all EU citizens in the UK have found that they must apply to remain in their homes. Meanwhile, British citizens have lost their rights of free movement in the EU.

The right of an EU citizen to live in the UK came from EU law. If EU law was no longer to apply after Brexit, it followed as a matter of law that EU citizens would have no legal right to live here. The official Vote Leave campaign had rather dishonestly sidestepped this inconvenient truth by asserting, as if it were fact, 'There will be no change for EU citizens already lawfully resident in the UK' and 'EU citizens will automatically be granted indefinite leave to remain in the UK and will be treated no less favourably than they are at present.'[32] Vote Leave was not campaigning for office in a general election and was never an incoming government-in-waiting, so this assertion had no real force.

When Theresa May took over as Prime Minister in 2016, her

government adopted a very different approach. Instead of an automatic grant of status, every EU citizen would now have to apply for new immigration status or else become unlawfully resident once the deadline had expired. The application would either lead to five years of permission to stay or, if the applicant could prove five years of previous residence, it would lead straight to settlement. Proving five years of residence would require the algorithmic cross-checking of selected government databases or the submission of physical documents as proof. Initially, a fee of £65 was to be charged to EU citizens who had been permitted no vote on their future and now had to make an application to stay in their own homes, but this was belatedly dropped in the first weeks of the application process. It was very much not the automatic process that had been promised – although it is fair to say that it was a considerable improvement on the normal nightmarish immigration application process for non-EU nationals.

Critics have warned that no registration or application exercise has ever or will ever achieve 100 per cent success: there will always be some eligible people who do not apply. In this case though, where very large figures are involved, an apparently small percentage of people not applying has the potential to translate as a huge number of individuals, especially given that there are an estimated three to four million EU citizens currently living in the UK. Even if 90 per cent of people applied, which would be far better than any previous comparable exercise around the world, there could still be 400,000 EU citizens left unlawfully resident as a consequence. The final number will probably prove to be higher, although we may never know for sure because there is no register or list of EU citizens living in the UK against which to compare the final tally.

Oxford-based Migration Observatory researchers identified certain groups of EU citizens to be at particular risk of being left behind by the process.[33] Firstly, there may be a significant number of people who do not know that they need to apply: children whose parents do not apply for them, perhaps because they wrongly think they are already British citizens; long-term residents who are elderly or wrongly believe they already have permanent status; those who already have permanent residence under EU law; and people who wrongly believe they are ineligible, for example. There will also be some vulnerable individuals who struggle to complete the process, such as victims of domestic violence, victims of exploitation and victims of modern slavery. Barriers such as lack of English language proficiency, age, disability or lack of computer literacy may well mean that some people do not know they need to apply, or even if they do, they may struggle to complete their application. Lastly, there will be a number of people who fail to prove five years of residency and thus end up with only five years' permission to stay. Later, they may fail to apply at the end of that period or may accidentally render themselves ineligible as a result of being outside the UK for six months out of any twelve, for example on a gap year, work placement abroad or caring for relatives.

Comparisons have been made with the Windrush scandal that emerged in 2018. The comparison is apt but there are important differences. As we have seen, the Windrush scandal arose from a decision to confer lawful status automatically on a large cohort of people without issuing them with papers. This was done for the very good reason of ensuring everyone eligible was automatically lawful, but it also meant that they did not necessarily have a way to prove it. This became a major problem following the introduction of the hostile environment. The problem facing EU citizens is arguably worse. Instead of a declaratory system in which everyone is lawful but some people lack proof, EU citizens are being forced to apply. Those who fail to do so will be illegally resident and will also, obviously, lack proof of lawful status. It will not be well-educated professionals who are caught out, but low-skilled workers with poor language skills and other vulnerable groups. There will be no easy route back to legality, either, as the government says that 'good reason' will be needed for not applying before the deadline. Not realising that you had to apply is never going to constitute a sufficiently decent reason, I suspect.

This is where Lilley's crusade against benefit tourist bogeymen and Johnson's witty Euromyths have brought us: out of the European Union in which British citizens were one of the biggest national groups benefiting from free movement rights, and into a situation where EU citizens in the UK have to apply to stay in the country they moved to as legal citizens, or else face uncompromising deportation.

CHAPTER 10

DEPORTATION, EXILE AND MODERN TRANSPORTATION

Shannoy McLeod grew up and attended primary and secondary school in Lewisham in south London. He committed a handful of minor non-violent offences and in 2017, aged twenty-one, he was caught by police carrying enough cannabis to trigger an intent to supply charge, as well as driving a moped while disqualified. He was given a fifteen-month prison sentence. To his horror, he then also received a letter from the Home Office declaring that they had decided to deport him. Unluckily for Shannoy, he had come to the UK from Jamaica at the age of four. He could barely remember his life there, and he had lawful, settled status in the UK alongside his three siblings, all of whom were British. He himself had been eligible to apply for British citizenship but had not done so because it was expensive and seemed unnecessary at the time; this turned out to be a terrible mistake.[1]

Perhaps even more stark was the case of Remi Akinyemi. He was born in the United Kingdom in June 1983. As we will see when we turn to British citizenship laws in Chapter 12, had he been born a few months earlier, in 1982, he would have been a British citizen, and indeed his elder brother was British from birth. Like Shannoy, Remi was eligible to be registered as a British citizen or could later have naturalised as British, as his father and younger brother had. Everyone already thought he was British, so there seemed to be no need. His mother died when he was fourteen and he struggled with mental health problems and depression from a young age. After a series of suicide attempts, now on anti-depressants and anti-epilepsy medication and belatedly receiving counselling, he settled down with a partner. The problem was, he was by now classified as a 'foreign national offender'. A Nigerian national by descent, he had committed a string of criminal offences, some of which were very serious. In 2007 he was sentenced to four years in prison for causing death by dangerous driving and in 2013 he was sentenced to three and a half years for Class A drugs offences. The Home Office decided to deport him in 2014. He fought the case through the courts, but because judges kept making legal mistakes on his case, he was still going through the courts as this book went to press.[2]

In the United Kingdom, 'deportation' means the exclusion of a foreign national from the country. Not only is the person physically removed but he or she is also banned from returning. It is a legal power that is most often used against foreign criminals, though it can also be used both against a person who does not have permission to stay in the UK and against somebody who does. Even someone with settled status can therefore be deported. Lawyers get hung up on the difference between deportation and mere removal, where a person who does not have permission to stay in the UK is physically removed but can sometimes apply to come back again. The distinction only really matters to lawyers. In public discussion, 'deportation' and 'removal' are generally considered to be interchangeable terms. But deportation feels like a more evocative, meaningful word.

Shannoy grew up in the UK, he was educated here, all of his friends and everything he knew was here, he had strong family links with his mother and three siblings living here, his offending was non-violent and he seems to have been rather unlucky to get a sentence as long as fifteen months. He could remember nothing about Jamaica and had no idea how he would live there. And even if his conduct *was* serious enough to justify deportation, why should it be Jamaica that hosts him in the future, given he is very much a product of the United Kingdom? Similarly, Remi was born in the United Kingdom and had never left the country. He could and should have been British, except that his parents had not paid to register him as such. His offending was serious, but he also came from a very disturbed background for which he was not at fault. Furthermore, his only link to Nigeria was a legal inheritance of citizenship through his father; he did not know Nigeria at all and had never even been there. These are examples not of deportation but of exile.

THE GREAT DEPORTATION SCANDAL

Deportation was a niche area of immigration law until, on 25 April 2006, then Home Secretary Charles Clarke publicly admitted that the Home Office had failed to consider the deportation of over 1,000 foreign criminals who were coming to the end of their prison sentences, that this had been going on for years, that some of the offenders were rapists and murderers, that some had re-offended after their release and that the Home Office had lost track of most who had been let go. Even very serious criminals who had committed awful crimes and served long sentences were being released into the community without any consideration for whether they could or should be deported; they were simply allowed to stay. Prisons were failing to inform the Home Office that foreign nationals were due to be released, and even where they were, the Home Office was doing nothing about it. A subsequent report by the House of

Commons public accounts committee blamed a 'parochial culture' within different teams at the Home Office and 'a lack of leadership and strategic oversight, a failure to acknowledge that departmental procedures were not keeping pace with demand for the service, and the tacit acceptance of backlogs and delays'.[3] It is hard to imagine more damning criticism, although similar things continue to be said about the Home Office today.

The fault was arguably that of officials at the Home Office, who were failing to operate the machinery of government. Ultimately, though, the doctrine of ministerial accountability means that a minister is responsible for the actions of their officials. In this case, perhaps the responsibility was real as well as theoretical. The New Labour government was obsessed with asylum and economic migration and it turned out that this was almost to the exclusion of all else. The number of officials working on deportation cases rose from 100 before the foreign criminals scandal to 550 by 2010 and then, during a period when the overall headcount at the Home Office fell, to over 900 by 2014.[4] Even today politicians continue to manage a crisis at the Home Office by reallocating resources from one area to another. As the chief inspector of borders and immigration puts it, 'The response to the latest priority or crisis is typically at the expense of performance elsewhere.'[5]

The fault was certainly not that of the law. The failure was an administrative one. It was not that deportation was legally difficult or that there were insuperable legal barriers; foreign criminals were not even considered for deportation by immigration officials in the first place. The Immigration Act 1971 had given the Home Secretary a huge level of discretion when deporting foreign criminals when he or she considered it to be 'conducive to the public good'. There was no real statutory limit or definition to this power, meaning the Home

Secretary of the day could interpret 'conducive to the public good' as widely or as narrowly as he or she chose. The Immigration Rules included several paragraphs on deportation, but these also imposed no real restriction on the power to deport, being instead just a list of relevant and common-sense considerations, such as the seriousness of the offence, length of residence and family connections. The Human Rights Act 1998 and the European Convention on Human Rights might impose some restrictions on deportation because a criminal's right to a private and family life had to be considered before he or she was deported. But most cases had not been reaching that stage, and human rights laws certainly do not prevent the deportation of serious criminals or those with weak connections to the United Kingdom.

The media narrative meant that the scandal needed to be somebody's fault. A crisis of this scale demanded a scalp. The government could have collectively admitted that it had been distracted by the increase in asylum numbers and the growing backlog that came as a result, but this would have put Prime Minister Tony Blair in the frame. Charles Clarke was the current Home Secretary and had been for a year and half. The problems at the Home Office went back further than that, but Clarke was, after some initial prevarication, sacked by Blair on 5 May 2006.

AUTOMATIC DEPORTATION

To try to show something was being done beyond the defenestration of Clarke, Blair had rather unwisely pledged at Prime Minister's Questions on 3 May that he would radically overhaul the existing system, 'so that those who are convicted of a serious criminal offence are deported automatically'.[6] On the face of it, this sounded like it would actually deal with the problem that had arisen, which was the failure even to initially appraise foreign criminals for deportation.

Blair went further, though, pointing out that even where foreign criminals were considered for deportation, they were not necessarily removed from the country as a result. He implied that the law was at fault and attempted to deflect blame onto previous governments for failing to legislate properly. He wanted to move the discussion on from poor management of the Home Office. But pledging to deport foreign criminals automatically, come what may, no matter what their links to the UK, was to pledge the impossible. The law protecting criminals from deportation was not strong, but it did exist. The pledge soon morphed instead into a commitment to introduce a rebuttable presumption of deportation; the law would assume that a person would be deported unless they could persuade officials or a judge otherwise.

The resulting legislation was the UK Borders Act 2007, which remains in force today. Section 32 is entitled 'Automatic Deportation'. It states that a deportation order must be made against any foreign national who is convicted and sent to prison for twelve months or more. But any lawyer reading the Act will immediately see that Section 33 is entitled 'Exceptions'. In reality, deportation is anything but automatic. The exceptions include recognised refugees, certain EU citizens and cases in which human rights laws would be breached by deportation. Oddly, this legislation did not replace the original Home Office power to deport foreign nationals contained in the earlier mentioned Immigration Act 1971. Instead, it supplemented the original power and in effect defined some of those whose deportation the Home Office would in future consider to be conducive to the public good.

If anything, though, the original 1971 power to deport foreign nationals was wider and more draconian than the new legislation. What about foreign nationals who committed a string of offences, receiving a sentence of less than twelve months on each occasion? Or a foreign national who was not actually convicted of a crime but where there was some other compelling reason to deport him or her? In these cases, the Home Office still needed to rely on 1971 powers rather than the new, quite complex scheme of 2007. Meanwhile, the Home Office often found a way not to apply the theoretical exceptions. Recognised refugees had their asylum status revoked on the basis it was now safe for them to return, for example. Those with long residence in the UK since birth or childhood, and even those with British children, were told that their private family life was outweighed by the public interest in their deportation. They could maintain their relationships from afar by (that phrase again) 'modern means of communication', they were told, over and over again.

The number of deportation cases coming before the courts dramatically increased. This was not directly because of the new legislation; the Home Office could have used existing powers to bring more deportation cases after all. The increase was due to the Home Office starting to take deportation work seriously. Some of the cases involved very serious criminals convicted of drugs, sex and violence offences, and sometimes the criminals had few links to the UK. In those cases, few tears were shed other than by those directly affected. As Stephen Sedley, one of the wisest judges of recent years, said in one such case, 'The tragic consequence is that this family ... will be broken up for ever because of the appellant's bad behaviour. That is what deportation does.'[7] But in many other cases, the hard-and-fast rule that any sentence of twelve months or more triggered automatic deportation action started to lead to questionable results.

Young men like Shannoy McLeod, men who had grown up in the UK and whose convictions were comparatively minor, faced exile to countries they simply did not know – as did some like Remi Akinyemi who had even been born in the UK. Mothers and fathers were told that their sons and daughters would not only serve time behind bars, but they would also be deported to another country, probably never to see their parents again. To have to begin again in a new country with no friends, no family and no resources is a very harsh sentence. Indeed, it is essentially a modern form of transportation punishment, when minor criminals were sentenced to permanent exile in Australia in the nineteenth century.

OF CATS AND JUDGES

Judges stand at the line between the policy and the person. It is easy for a newspaper columnist or politician to advocate a policy of deporting every foreign criminal no matter what. They never have to meet the people concerned or their families. It is almost as easy for a remote official in a Home Office tower block in Croydon to consign to exile the subject of one more file, sending them to an unknown country away from their children. The officials do not see the recipients of their decisions as actual people, but rather as cases. A witness statement, a letter of support or yet another photo of some smiling children is all too straightforward to disregard when the author or subject is absent.

It is quite another matter to swear a judicial oath to uphold the law, which includes the Human Rights Act 1998, and then look that person in the face, meet their children and tell them they must live in different countries. The number of deportation appeals increased rapidly after the problems of 2006 and doubled from around 1,000 to around 2,000 per year between 2012 and 2015. Some judges were horrified at what the Home Office decisions really meant for the people coming before them, but the actual success rate for deportation appeals remained the same, at around 35 per cent.[8] Judges had to be mindful of the need to balance the public interest in deportation against the private and family lives of the individuals affected by such decisions.

Nevertheless, in response to a trickle of stories about serious criminals alleged to have won their cases because of the way judges interpreted the Human Rights Act, Theresa May went on the attack at the Conservative Party conference in 2011:

> We all know the stories about the Human Rights Act. The violent drug dealer who cannot be sent home because his daughter – for whom he pays no maintenance – lives here. The robber who cannot be removed because he has a girlfriend. The illegal immigrant who cannot be deported because – and I am not making this up – he had a pet cat.[9]

She went on to say that the meaning of human rights had been 'perverted'. Pledging to rewrite the Immigration Rules to prevent 'misinterpretation' of the right to a private and family life, she promised to clear up any 'misconception' judges might have about what it meant.

I have represented many foreign criminals in deportation cases over the years and it is not exactly my favourite aspect of working as an immigration lawyer. But I have never seen a violent drug dealer who has no relationship with his daughter win a case, nor a robber succeed in resisting deportation because of a girlfriend, nor anyone ever get to stay because of their pet cat. In fact, it turned out that the pet cat was a reference to a real case, but one where the presence of said cat had been irrelevant to the outcome. Instead, the migrant had won because the Home Office had failed properly to consider the case until the day of the hearing.[10] The Judicial Office for Communication even put out a statement saying, 'The cat had nothing to do with the decision.'[11]

Theresa May, or at least her speechwriter, *was*, in fact, making it up, as it transpired. She was not alone on her crusade against the judges, though. Certain sections of the media, principally the *Daily Mail* and the *Telegraph*, ran a series of stories in 2012, attacking judges for allowing too many deportation appeals. In an 'investigation' supposedly showing that 'some judges rule far more often than others in favour of offenders seeking to avoid deportation', three immigration judges were singled out by name in one article by the *Telegraph*.[12] The fact that these appeal judges were ruling not on the merits or final outcomes of the cases but only on whether a junior judge had committed an error of law seemed to have passed the journalists by. A piece in the *Daily Mail* shortly afterwards attacked another named judge for allowing an appeal against deportation by a rapist.[13] A paparazzi-style photo of the judge getting into his car in casual clothes accompanied the article. Another judge sent me the full decision in question a few days later and, in reality, a Home Office lawyer had agreed in court that the appeal must be allowed.[14] Yet that had not prevented an unnamed aide to Theresa May disingenuously telling the paper, 'We are at the mercy of the courts', and a spokesman for the Home Office saying, 'We do not believe this individual needs or deserves refuge in this country.'

DEPORT FIRST, ASK QUESTIONS LATER

In July 2012 the Home Office unveiled radical new immigration rules on deportation. These set out yet more rules on when a person should be deported. A new categorisation was created for serious offending (those sentenced to four years or more), medium offending (those sentenced to more than one year but less than four years) and lower level offending (those sentences to less than one year, but designed for persistent offenders or offending causing 'serious harm'). This was arguably sensible. The problem was, very narrow exceptions to deportation were also specified at each individual level.

One such exception was applied if a person had been lawfully resident for most of his or her life and was socially and culturally integrated into the UK, and if there were significant obstacles to the person integrating into the country of return. These tests may sound sensible to some. In practice almost no person facing deportation could meet the cumulative combination of these tests. 'Most of life' was a mathematical calculation and many failed it. The Home Office argued that any person who had offended had not been integrated into the UK, whether or not he or she might have been brought up here. And any person who was fit and well and had even a hint of an ability to speak the relevant language was argued by the Home Office to be able to adapt, and therefore integrate, into the receiving country.

Another exception was on the basis of family links. If a parent facing deportation had a 'genuine and subsisting parental relationship' with a child who was British or had been resident in the UK for at least seven years, and could show both that it would be 'unduly harsh' for the child to leave the UK with the parent and for it to remain in the UK without them, only then would deportation not be pursued. Similarly, if a partner had a genuine relationship with a British or settled person in the UK and it would be unduly harsh for the partner to leave the UK or remain in the UK without the deportee, then deportation could be avoided. The problem with these exceptions were that the words 'unduly harsh' were interpreted by the Home Office as meaning something 'excessively severe or cruel', which is over and above 'very serious hardship' and is certainly more than an 'insurmountable obstacle'.[15] These final words reveal the truth of the test: it is literally more than insurmountable and the game cannot be won. Unsurprisingly, it is a test that is never satisfied as far as the Home Office is concerned.

These two exceptions described above apply to medium and lower level offenders. For the most serious category of offender, those sentenced to four or more years of imprisonment, there must be 'very compelling circumstances' that are over and above the illusory, impossible exceptions we have already considered.

But even these rules were insufficient. After refraining from primary legislation for the first years of the coalition government, the Immigration Act 2014 was an opportunity to tighten the law yet further. Very similar – but for pedants like me frustratingly not quite identical – provisions to the 2012 rules were introduced as an Act of Parliament. This time the requirements were aimed at the judges themselves. No one, but no one, working in immigration law would have said that judges had previously been ignoring the 2012 rules, but nevertheless they were instructed by the new Act that they 'must' have regard to them.

To sidestep these pesky judges and stop them from having the chance to allow appeals, changes were also made to the appeal process. The most important of these were new 'deport first, appeal later' rules, which prevented a foreign criminal from appealing his or her deportation until after he or she had actually been deported. Introduced late in 2014, these new rules led to a dramatic decline in the number of appeals brought against deportation. This was no surprise: after removal it is hard to find, pay for and talk to a lawyer in another country, and it is very hard to get together the evidence you would need to win your case. The narrative of the case is changed from one in which you are a resident fighting deportation to one in which you are struggling to get back into the country having already been deported.

Eventually, in June 2017, the Supreme Court found that the way the Home Office was operating the new system was unlawful.[16] Of the 1,175 cases in which the powers had been used, it was found that only seventy-two individuals had attempted to pursue an appeal from abroad. None succeeded. The success rate seemed to have been reduced from around 35 per cent in deportation cases to literally 0 per cent. Neither the Home Office nor the Ministry of Justice had been willing to assist with setting up video links for appeals, thereby effectively preventing appellants from giving oral evidence in their own cases, as well as thwarting their attempts to prepare and present expert evidence in support of their cases. The policy was clearly a success from the point of view of the government, but Lord Wilson, giving the judgment of the court, held that the policy violated the basic rule of law. 'When we are afforded a right of appeal,' he said, 'our appeal should be effective.'

In parallel with the changes to the law to undermine legal challenges to deportation, the Home Office worked to increase the number of migrants it targeted for deportation. The previously mentioned Operation Nexus, as it was known, began in London in 2010 as a targeted plan to deport suspected gang members. The high standard of proof beyond reasonable doubt, plus various procedural protections, had made it difficult to secure criminal convictions in gang-related cases. Rather than work harder to put violent criminals behind bars, the police worked with immigration officials to use immigration laws as a method of taking suspects out of circulation, whether or not there was sufficient evidence to secure a conviction in the criminal courts. Quite often the alleged gang members had grown up in the United Kingdom. They might well have lawful status but had never applied for citizenship. And as non-citizens, they could fairly easily be removed and made some other country's problem instead.

FRUSTRATING DEPORTATION

With the exception of the effective abolition of a legal challenge, most of these measures were just noise. The absolute number of people subject to deportation action certainly increased. However, the success rate of their appeals crept up slightly, which was the opposite effect to that intended. Crucially, the number of foreign national offenders actually being deported at the end of it all did creep up from below 5,000 per year to just over 6,000 between 2011 and 2016, but has since then fallen slightly again. Over that same period, the composition of those being deported also changed rapidly from being mainly non-EU nationals to mainly EU nationals. And at the same time, the number of deportees assessed as being of the 'highest harm' almost halved. The Home Office was basically using low-harm offenders and EU nationals to plump up the numbers. And even then, the overall numbers have still fallen in the past couple of years.

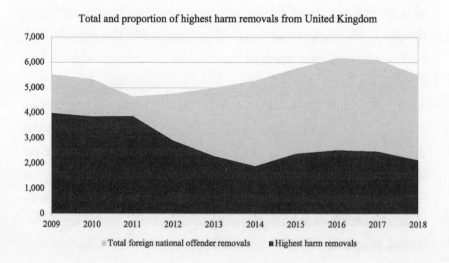

Total and proportion of highest harm removals from United Kingdom

Total foreign national offender removals   Highest harm removals

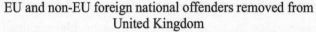

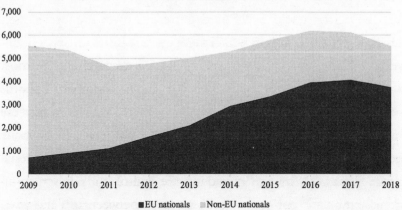

Source for both graphs: Home Office quarterly statistics year ended June 2019 (2nd ed).
Tables Rt_06_q updated with figures from September 2019 tables Ret_02.

The reality is that it is hard to deport foreign national criminals and that judges have little if anything to do with it. The foreign criminals themselves often resist deportation, for example by failing to provide the information needed. It is hard to get some other countries to accept criminals back. It is hard to break apart families, not least because many of those families do everything they can to resist. It is hard to balance encouragement with compulsion. But arguably the biggest barrier to the deportation of foreign criminals is the Home Office itself.

One of the key obstacles to deporting foreign national offenders is obtaining what is called an 'Emergency Travel Document'. Where the deportee does not possess a current, valid passport (which is in the majority of cases), this travel document or an equivalent is needed to persuade immigration officials in the receiving country to allow the person onto their territory. Without one, the deportee will simply be returned to the United Kingdom. In a 2014 report into the management of this delicate process, inspectors found that officials were applying for travel documents in cases for which it was unlikely that the person could really be deported, and yet they were often failing to progress cases in which there was a realistic prospect of deportation. The inspectors wrote, 'The practice of detaining [Foreign National Offenders] for months or years in the hope that they will eventually comply with the [Emergency Travel Document] process is not only potentially a breach of their human rights; it is also poor value for money for the taxpayer, given the high costs involved.'[17] The National Audit Office also looked into the issue in the same year and likewise found a host of problems, including unnecessary delays in starting cases, inefficient information-gathering, communication delays, processing delays, failure to prioritise on the basis of removability and failure to carry out cost–benefit analyses.[18]

Three years later, in 2017, inspectors found old problems continuing as well as various new issues. The risk of foreign national offenders re-offending after release had actually been increased by hostile environment measures and, to make matters worse, the Home Office was losing track of the individuals concerned because it was refusing to provide accommodation to them, potentially also making it impossible to deport them later. Home Office record-keeping was similarly heavily criticised – a theme of almost all inspection reports – and 'major inconsistencies' were found in the ways in which Home Office officials had dealt with reports of absconding. Inspectors commented that there was 'no indication of any central oversight or co-ordination' to ensure that previous recommendations for improvement might actually be implemented.[19] Nevertheless, the follow-up report a further two years later in 2019 found that previous recommendations still remained outstanding. The management of contact with foreign national offenders after their release was found to have 'little value', but the inspectors went on to say that 'the greater concern is the failure to grip the absconder process effectively' and that the issue 'deserves to be treated with considerably more urgency than the Home Office has shown to this point'.[20]

So, the present position is that automatic deportation applies, even to those who were born in the UK or brought here as small children, if an offender receives any sentence in excess of twelve months, with very limited exceptions that will often not apply in practice. Children are left without parents and families are torn apart by these rules. Meanwhile, the number of deportations of foreign national offenders convicted of very serious crimes and assessed as being of high risk to the public has fallen considerably since 2011. This fact is obscured in the overall deportation statistics by a sharp increase in the number of low-risk EU citizens who have committed minor offences being deported. Officials at the Home Office, presumably as a result of targets, focus on easy-to-remove, low-risk criminals, but are failing to progress the removal of more serious criminals. This leads to more serious criminals being detained for very prolonged periods, and at considerable public expense, before they are eventually released back into the community. This makes their detention entirely pointless from a practical point of view, of course. And when they are released, multiple reports have shown that their monitoring is ineffective, that they are now unable to work or claim benefits and that some are made homeless because the Home Office refuses to provide accommodation – all of which increases the risk of re-offending. Where external observers like the National Audit Office or chief inspector of borders and immigration examine Home Office practice and procedure in this area, they almost universally make recommendations that officials then fail to implement.

Politicians must stop blaming judges and laws for their own

failings. If they are serious about removing foreign national offenders, rather than merely posturing on and exploiting the issue for political gain, they should focus on serious and high-risk cases where the person genuinely has weak links to the United Kingdom, or at least where he or she has made a conscious choice to come to the United Kingdom as an adult. In short, the rules on automatic deportation need to be scrapped; they lead to grossly disproportionate action that is felt almost exclusively by black and minority ethnic families and communities. Of course, it is politically extremely difficult to go down this road and it is easy to imagine the reaction of the tabloid press, but the present situation is a morally unacceptable, poor public policy.

CHAPTER 11

IMMIGRATION DETENTION: ENFORCING CONTROL

Alois Dvorzak was a Canadian national detained for nineteen days in early 2013. He died in detention and was wearing handcuffs when he took his last breath. He was eighty-four years old and suffering from Alzheimer's. The initially anonymous details of his treatment emerged only months later in a report by Her Majesty's inspector of prisons, then Nick Hardwick, in which he criticised the 'excessive and unacceptable' use of handcuffs in a case 'where a sense of humanity was lost'.[1] *Channel 4 News* followed up the story and broadcast a poignant investigation into Dvorzak's life.[2] The full, even more horrifying, story was detailed later at the inquest into the death, which was diligently reported by Phil Miller for the website Open Democracy.[3]

THE HUMAN COST OF DETENTION

Dvorzak had been trying to visit his estranged daughter in Slovenia but gave confused answers to immigration officials as he passed through Gatwick Airport on his way. He was refused entry to the UK on 23 January 2013 and the frail 84-year-old man slept his first night in this country across some fixed chairs in a holding room at the airport. The Canadian High Commission was contacted, and they suggested Dvorzak be sent to a hotel or a hospital. He was duly sent by immigration officials to East Surrey Hospital, where he was assessed as fit for detention and fit to fly. For Dvorzak's second night in the UK, though, a hospital was found while immigration officials waited for a place to become available in an immigration detention centre. His third night was spent at Harmondsworth detention centre, a grim and imposing prison-like building situated in a 'wasteland of motorways and outposts of the air terminals beyond Heathrow', as an earlier visitor, Amrit Wilson of the Joint Council for the Welfare of Immigrants, put it in 1975.[4] Unfortunately, I know it well myself, from my visits to clients being detained there. Situated at an abrupt turn-off from the Colnbrook bypass, its huge scale and razor wire cornicing is severe on the outside, while the interior exudes sanitised violence. The on-site duty doctor filed an official report stating that Dvorzak was not fit for detention. She even made a point of calling the detention centre manager and the Canadian High Commission herself. Dvorzak stopped taking his heart and dementia medication and everyone who came into contact with him was worried about his frailty and health. One clinician noted in writing that Dvorzak was 'at high risk of death in detention'. Nevertheless, his detention continued.

'I haven't got much time, I need to go to see my family,' a tearful but, as always, smartly dressed Dvorzak told Vernon Simmonds-Dunne, the older persons liaison officer at Harmondsworth. Officials attempted to remove him to Canada, but the removal was aborted because Mr Dvorzak became distressed, banging the side of the detention van and constantly shouting, 'NO, NO, NO.' Twice, he was taken to hospital from the detention centre as he complained of chest pains, and on both occasions he was handcuffed and chained to a security guard because he was, incredibly, assessed to be an escape risk. The private contractor responsible for the day-to-day running of the detention centre, Firat Loveridge, admitted at the inquest that when he saw Dvorzak in the ambulance in handcuffs he realised restraints were unnecessary, but he said, 'There was no room for discretion,' and removing the cuffs would have slowed Dvorzak's going to hospital, he thought. This was a model example of what Hardwick would describe in his later inspection report as 'a lack of intelligent individual risk assessment'.

On his second visit to hospital, on 10 February 2013, Mr Dvorzak died. He was still wearing the handcuffs. They were only removed after his heart and breathing had stopped as medics attempted resuscitation. He had been handcuffed for five hours by the time of his death. It was a miserable, ignominious end.

The case is a distressing one and it is unusual for featuring an elderly, ethnically white citizen of a rich country, whose detention only ended because he died. Academic Mary Bosworth spent 2,400 hours, equivalent to three days per week for twenty months, observing inside immigration detention centres around the United Kingdom with unprecedented access. In that time, she met one white Australian, one white Zimbabwean, one white South African and no New Zealanders or Canadians.[5] But, up until almost the end, what happened to Alois Dvorzak was in many ways typical. Detention is only supposed to occur when there is a realistic prospect of removal. Dvorzak was, in reality, never really removable, at least not without very considerable care or planning. And there was no hint whatsoever of either care or planning in the nineteen days for which Dvorak was detained.

So why was he detained at all? His case was clearly a challenging one but that is no excuse for what was inflicted on him. What was supposed to be a short period of detention ended up going on for almost three weeks, in an ordeal ended only by death. One wonders what else, if anything, might have finally brought Dvorzak's detention to a conclusion. A series of private contractors working for the company GEO, which profited from immigration detention by providing the facilities to the Home Office under a commercial contract, made critical decisions concerning Dvorzak's welfare, from the choice to handcuff him to the judgement to abort his attempted removal. Multiple doctors certified that Dvorzak was unfit for detention using the official 'Rule 35 report' form and yet detention continued. The healthcare Dvorzak received was obviously inadequate and far below that which could be provided by normal NHS services, and Dvorzak was clearly extremely distressed by his experience. There was no single person who was responsible for him, as the sheer number of witnesses from the detention centre who gave evidence at the inquest testifies. Yet, officials and private contractors consistently followed the line of least resistance, even though Dvorzak suffered appallingly as a consequence.

All of these were and still remain standard operating procedures in immigration detention. The effects on detainees are awful and the law reports are replete with examples. Take Xiao Yun Xue, who was detained for over two years before being released back into the community, having been irreparably damaged by her experience. Mrs Justice Laing ultimately found that she had been unlawfully detained.[6] 'The longer her detention went on, the more vulnerable she became,' found Laing. 'Her physical health has been significantly compromised, probably permanently. Her mental health also declined in detention. She eventually fell down a stairwell and broke her back.' Officials, it was found, had ignored the copious medical and psychiatric evidence that was sent to them. In the meantime, Xue self-harmed repeatedly, became psychotic and, owing to side effects from her medication, became physically unable to urinate. She had to be issued with and taught to use a catheter. All this because she had no right to be in the UK and had committed a string of minor offences – but at no time does there seem to have been any real prospect of removing her. What was the point of the suffering she endured and the financial cost of detaining her?

In another example from the law reports a young woman, known only as MD, came to the UK from Guinea to join her refugee husband. She entered lawfully with a visa but was detained on arrival after giving confused answers to an immigration officer. Officials suspected that she might be a child but nevertheless kept her in an adult detention facility, and even after they realised their mistake, her confinement dragged on and on. In the end, she was detained for eleven months. MD had no mental health difficulties before going into detention but her mental state deteriorated to the point that she suffered both major depression and PTSD after being released. The judgment makes extremely distressing reading:

She made superficial scratches on her chest and abdomen on the 26th August 2011. Similar incidents continued to take place. She was restrained, removed from association with other detainees and handcuffs were used to stop her harming herself. The Claimant self-harmed on at least eleven occasions between August and November 2011 including occasions when she cut her forehead with the top of a sardine tin, when she again cut her forehead and the right side of her face this time with pieces of china, when she tried to strangle herself using a mobile telephone cable as a ligature and placed a pillow over her head, when she banged her head against the wall, when she cut her neck using pieces of china and occasions when she cut her stomach, neck and arm.

Hearing her case, Judge Price Lewis QC accepted that MD's mental collapse was caused by her continued detention and the lack of any satisfactory medical treatment at Yarl's Wood detention centre. He ruled that her detention was unlawful, found that the detention amounted to inhuman and degrading treatment and ordered that damages be paid.[7]

These are not isolated examples of an otherwise humane system now and then malfunctioning. At the time of writing, the charity Inquest had recorded thirty-seven deaths in immigration detention centres since 2000 and a further fourteen deaths of immigration detainees held in prisons under immigration laws. In total, twenty deaths were non-self-inflicted and twenty-six were self-inflicted. In fact, nearly thirty people have died in immigration detention since Alois Dvorzak's death in 2013.[8] A 2017 study into the mental health of immigration detainees in the United Kingdom found that more than half of detainees suffered from depression, more than one-fifth experienced PTSD, one in ten faced psychotic or depressive affective disorders and one-third had some sort of personality disorder.[9]

The human cost is clearly borne first and foremost by the detainees. But it also takes a toll on those employed to enforce the system, who sometimes take it out on those placed in their care. Most detention centres are run by private companies under secretive contracts with the Home Office. During her earlier mentioned research work, Mary Bosworth interviewed many detention centre staff.[10] Detention custody officers need a minimum qualification of one GCSE and normally start on a salary in the mid-£20,000s. They come from a wide range of backgrounds, including straight from school, the armed forces, the prison service, retail, homemaking and security work such as nightclubs and airports. After six weeks of training, much of which is on the job, they work long shifts, with limited job security and few opportunities for career advancement. Staff turnover is high, and it is not hard to see why.

Jane, who worked at Morton Hall Immigration Removal Centre, expressed her frustration at her own lack of agency and self-determination. 'Everything is governed by the Home Office,' she complained. 'Mentally, it's very, very, very challenging. Because you don't make a difference to [detainees], really. You make no difference. Whereas with a prisoner, you feel as though you're working towards something, you don't have that kind of satisfaction, really ... We make no difference whatsoever.' Of course, her frustrations are nothing compared to what the detainees experience. But, indirectly, we get an inkling of how utterly powerless they might feel.

Another of Bosworth's interviewees, Imran, is a manager at Harmondsworth and seems unaware at a conscious level of the impact his work has on him or his charges. 'To start with, seeing self-harm affected me, yes. I was a bit shocked, but now, I've got to say, no. Once I've dealt with it I move on. I have to, you know.' It seems unlikely that he could really just 'move on' – unless he has distanced himself so far from the detainees he is supposed to look after that he has no concern for their welfare at all.

Immigration detention centres are not therapeutic, healing environments but ones of coercive force that drive detainees to harm themselves. Detainees are not willing participants; they are imprisoned against their will with the threat of violence hanging over them if they do not comply. Some detention centre staff, themselves brutalised by their experience of carrying out this state-sanctioned violence, react with abuse, aggression and violence, as was revealed in an undercover investigation by BBC *Panorama* in 2017. Video footage secretly recorded by 21-year-old whistleblower Callum Tulley showed a guard choking a detainee. Other guards recounted

violent acts they had committed against detainees, including banging one's head and forcing another's fingers back against his hand.
One claimed, 'If I killed a man, I wouldn't be bothered.'[11]

INDEFINITE DETENTION

These anecdotes and statistics are all very well, but it is hard to really
understand the impact of being detained under immigration law
powers without visiting a detention centre yourself, or at least spending time with those who have experienced it. Michael Darko was
detained for two and a half years before being released back into the
community. He says that it was like prison, except 'the only difference
here was that there was no end to your detention'. His experience was
a form of 'mental torture', he said, leading him to campaign for an
end to the system that scarred him. He is a member of Freed Voices,
a group of former detainees who speak out about their experiences
in the hope that the system will change, and others will not have to
go through the same experiences.

In interviews with those who have had anything to do with immigration detention centres, the single, stand-out worst thing seems
to be that it is indefinite. There is no defined maximum period, and
a detainee has no idea for how long they will be kept there against
their will. This marks it out as a very different experience to spending
time in prison as a result of a criminal sentence, for which there will
be a known release date. 'You don't know what you are doing there,
you don't know how long you will be there,' says Rabah, an Algerian
national who was detained for two years. 'Sometimes it feels like you
will be there for ever.' Another detainee said, 'While I was an immigration detainee in prison, I didn't know I had the right to apply for
bail. I really believed the UKBA could hold me there for as long as
they wanted. I thought they had the power to do that.'[12]

Detainees feel helpless and powerless, and with good reason. They have no idea if or when they might be either removed from the UK or released into society and, as we will see, many are unable to do anything to bring about either outcome. They can ask to be released but their requests are often refused.

Home Office ministers have consistently rejected claims that the United Kingdom has a system of indefinite detention. As immigration minister in 2015, James Brokenshire argued that it was wrong to say immigration detention is indefinite because there are some legal constraints on the power to detain, and the phrase 'implies detention that cannot be brought to an end'. It is certainly true that there are legal constraints, but they are vague in nature. There is nothing in the Immigration Act 1971 or any other legislation that explicitly limits the power to detain. In a case known as *Hardial Singh*, back in 1983, Mr Justice Woolf held that there must be some implied limits.[13] Mr Singh had been detained for three months at HMP Durham and the legal action was an application for *habeas corpus*, an ancient form of request to be released from detention dating back to the Magna Carta of 1215. Woolf decided that the implicit limits must be:

1. The Secretary of State must intend to deport the person and can only use the power to detain for that purpose.
2. The deportee may only be detained for a period that is reasonable in all the circumstances.
3. If, before the expiry of the reasonable period, it becomes apparent that the Secretary of State will not be able to effect deportation within a reasonable period, he should not seek to exercise the power of detention.
4. The Secretary of State should act with all diligence and expedition to effect removal.

The Hardial Singh case has been followed by other judges ever since, but these principles remain the only restrictions on the power of immigration detention. There is no specific maximum time limit for which a person can be detained, as long as it is seen to be 'reasonable in all the circumstances'. Unfortunately, this is very much a matter for debate in each and every case.

The dictionary seems to be on the side of campaigners. My favoured dictionary of choice, *Chambers*, defines 'indefinite' thus:

indefinite /*in-def-i-nit*/
1. Without clearly marked outlines or limits
2. Not clearly distinguished in character
3. Not precise, clear
4. Undetermined...

That exactly describes immigration detention in the United Kingdom. There is no real, proper time limit after which a detainee must be released, unlike in every other European country. In France, for example, the limit is ninety days. In Germany it is eighteen months. In Portugal it is sixty days.[14] In the minimum standards set by the EU Returns Directive, which the United Kingdom never opted into, the limit is six months, though this can be extended by a further twelve months in some circumstances.[15] Around one-third of detainees in the UK are detained for twenty-eight days or more and in any given year around 500 are detained for six months or more. Worse still, between 2010 and 2018, thirty-three migrants were detained for more than three years, and the longest period spent in detention was just over six years.[16] By comparison, a prison sentence of even a day would usually be considered a severe and humiliating punishment by most citizens, if it were inflicted on them as a sanction.

THE BUSINESS OF DETENTION

In the 1980s, at most one or two hundred migrants might be detained under immigration powers, mainly in prisons.[17] Since then, dedicated facilities detaining migrants in prison-like conditions have proliferated. Harmondsworth was the first in the 1970s and it was substantially rebuilt in the 1980s. Then, later in that same decade, the prison at Haslar near Portsmouth started to house migrants in a separate wing. With the government of the day unafraid of or indifferent to accusations of using a Napoleonic-era floating prison hulk, the MV *Earl William*, a former cross-Channel ferry, was drafted into service to house up to 240 migrants between May and October 1987. It broke free from its moorings during a storm and forty Tamil asylum seekers had to be rescued. Tinsley House near Gatwick and Campsfield House near Oxford followed in the 1990s. Dover Castle, Lindholme in Yorkshire, Oakington near Cambridge (where I later got my first job in immigration law as an on-site legal adviser), Dungavel in Scotland, Yarl's Wood near Bedford, Colnbrook next to the existing detention centre at Harmondsworth and Brook House near Gatwick all followed between 2000 and 2009. Some were custom built from scratch and others were converted from prisons or military barracks. A special detention facility for families with children was opened at The Cedars in West Sussex in 2010, Morton Hall in Lincolnshire was opened in 2011, and The Verne on Portland followed in 2014.

Despite all these new facilities, prisons are still in use today as homes for migrants detained under immigration powers, with as many as 1,000 immigration detainees held in this way at any one time.[18] Private contractors from different companies run most of these facilities under detailed contracts with the Home Office and all are governed by the Detention Centre Rules. The physical environment, regime and culture varies considerably between the different detention centres, though. Dungavel, Campsfield and Tinsley House were preferred by male detainees, while Colnbrook and Brook House, built to exacting Category B prison security standards and with very limited internal movement or mixing by detainees permitted, were very unpopular.[19]

This extensive building programme suggests a massive growth in the use of immigration detention powers. The publicly available Home Office statistics on immigration detention only date back to 2009 and they do confirm a seemingly inexorable rise in the number of detainees until 2015, but it has fallen back since then, with several detention centres being closed.[20] At its peak in 2015, the 'immigration detention estate', as it is known, held around 3,500 migrants at any one time and over 30,000 were experiencing immigration detention per year. At the time of writing, following a number of scandals and a major review by the Home Office, the number had fallen back to fewer than 2,000 being held at any one time and fewer than 25,000 experiencing detention per year.

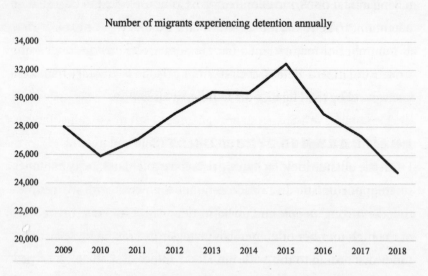

Number of migrants experiencing detention annually

Source: Home Office quarterly statistics year ended June 2019 (2nd ed).
Table dt_01 updated with figures from September 2019.

We do not know the cost of the mammoth building programme or the profits that the various private contractors make from running their private detention centres, though it is estimated that the Yarl's Wood facility alone cost around £100 million at the time it was built.[21] We do know that, in 2019, the basic cost of immigration detention for one person for one day was £87.71. The annual upfront cost of immigration detention for the year ended March 2018 was £108 million. However, even aside from the human cost, that is not the whole, true financial cost. The charity Bail for Immigration Detainees points out that this figure does not include 'administrative costs, the cost of opposing bail and other legal costs which could amount to thousands of pounds per detainee, nor do they include the costs the Home Office has paid out in compensation for unlawful detention.'[22] Between 2011 and 2019, for example, the government paid out well over £43 million in compensation to people wrongfully apprehended in immigration detention. For the financial year 2018/19, the Home Office reports paying a total of £8.2 million compensation for 312 cases of unlawful detention.[23] The totals for coming years are likely to be even higher, as a number of major claims for damages are known to be pending from EU citizens detained under Home Office projects that were later found by the High Court to be unlawful.[24]

ARBITRARY AND OPPORTUNISTIC

From the outside looking in, initial decisions to detain a person often seem opportunistic and random rather than strategic. The result is that the 'wrong' people end up being detained. We know this because of the high number of vulnerable people being detained who should not be according to the government's own policies, the high level of compensation payments being made for unlawful detention, and the fact that the proportion of detainees released into the community from so-called 'removal' centres now stands at over 50 per cent – a proportion that has increased significantly in recent years. How can it be, then, that in 2012, a joint inspection report on immigration detention casework by HM inspector of prisons and the chief inspector of borders and immigration found that most decisions to detain were 'reasoned and defensible', and only around 10 per cent were not?[25]

First of all, when a country is detaining around 25,000 people per year, a 10 per cent rate of error is still 2,500 people. Secondly, it can be said that detention causes vulnerability, particularly if prolonged; as we have seen, the mental and physical health of detainees can deteriorate rapidly in immigration detention. As a high-level review of previous research by eminent doctors in 2018 concluded, 'Detention should be viewed as a traumatic experience in and of itself.'[26] Thirdly, the pathways into detention generally rely on happenstance rather than planning. Officials are not identifying high-risk migrants, planning their removal, putting the documents in place to ensure their expulsion and then detaining and removing them. Rather, migrants are 'encountered'. Foreign national offenders reach the end of their sentences, individuals claim asylum and unauthorised migrants are discovered in enforcement raids or by the police.

Worst of all, migrants of any given nationality are often rounded up solely because of their nationality for group removals on chartered flights. Around 2,000 migrants are expelled in this manner each year, which is about 15 per cent of the total number of removals. When a date for one of these charter flights has been set, officials will look through their case files for migrants from that country and detain them with a view to including them in the group removal, with the emphasis being on their nationality rather than any other factor. To make the situation even graver, a greater number of detainees than can physically be boarded onto the plane will be apprehended, with a view to filling the spaces vacated by last-minute legal reprieves, in a practice that has been repeatedly condemned. Charter flights to Nigeria, Ghana and Pakistan in particular are routinely massively overbooked by the Home Office, raising questions of racial bias.[27] Although it is a cost-effective method of immigrant removal, this practice causes huge and largely pointless distress to those who are detained. Overbooking for charter flights has been repeatedly criticised by HM inspectorate of prisons and the original Shaw Review in 2016 strongly recommended that it cease, with Shaw writing that he found 'the whole practice to be unsavoury and inconsistent with a welfare-centred approach'. The recommendation was rejected by the Home Office, however, and overbooking continues today.

Most fundamentally of all, even if each individual decision was reasoned and justifiable on its own facts alone, every decision to detain is made inherently arbitrary when similar cases are treated differently. Every time an unauthorised migrant is detained, he or she was simply unlucky, it seems; after all, there were many other unauthorised migrants who could justifiably have been detained but were not. As we have seen, recent attempts to guess at the number of unauthorised migrants living in the United Kingdom today range between around 600,000 and 1.2 million.[28] Decisions to detain and remove particular individuals within the group are therefore almost inevitably arbitrary. Worse still, the selective nature of the exercise allows for, and perhaps even encourages, discrimination and could perhaps explain the prevalence of certain nationalities and racialised groups in immigration detention. How is it fair that unlawful resident X is detained for removal because of his or her unlawful residence but unlawful resident Y is not?

As Hiroshi Motomura puts it in the context of the United States, 'The letter of the law creates a large removable population, but whether an individual is actually targeted for removal has long depended on government discretion and bad luck.'[29] The discretion exists at what Motomura describes as a macro level, deciding what resources to put into enforcement, how to deploy those resources and which categories of unlawful migrant to target. For example, how should resources be divided between policing the borders to prevent illegal entry and detecting existing unlawful residents? Is targeting certain nationalities the way forward in accordance with the level of co-operation provided by that country's embassy staff, or should the focus be on targeting homeless migrants, or foreign criminals, or failed asylum seekers, or sham marriages, or conducting workplace raids, or dawn raids on families, or some other priority? Discretion also exists at a micro level, because even within these broad resourcing decisions, the power to detain must be exercised on specific individuals and there are many from whom to choose.

This gets to the heart of the problem with immigration detention: it is a policy aimed at managing broad groups, not simply a judicial measure targeted at a particular individual. In this context, singular decision-making is unimportant. What matters is that some, any unauthorised migrants are detained. What the justification might be in each specific case is ultimately of little import.

CHECKS AND BALANCES

As well as questionable judgements being made to detain migrants in the first place, the Home Office is often very reluctant to release detainees once that decision has been made. This is partly bureaucratic inertia and partly an institutional reluctance to admit error. Even in cases where it would be clear to any rational person that a mistake has been made, officials still search for excuses to maintain detention. One example, which lawyers like me will recognise as typical, was given in a joint report by the chief inspectors of prisons and borders and immigration. It was cited as an example of the poor assessment of the likelihood of removal: 'Subject to the outcome of the appeal hearing of the further representation/new claim being refused and he becomes appeals rights exhausted, his removal can be made within a reasonable timescale when the Iraqi authorities resume referrals for agreeing removal on an EU letter.'[30] As you will probably have detected, the assessment was nonsense. This particular detainee has already been detained for seventeen months and might be waiting weeks or months for an appeal at the immigration tribunal, after which there may well be further legal appeals. Even if the appeal had been dealt with quickly, the memo itself admitted that it was still impossible to remove the detainee to Iraq anyway, at least pending a further decision by the Iraqi authorities, which might never come. Removal could never rationally be described as imminent in this example, yet the officials proposed to carry on detaining the person anyway.

The checks and balances on the arbitrary power of detention are very weak, meaning this sort of poor decision-making goes unchallenged. The Home Office does review its own decisions at set intervals of at least once per month, and there is a hierarchy of decision-making, with more senior officials having to approve cases of long-term detention and decisions to release. However, these reviews are quite literally tick-box exercises, where the official checks off one of several standard reasons. Other material is routinely 'cut and pasted' from other cases or from previous reviews. The reviews are not independent and simply do not work.

Instead of waiting for a review, there is an option for a detainee to herself ask the Home Office for release. Unsurprisingly, this seldom works. It would be an admission, after all, that an incorrect decision had been made. To up the ante slightly, a detainee could ask a lawyer for help. There is a duty scheme run by the Legal Aid Agency for lawyers to visit detention centres; although there are concerns about the availability and quality of this advice, it is certainly better than nothing.[31] The duty scheme does not extend to prisons, however, where at least several hundred people are held under immigration powers at any one time in a wide variety of jails across the country.[32] Perhaps more fundamentally, legal aid was abolished for immigration cases in 2013, and the first contact some migrants have with a lawyer is after they are detained, at which point it may finally emerge that they have a good case for remaining in the UK. Only funding legal advice *after* detention is surely not a sensible policy, though.

Another option for detained individuals is that a bail application can be made to an immigration judge. The detainee can try to make the application herself or seek help. The process is not straightforward and even where detainees are aware that they can make such an application, in practice many are unable to do so without assistance. Around one-third of bail applications succeed, but too few such applications are ever made in the first place.[33] A charity called Bail for Immigration Detainees does what it can to help and their experience is that just applying for bail in the first place will often cause the Home Office to release a detainee. This calls into question why the detainee was being held in the first place, why she was still being held until the point of her application and just how many others who do not apply for bail are simply left to rot for no good reason.

ATTEMPTS TO REFORM

The year 2015 marked a turning point in the number of people being detained. The numbers were going up and up at the time, and since then have been falling. The change of direction was brought about by what became known as the Shaw Report into the welfare of vulnerable immigration detainees.[34] Conducted by Stephen Shaw, a former prisons and probation ombudsman, the report was commissioned by Theresa May when she was Home Secretary, following several cases, like that of MD, in which the courts found that detainees had been subjected to inhuman and degrading treatment. Amongst other things, Shaw found that the mechanism supposed to protect vulnerable detainees was ineffective and that there was a culture of disbelief amongst healthcare staff. He recommended that there should be a ban on detaining pregnant women, an upper age limit for the detention of the elderly and a presumption against detention for vulnerable detainees including transsexuals, victims of rape and other sexual or gender-based violence, those suffering from PTSD and those with serious mental illness or learning disabilities. Finally, he concluded that Home Office policies on who was considered vulnerable and whether they should be detained should be re-written.

Most people reading these recommendations might well be surprised, or even horrified, that they needed to be made at all. What on earth was the Home Office doing detaining pregnant women, for example? Yet it certainly happens in practice; a report by HM inspector of prisons revealed that ninety-nine pregnant asylum seekers were detained in 2014. To make matters worse, 90 per cent of them were then released back into the community again, making their detention particularly cruel and pointless. When Mark Harper was minister of immigration in 2013, he gave some insight into the mentality governing this policy:

If we were to ... have a blanket policy of not detaining [pregnant] women, first, having read many cases, I fear we would find quite a lot of people saying they were pregnant as another method of delaying their departure from the UK ... I do not want this to be an excuse that women who are not pregnant dream up in order to throw a legal obstacle in the way.[35]

That the minister in charge of immigration can say out loud in Parliament that women might pretend to be pregnant in order to avoid detention tells us a great deal about the culture of cynical disbelief that prevails at the highest levels of the Home Office.

Following the Shaw Report, the Home Office introduced a new policy for detaining vulnerable adults. Although the total number of people being detained fell as a result, the new policy seems to have led to a higher rate of detention for those who are the most vulnerable. A record seventeen migrants died in immigration detention in 2017. One of them was Carlington Spencer, a 38-year-old man who suffered a stroke at Morton Hall but was denied potentially life-saving emergency care because detention staff wrongly presumed that he had taken illegal drugs. The coroner criticised the 'confirmatory bias' by staff.[36] HM chief inspector of prisons also highlighted the case of a wheelchair user who had tried to set himself on fire after being held for fifteen months, and that of a blind detainee who was held for over a year.[37]

'Detention too often appears to be the default position', wrote Shaw in his 2018 follow-up report. While researching the new report, Shaw encountered a 77-year-old woman detained at Colnbrook who had complex health needs and a 71-year-old man who had been initially detained at Brook House, but then moved to Tinsley House for a proposed return on a charter fight. 'Having made further enquiries,' Shaw wrote, 'I did not see how either of these detentions was possibly justified.' He was 'utterly bemused and appalled' by the detention of the 77-year-old in particular, and enquiries revealed that a total of fifty migrants over the age of seventy had been detained between

September 2016 and November 2017.[38] A parliamentary committee found in 2019 that the new policy 'has not only failed to mitigate the harmful impact of detention on vulnerable people but has failed to deliver a reduction in the number of vulnerable people in detention'.[39]

To make this system work, the officials at the Home Office who are responsible for decisions to detain or release are kept separate from those whose lives they govern. They are, as Mary Bosworth writes, 'sequestered from the potentially destabilising effects of facing up to those they wish to remove'. One official who had, unusually, visited a detention centre told Shaw, somewhat ruefully, that her 'job had been easier before the visit as it had been possible to consider detainees just as case files rather than as people'. One has to wonder what sort of human being would have made a positive decision to keep Alois Dvorzak, Xiao Yun Xue or MD in detention if they had actually met them, for example. The separation of officials from detainees is not only 'bureaucratically effective', as Bosworth puts it, militating in favour of detention, but it also creates uncertainty and despair amongst detainees and, to a lesser extent, amongst detention centre staff. The distant decision-makers are made to seem remote, unknown and ineffable, with an almost God-like power over the lives of detainees. One of Shaw's recommendations – arguably his most important – was that the caseworkers making detention decisions should actually meet those they decide to detain. The recommendation was rejected by the Home Office.

THE PURPOSE OF DETENTION

What is driving this large-scale and cruel system of human ware-housing? No one seems to want it, and even by the Home Office's own logic it all seems to make no sense given that ever fewer detainees are actually removed from the country as a result. The immigration detention system seems to have a life of its own, driven onward by its own momentum.

The legally permissible purposes of immigration detention are supposed to be to interview migrants on arrival, to investigate their cases and, ultimately, to remove them. Where a migrant has committed a criminal offence, detention can also be used for the purpose of protecting the public, although even then detention cannot go on if there is no realistic prospect of removal. Some migrants are detained for a very short time, usually on their arrival to the UK. They may be refused entry and then held for a few hours or overnight before being sent back to their country of origin on another flight. Long-term detention is most often utilised in cases involving the attempted removal of foreign criminals who have already served a prison sentence but who, at the end of it, are taken straight into immigration detention rather than being released. This is not always so, as the case of MD from Guinea showed. In that case, she was detained on arrival and kept in detention for eleven months.

Some detention decisions are driven by the fear of generating stories in the press. Foreign criminals reaching the end of their sentence will be detained under immigration powers come what may and no matter what the chances of their removal within a reasonable time period. In 2012, a joint report by HM inspector of prisons and the chief inspector of borders and immigration found that decisions to detain foreign criminals could be made at a junior level, while decisions to release had to be referred to very senior management, setting up a system in which it is both easier and simpler for an official to detain rather than release. The inspectors found this was 'clearly inconsistent with the presumption in favour of release'.

Abdulrahman Mohammed was a career criminal with offences ranging from the petty to the serious: from disorderly behaviour and shoplifting to robbery, burglary, and possession of an offensive weapon. He was detained repeatedly by the Home Office, despite there being no realistic prospect of his being removed to Somalia, which was a war zone at the time. One of the official reasons stated for his detention was unusually candid: 'If you are released from detention, our actions can lead to a negative view of the Home Office by the general public who may see the department as failing in its duty to protect them from criminals and therefore there is a high risk of harm to the public.'[40]

Protecting the reputation of the Home Office is definitely not one of the lawful, permissible reasons for detaining someone. Mohammed was awarded £78,500 in damages as a result. The case highlighted a worrying trend in deportation and detention decision-making. Government officials are supposed to follow and obey the law and judges should be a last resort. Instead, foreign criminals are frequently issued with deportation orders and detained come what may. Judges are then blamed by the media and even the Home Office for upholding the law.

The huge expansion in detention centres that we considered earlier was initiated by the 1997 to 2010 Labour government. In the four years between 1997 and 2001 alone, the number of detention places trebled from around 900 to 2,800. The rationale was never stated clearly, though a whole chapter was dedicated to detention in the first Labour White Paper on immigration: 'Fairer, Faster, Firmer'.[41] Here we are told that 'effective enforcement of immigration control requires some immigration offenders to be detained' and that 'detention is necessary to ensure the integrity of our immigration control'. What we are not told is how detention will achieve this, other than that it would 'support an increased number of removals'. But would *all* 'immigration offenders' be detained and removed? If not, what percentage might be? If a small percentage, which is inevitable without a programme of mass detention and removal being put in place, how does that really make immigration controls 'effective' and ensure their 'integrity'?

In the second Labour White Paper, 'Secure Borders, Safe Haven', a new pledge was introduced to remove as many as 30,000 failed asylum seekers per year, or 2,500 per month, by the spring of 2003.[42] To help achieve this detention, capacity would be increased by a further 40 per cent to 4,000 places and detention centres were to be re-titled 'removal' centres, in order to signal their real purpose: to 'facilitate an increased rate of removal'. Within months, David Blunkett, then Home Secretary, had to abandon the removals pledge as being completely impractical.[43] Despite this, the detention centre building programme continued. In September 2004 Tony Blair introduced yet another commitment, this time to remove more failed asylum seekers than new applicants by the end of 2005, 'and so restore faith in a system that we know has been abused'.[44] The nature of the target seemed to imply that all, or at least most, failed asylum seekers could and would ultimately be removed. In 2006, the Public Accounts Committee also seemed to be entertaining this hypothetical possibility when it concluded, 'It would take between ten and eighteen years to clear the existing backlog' of removals even if no new applications were made.[45] To be fair, their comments can certainly also be read as ridiculing the possibility.

Following Blair's speech, removals did increase to over 21,000 per year, but only before falling back again year-on-year after that. (The Home Office statistical series does not extend back further than 2004, but press reports indicate that the totals were lower in previous years.) Today, the number of enforced removals per year stands lower than at any time since the turn of the millennium: fewer than 8,000 per year.[46]

The reality is that detaining and removing all unauthorised migrants would have required huge resources and been hugely controversial. This was implicitly recognised by Labour, as the pool of people subject to detention and removal was reduced by means of a regularisation programme for families around 2003. This was in all but name an amnesty, involving granting legal status to a significant number of the failed asylum seekers that the government judged it would be hardest and perhaps cruellest to remove. The decision not to impose controls when the European Union expanded in 2004 had the effect of regularising a further tranche of migrants from Eastern Europe, who had until then been unlawfully resident. A 'legacy backlog clearance exercise', another amnesty in all but name, involving the grant of status to thousands more unauthorised migrants was also carried out between 2006 and 2010.

Since 2010, governments have abandoned regularisation paired with detention and enforced removal as a means of reducing the size of the unauthorised population. Instead, governments have purported to rely, without any evidence that they are effective, on the 'hostile environment' policies discussed in Chapter 3. Following what seems to have been some genuine introspection about which migrants are detained and why, the Home Office stated in 2018 that detention is part of its broader immigration enforcement strategy in support of its vision 'to reduce the size of the illegal population and the harm it causes'.[47] But as Stephen Shaw observed in his review, it is unclear how immigration detention will be used as part of this plan, why the current high number of places available is needed for the strategy to succeed and why, if there is a broader strategy, the number of detainees appears in reality to be determined by the number of places available.

There are two ways in which immigration detention can

arguably be used to achieve 'effective enforcement'. One is detention as literal enforcement, with all, or at least a very high proportion of, unauthorised migrants being detained and removed. We can see this strategy being attempted in the United States, where a wall is being built, border patrols have been massively expanded, there are over 50,000 detention places and half a million migrants are detained each year.[48] Years earlier, Labour seemed at times to be pursuing this enforcement policy in tandem with occasional targeted amnesties. The other possibility is detention as deterrent. It is possible that un-authorised migrants might think twice about coming to the United Kingdom if they perceive a real risk of being detained and removed, and existing unauthorised residents might decide that the trauma of detention is too risky and therefore decide to leave. This may be the rationale behind current government policy, although if so, it has not been publicly stated. It would certainly match with the overall prevailing policy of immigration deterrence that has been pursued since around 2012, though.

The current approach to immigration detention achieves neither of these potential strategies. In fact, it is quantifiably failing even at the basic justification of facilitating removal. Over half of detainees at so-called 'removal' centres are released back into the community rather than being removed, for instance. The proportion of detain-ees pointlessly held in this way and then released has actually been increasing in recent years. The problems with literal enforcement are that it is extremely expensive, the human cost to those removed and their families and communities is immense, and its effectiveness is unproven given that it has never really been attempted before. As previously mentioned, the UK's unauthorised migrant population that these measures target is currently estimated to number between 600,000 and 1.2 million. Detecting and removing that many people would be impractical, even aside from any moral or legal objections we might have. Even if it was possible, there is no public or political appetite for such a radical programme in the United Kingdom. Similar problems arise with any genuine attempt at deterrence. With less than 8,000 enforced removals per year currently, the percentage of the unauthorised population being removed is somewhere between 1.3 and 0.7 per cent. That does not look like a real risk of detention and removal that would be sufficient to have a deterrent effect. Besides, as we saw in Chapter 6, all the available evidence suggests that country-specific policies and practices are irrelevant to migrant decision-making.

The only purpose that the immigration detention system seems to be performing at present is to serve a sense of moral righteousness. Unlawful residence is, obviously, in breach of the law. Breaking the law should be penalised because otherwise the law is meaningless and public opinion is certainly not willing to countenance the idea that immigration laws are meaningless. Criminal law sanctions against those who breach immigration laws are available but would be highly expensive to enforce. It would also serve no useful purpose to detain a migrant in prison for weeks or months, only to remove him or her at its conclusion; why not simply remove them in the first place? And this is all before taking into account that criminal law enforcement is even more impractical and expensive than the enforcement of administrative removals.

Seen like this, the purpose of immigration detention seems to be to punish. But not all unauthorised migrants can be punished in this way, so current immigration detention policy says that it is better to punish some rather than none at all. This might explain why all attempts to reform the system have failed; realising that it performs no useful direct policy function, those officials who operate the system intend it to be punitive in nature. Whatever the intention, this is certainly how detainees themselves experience the system, and their insights should not lightly be disregarded. Attempts to persuade the Home Office as an institution, and officials as humans, to exercise restraint and properly to care for the welfare of detainees miss the point. At least as far as those responsible are concerned, the reason detainees are in detention is because they deserve it.

CHAPTER 12

CITIZENSHIP, NATIONALITY AND INTEGRATION

We have considered all aspects of immigration policy; it is now time to turn to the issue of citizenship. After a person has migrated to the United Kingdom, under what circumstances do she and her family become British? And what does it mean to be 'British' anyway? For a lawyer like me, a superficial answer to this last question is easy. A British citizen is a person on whom that status has been conferred, either automatically by law or by administrative action exercised under the British Nationality Act 1981. But once we start really thinking about this, things get very complicated very quickly, because there are other forms of legal status that either are or were also considered 'British'.

Firstly, we can look to the past and how the meaning of 'British' has changed in law over the last century. Working backwards from the present, there was no such thing, legally, as a 'British citizen' before the 1981 Act came into effect on 1 January 1983. There was such a thing as a 'British subject', but this status applied to every single citizen of a Commonwealth country around the globe – some 600 million souls. The principal nationality and citizenship status for residents of the United Kingdom specifically was that of a 'citizen of the United Kingdom and Colonies'. This status was the creation of the British Nationality Act 1948 and if a person had talked about 'British citizens' or 'the British' at that time, this was the closest thing there was in nationality law terms. But, as the very title suggests, it was a status held not just by residents of the United Kingdom but also by residents of the colonies. As we saw in Chapter 1, from the time of the Commonwealth Immigrants Act 1962, many people in possession of this citizenship who had not been born in the UK did not actually have the right to live in the country of which they were nominally considered citizens. Going further back in history, before the 1948 Act came into force the only form of British legal status was that of the British subject. This ancient common law status applied to all, or at least most, residents of the British Empire.

So, until the 1981 Act, it made no sense in legal terms to use the word 'British' to describe residents of Great Britain; all the available legal meanings of 'British' described a far, far wider group of people.

To confuse matters further, there are other forms of British legal status, aside from British citizenship, that still exist today. The 1981 Act also established two further forms of British nationality: British dependent territory citizenship and British overseas citizenship. And there are still other residual forms of British nationality as well, from other statutes and common law: British nationals overseas, British protected persons and British subjects. These British nationals generally live outside of Britain because none of these forms of nationality or status actually imbue the holder with a right to live here – a feature we might expect to be rather closely linked with 'Britishness'.

There is no central register of the holders of any of these forms of British nationality, so nobody knows exactly how many there are of each. A passport is evidence of nationality but does not confer it; or, to put it another way, some people holding British nationality will have passports to prove it, but by no means will all of them. At the end of 2015, the Home Office reported that there were 48,821,200 British citizen passports in circulation.[1] In comparison, the total population of the United Kingdom is something like sixty-five million, and we also know that some of those passport holders live outside the United Kingdom. One of the reasons for the difference between the number of passport holders and the number of residents is the fact that there are many British citizens who do not have passports.[2] They may be children whose parents have not yet applied for their passport or adults who have never had cause to apply, perhaps because they have never travelled abroad, for example. The total number of British passports issued to the other types of British national noted above was 210,700 in 2015, the majority of which were given to British nationals overseas in Hong Kong.

LONG-TERM RESIDENTS WITHOUT CITIZENSHIP

So far, we have only considered 'Britishness' in narrow, purely legal terms. As the Windrush scandal of 2018 highlighted, though, there are many long-term, lawful residents of the United Kingdom who would be thought of by most as British and as 'citizens' in the wider colloquial sense. They may well also think of themselves as British, despite in fact now not being so – at least in the eyes of the law. To complicate things further, they may well have arrived at a time when they were actually considered British subjects (and perhaps even citizens of the United Kingdom and Colonies). In 2018, the researchers at Migration Observatory estimated that there were around 57,000 such long-term resident Commonwealth nationals in this position, who had entered the UK before 1971 but had not acquired British citizenship.[3] These residents would normally possess a status formally called Indefinite Leave to Remain ('ILR' is the acronym beloved of lawyers and officials) but also variously referred to as settled status, settlement or permanent residence. There are also an unknown number of other residents who have arrived from all over the world since 1971 and who have been granted settlement, but without acquiring British citizenship. For example, those EU citizens living in the UK who apply for it are being granted settled status under the EU Settlement Scheme, meaning they will have secure residency after Brexit. It is not the same as British citizenship or nationality, though.

Those who have been living in the United Kingdom for a long time may not have any current, up-to-date proof of their status. Their passport, into which a stamp or sticker vignette was placed as proof, may have expired or been lost and a new one not issued, for example. If they were resident before 1 January 1973, they may never have been issued with a proof of their status in the first place, as back then it was conferred on them automatically by law, without the need for documentary proof. This is why some members of the Windrush generation were denied employment, benefits, healthcare and threatened with deportation from around 2014 onwards: new laws meant they needed proof for the first time and they could not persuade the Home Office to issue them with it.

Then there are other non-citizen residents who were born in the UK or moved here at an early age and who have lived here all their lives. Automatic birth-right citizenship for anyone born in Britain was scrapped by the British Nationality Act 1981 with effect from 1 January 1983. Whether a child born in Britain is a British citizen now depends on the status of their parents at the time of their birth, or the actions of their parents since. As a result, many children in this position lack any kind of lawful status at all. This matters little while they are at school and they may not realise that they are different to their friends until their teenage years. Then, some find they cannot go on school trips abroad. Others only find out when it comes to applying to university, because they have no proof that they are a 'home student' who is exempt from the high fees that foreign students are required to pay. As we saw in Chapter 10, some end up being deported to countries in which they have never set foot or of which they have no memory at all. They seem British and sound British, their cultural reference points are all British and all their experiences and friends are British, yet they are unable to get a job, rent a property, open a bank account, claim benefits or local authority assistance, drive, marry or vote. The numbers are significant and will only grow over time, unless something is done.

In early 2020, a study by the Institute of Community Research and Development at the University of Wolverhampton estimated that there were 215,000 children living in the United Kingdom without immigration status, half of whom were born in the country.[4] Some may be able to secure some form of status, but it can be prohibitively expensive – and they often have no means to pay lawyers or application fees – and tortuous. The application fee for a child born in Britain and resident for the first ten years of her life to register as a British citizen was, at the time of writing, £1,012. This is simply unaffordable to many families. To rub salt in the wound, the cost to the Home Office of processing each application is only £372; the difference is essentially profit, used to fund other aspects of the citizenship and immigration system. In 1983, when it was first introduced, the fee was £35. Even in cases where parents are aware that an application can be made for their children, those on low incomes either cannot afford the modern fee at all or have to choose which of their children to register. What are those children who are effectively excluded from citizenship by these fees supposed to do? They are unlikely to leave Britain, their home country, voluntarily because they would have no right of re-entry and they know no other country. Instead, they face the vulnerable, exploited, destitute lives on the margins of British society.

RIGHTS AND RESPONSIBILITIES

Perhaps surprisingly, there is almost no right or responsibility set out in law that is unique to British citizens over British nationals and long-term residents. Instead, we see huge overlap between these different forms of status.

If we start with the right to live and work long-term in the United Kingdom, the 'right of abode' was created by the Immigration Act 1971 and is an exemption from immigration control, meaning an immigration officer must only let into the country a person who can prove they possess this status. British citizens have this right, but so too do some Commonwealth citizens and their family members. Other groups have similar but legally slightly different rights: EU citizens will also be exempted from UK immigration control until the end of the Brexit transition period; Irish citizens have the right to live freely in the United Kingdom; and there are hundreds of thousands of long-term UK residents with a form of permanent residence called indefinite leave to remain.

We might expect the rights to vote and to stand in elections to be restricted to citizens alone, but in fact the Representation of the People Act 1983 also confers these rights on settled Commonwealth and Irish citizens. Prior to Brexit, EU citizens had the right to vote in local elections. There are no welfare benefits that are specifically restricted to citizens alone. Abroad, the British government can offer its citizens help in the form of diplomatic protection and consular assistance. Both are discretionary rather than as of right – the government is not required to do anything by law – and both are provided to all types of British national, not just British citizens. Consular assistance is also provided to Commonwealth citizens whose government is not represented in that country.

The same picture emerges if we look at what might be thought to be the responsibilities of citizenship. The obligation to serve on juries is the only potential shared, performative obligation of citizenship. It is tied to the right to vote in local and general elections, meaning that UK-based Commonwealth and Irish citizens (and EU citizens prior to Brexit) are also obliged to perform jury service. There is no longer a clear legal obligation of loyalty that applies to British citizens or nationals. Treason laws still technically exist on the statute book, but the Treason Act 1351 is widely considered unenforceable in its antiquated state. Prosecutions for treason have been virtually unknown since the Second World War, despite the issues of loyalty that have been thrown up by British citizens travelling abroad to fight as enemy combatants over the past twenty years. Even the power to strip British citizens of their status as citizens and exile them abroad is expressed in exactly the same language as the test for deporting foreign nationals: whether it is 'conducive to the public good'.

For completeness, there was until recently one right that was genuinely unique to British citizens. Only British citizens, and not other types of British nationals or other long-term residents of the United Kingdom, qualified as citizens of the European Union. The right of free movement attached to this status enabled British citizens to travel, work, study and live anywhere in the European Union without applying for visas. As a result of Brexit, British citizens lost this status on 31 January 2020, although free movement rights are due to continue until the completion of the transition period at the end of 2020.

In a healthy democracy, long-term residents become citizens. Without citizenship, most will not have the right to vote, they will be vulnerable to deportation, which is damaging to the fabric of their family and community, and perhaps more importantly, they will lack 'belonging'. As American legal academic Hiroshi Motomura writes, 'Democracy is impaired by having a large group of marginalised residents who are governed but cannot acquire a voice in governing.' He argues that the less it means to be a citizen, the more other forms of belonging will emerge, 'many of them more parochial and less cosmopolitan or democratic, and more closely tied to the exclusionary workings of race, ethnicity and class'.[5] In the United Kingdom, the similarities between citizenship and permanent residence mean that there is little incentive for permanent residents to naturalise. In fact, the fee acts as a significant disincentive. This is particularly true for Commonwealth and Irish citizens, who as noted above have the right to vote in parliamentary elections. While it would be retrograde to start removing long-held rights from long-term residents, there is a case for making citizenship an attainable and more attractive proposition in order to encourage more widespread adoption.

BECOMING BRITISH

There are essentially three ways to become British: by birth, by descent and by application. There are also some routes to acquiring citizenship that are a blend of these. The rules for each route can be complex and not everyone we would hope or expect to have acquired citizenship actually does so. What follows is not a full explanation of all the routes to becoming British but is an outline of those main paths.

A child born in the United Kingdom will automatically be born a British citizen if at least one of their parents is settled – meaning that they are in possession of indefinite leave to remain, permanent residence, the right of abode or British citizenship – at the time of their birth. No application needs to be made and no fee is payable. If or when such a child wants or needs a British passport as proof of their citizenship, they can apply for the passport and send in proof that they qualify. Before the British Nationality Act 1981 came into force, the simple fact of being born in the UK was sufficient to make the child British (or, more accurately, a citizen of the United Kingdom and Colonies possessing the right of abode).

There are two other principal routes by which a child born in the United Kingdom can become British after birth. One is where the child lives continuously in the country for the first ten years of her life and then makes an application for registration as a British citizen. The other is where at least one of the child's parents becomes settled in the UK after the child's birth, and an application for registration is made. Neither of these routes is automatic, though. If the application is not made, the child does not become British. A fee must also be paid. And at the time of writing, the fee was £1,012.

All three of these routes include exceptions or gaps that mean not all children living long-term in the United Kingdom will become British. The requirement that one of the parents holds a certain form of immigration status means that not all children born in the UK are British, for example. This was clearly the intention at the time that the British Nationality Act 1981 was passed. However, the two additional routes – living here for ten years continuously or a parent becoming settled – were intended to confer British citizenship on children who would remain in the United Kingdom for a long time.

Neither route has been effective; at the time of writing there are estimated to be over 100,000 children born and living in the UK with insecure status.[6] The reasons for this are partly that parents do not know or understand that an application can be or has to be made, partly the complexity of the application process and partly the affordability of the fee. Families on low incomes literally cannot afford for their children to become British. And many of these families are from ethnic minorities. Insecure status, and the severe social and economic disadvantages that go with that, has unfortunately become generational.

A child born outside the United Kingdom is automatically born British if at least one of her parents was a first-generation British citizen at the time of her birth. However, if that child born outside the United Kingdom then has a child also born outside the country, citizenship is not automatically passed on any further. If such a child is born outside the UK and is then brought back to the country by her parents, there is normally no route by which that child can become British. Instead, she will need to wait until she turns eighteen and then apply as an adult.

The application route for adults to become British is called naturalisation. The rules differ slightly for those who are married to a British citizen and those who are not. Essentially, though, the requirements are that the applicant is of good character, has an intention to live in the UK, has lived lawfully in the UK for five years continuously and has settlement at the time of application and passes the citizenship test on knowledge of life in the United Kingdom. The 45-minute multiple-choice exam is based on the information in a booklet about Britain produced by the government. It has been compared to a bad pub quiz, with the booklet containing several hundred dates as well as odd trivia such as the height of the London Eye in feet and who started the first curry house and on what street.[7] Few existing British citizens are aware of these facts, which raises the question of why new British citizens should be expected to learn them. The overall pass rate for those sitting the test is around 70 per cent, but success varies considerably by country, with 97 per cent of Australians but only 40 per cent of Afghans getting through.[8] Where an applicant has committed serious criminal offences, the good character requirement may mean that she is permanently barred from applying in the first place, or for less serious offences a period of ten years must elapse before she can apply. At the time of writing the fee was £1,330, which is prohibitive for many.

Dual citizenship is where a person holds one or more nationalities. British nationality law is entirely relaxed about dual citizenship and permits its citizens to hold multiple nationalities. Some other countries force their citizens to choose, however, and several have laws that mean, if a person does acquire another nationality, their original nationality is automatically lost.

LOSS OF CITIZENSHIP

British citizenship is, in legal terms, merely a form of immigration status, and in recent years it has become a revocable one at that. Just as a settled foreign national can be stripped of his or her immigration status and deported on the grounds that to do so would be 'conducive to the public good', so too can a British citizen be deprived of his or her citizenship status on precisely the same basis. The power comes from different statutes – from the Immigration Act 1971 for foreign nationals and from the British Nationality Act 1981 for British citizens – but the test is expressed in identical terms.

Given that treason laws are now defunct, exiling a citizen is the strongest expression of disapproval available to the modern state. The deprivation power has existed in statute in one form or another since 1918, but for decades it was seldom used. The test for depriving a person of his or her citizenship went through various permutations in this time, including examinations of disloyalty and criminal behaviour. Between 1948 and 2010, only a handful of citizens were stripped of their status in this way – generally spies during the Cold War. In response to a handful of high-profile but exceptional cases, such as those of extremist cleric Abu Hamza and Guantanamo Bay detainee David Hicks, the power was expanded and the test lowered, so that by 2006 it was equivalent to the test for deportation. It also became possible to strip British citizens, who had been born as British citizens in Britain, of their citizenship if they happened to have inherited another nationality from their parents. Still, the power was still seldom used.[9] That changed in 2010, though, when the numbers began to creep up. Since then, hundreds of British citizens have been exiled on public good grounds.[10]

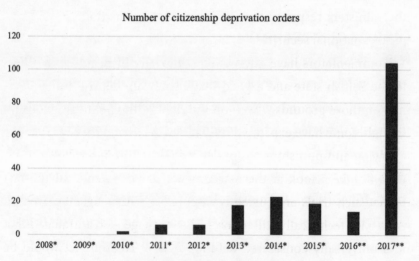

Number of citizenship deprivation orders

Source: FOI 38734; 'HM Government Transparency Report 2018: Disruptive and Investigatory Powers', July 2018.

Until the case of Shamima Begum highlighted this trend in 2019, there was little or no public discussion.[11] Begum was born in Britain and grew up in Britain, but aged fifteen she left the country and travelled to Syria to join the terrorist group ISIS. The British government, arguing that she had inherited Bangladeshi nationality through her parents, stripped her of her British citizenship in 2019, preventing her return to the UK. The fact that she had never even visited Bangladesh was irrelevant, it seemed, as was the fact the Bangladeshi government disclaimed responsibility for her.[12] So, she was left stranded in squalid, life-threatening conditions in a refugee camp in Syria, effectively stateless. It was reported in the press that she had given birth to three children, all of whom were British citizens by descent and all of whom died in infancy. Even now, the fact that hundreds of British citizens, primarily citizens of colour whose parents migrated to the United Kingdom, have been exiled abroad in unbelievably harsh conditions attracts little comment and no justification from the ministers responsible, other than that it was done in order to protect national security.

Commentators have questioned the loyalty of Begum and others to the British state and argued that citizenship deprivation is justified on those grounds.[13] Even on the right of the political spectrum, though, some have expressed unease and suggested that a better way of trying and punishing disloyalty would be through treason trials; we will take a look at these arguments in a moment, but the fact is that such trials are currently impossible.[14] Although the Treason Act 1351 is technically still in force, the language is so antiquated that it is universally considered defunct. A new Treason Act would be needed.

Whether or not Shamima Begum represents a threat to national security, her exile can be seen as opportunistic rather than principled. As a British citizen who was born and radicalised in Britain, she is the responsibility of the British government and should not therefore be foisted on Bangladesh or Syria or any other country. Other British citizens who had acted in the same way could not be treated alike because their parents did not come from abroad. Shamima Begum is a member of a new category of second-class citizens who have family origins abroad, and it cannot be ignored that they are therefore more likely to be from an ethnic minority. Her case and hundreds of cases like hers raise profound questions about the value and meaning of British citizenship. Some argue that the credible threat of taking something away increases its value. For example, prior to nationality law reforms in 2002, the White Paper 'Secure Borders, Safe Haven: Integration with Diversity in Modern Britain' argued that 'a corollary of attaching importance to British citizenship is that the UK should use the power to deprive someone of that citizenship'.[15] Others retort that the threat to remove citizenship, particularly when directed only against some citizens, only cheapens and trivialises it, turning it from an inalienable right into nothing more than another form of immigration status.

It might be argued in defence of deprivation that the protection of national security does not need to be principled, it just needs to be effective. But citizenship can be taken away on far wider than just national security grounds. In October 2018, then Home Secretary Sajid Javid announced that he would start to strip citizenship from serious criminals, as well as those who threatened national security.[16] The test case involved the notorious Rochdale sex trafficking gang, some members of whom had naturalised as British citizens as well as retaining their original nationality. It seems likely to be only a matter of time before other offences that attract public opprobrium, even those involving people who were born British, also trigger citizenship deprivation and exile. Now that the taboo against revoking citizenship has been broken, it will likely prove impossible for politicians to resist the temptation to use their wide discretionary powers.

BRITISH CITIZENSHIP POLICY

The whole concept of who is 'British', of who 'we' are, and of what it means to be British is therefore very confused. Some people who hold British legal status cannot live in Britain and some people who seem to be British and who do live in Britain do not hold any legal status at all. The rights and responsibilities of British citizenship overlap chaotically with other groups of residents and non-residents. The laws on nationality and citizenship often look like pragmatic policy choices made years ago as the United Kingdom withdrew from its empire. Depressingly, though, there are three entwined threads that tie together this apparent incoherence: the conception of citizenship as a privilege rather than a right, a desire to limit the numbers of citizens and a related racial dimension.

For a time during the 2000s, it seemed as if a positive citizenship policy might emerge linked to the idea of integration. The meaning of the word 'integration' has always been contested, and it was never clear if citizenship was a tool to promote and encourage the integration of migrants into British society, or if it was intended to certify that only after it had occurred. As Home Secretary, David Blunkett introduced a new citizenship test in 2002 that was intended to promote integration. The test was and remains still a multiple-choice exam based on a booklet about Britain. The content of the booklet has changed since the test's introduction, but the principle remains that migrants seeking citizenship need to learn the content of the booklet in order to pass the test. Setting aside the sometimes esoteric nature of the content of the booklet, in principle this does potentially perform an educative function for those who want to become citizens. However, it does nothing to encourage migrants to become citizens; if anything, it does the opposite, given that it acts as a barrier. Around 30 per cent of those who take it fail the test, and they must either resit and pass or accept their position as non-citizens with a less secure form of status. This is a strange way to integrate those who fail.

In 2008, the concept of 'earned citizenship' emerged and proposals were made to introduce a new status of 'probationary citizenship', which would last for between one and three years depending on whether the probationary citizen carried out a certain amount of voluntary or community work. The underlying principle was to be that migrants should earn their British citizenship – but this too looked more like an exclusionary than an integrationist approach. The reality was that citizenship would take longer to achieve and would be harder to obtain. The plan was an example of migrants being held to a higher standard than existing citizens, few of whom undertake community work other than as part of criminal sentences.

After the Conservative-led coalition government took power in 2010, the link between citizenship and integration faded away into the background. Leading politicians turned their attention to focus more on the circumstances in which citizenship is taken away, rather than the purpose for which it is granted in the first place. If there has been one idea driving developments over the past decade, it is that citizenship is exclusive and conditional. This conception of citizenship as something for which to be grateful has a long history, dating right back to the first introduction of the power of citizenship deprivation. The principle was initially only applied to naturalised citizens, though. Then Home Secretary George Cave, introducing the Bill that would become the British National and Status of Aliens Act 1918, justified the new deprivation power by explaining that, unlike the native-born citizen, 'a man who is naturalised here really gives a statement of good character, a promise to be of good behaviour, a promise of loyalty ... If these promises are broken it is only fair that the state should have the right to revoke a privilege given to him.'[17]

When use of the deprivation power had seemingly fallen into abeyance, the government of the day nevertheless wished to retain the option just in case. Lord Mackay of Clashfern, the Lord Chancellor, outlined the government's position:

> Citizenship is a privilege, and we think it reasonable that there should be power in the last resort to deprive someone who has voluntarily sought our citizenship ... and who then acts against the interests of this country or behaves in a way that brings discredit on the grant of citizenship to him.[18]

As previously noted, citizenship has become revocable for British citizens born British, as long as they have another nationality on which they can fall back. From that point on, in legal terms British citizenship has genuinely become a revocable privilege rather than an inviolable right, at least for citizens with a foreign heritage. The rhetoric took a few years to catch up with the law. As Home Secretary Jacqui Smith introduced the government of the day's 'earned citizenship' legislation reforming the criteria for naturalisation, she stated that citizenship was a privilege.[19] Lord West then made the same point for the government in the House of Lords a few days later.[20] In a sign of things to come, other parliamentarians on the right of the political spectrum explicitly and repeatedly stated during debates on the 2008 Bill not just that citizenship was a privilege, but also, more than that, that it was not a right.[21]

Under the 2010 to 2015 coalition government, this was sanctified as the official government position. Immigration minister Mark Harper used the 'privilege not a right' phrase when introducing proposals for the Immigration Act 2014 to enable even citizenship deprivation which would leave the individual stateless.[22] His successor as immigration minister, James Brokenshire, stated in 2015 that the government's position was: 'UK citizenship is a privilege for those who deserve it, not an automatic right for those who do not.' By this line of thinking, British citizenship is conditional even for those who are born British. It is the antithesis of political theorist Hannah Arendt's famous argument in *The Origins of Totalitarianism* that citizenship is both foundational and indispensable because it is the 'right to have rights', without which other all rights are meaningless. This is why citizenship-stripping is so momentous and why it is so concerning that ministers are increasingly willing to use the power against an ever-wider range of people. 'Denationalisation', as it is sometimes known, was once seen as the tool of regimes like Hitler's Germany and Stalin's Russia. Partly for this reason it was essentially abandoned as a practice after the Second World War. Today it is coming back into fashion.

As well as signalling censure, the modern penchant for citizenship-stripping in Britain also arguably reflects a desire to maintain a small rather than a large pool of citizens. There is popular pressure to keep the numbers of new citizens down, and the press commonly conflate immigration with nationality policy; perhaps unsurprisingly given that so too does the British government. When the numbers of residents naturalising rose by around 15 per cent in 2006, the *Telegraph* complained with a headline reading, '1 million new British citizens under Blair'. 'This is a direct result of their "no limits" immigration policy,' the chairman of anti-immigration pressure group MigrationWatch was quoted as saying. 'Immigration on this scale is changing the nature of our society without public consent. It is no longer acceptable.'[23] When the Labour government unveiled the earned citizenship proposals, the *Daily Mail* greeted the plan with the headline: 'The great passport giveaway: Up to 250,000 foreigners to get UK citizenship every year'.[24] This was not a cause for celebration, it seemed. After the Brexit referendum vote, as literally millions of EU citizens living in the UK wondered what their future held, *The Sun* splashed with: 'WE WANT TO BE LIKE EU: Thousands of EU citizens rush to get their hands on a British passport before Brexit, new figures reveal'. Lest readers miss the point, the subheading continued, 'Record numbers try and win right to stay and work in the UK once we leave the bloc in 2019'.[25] The article omitted to mention, however, that these EU citizens were required to have lived in the UK for at least five years to be eligible to apply for naturalisation. In some countries, new citizens are celebrated. Not so in Britain.

The obsession with numbers is official government policy and has been since at least 1981. This is not hard to deduce from the effects of various legal changes over the years, but the official intention to restrict numbers was confirmed in a revealing internal Home Office memorandum written in 2002. Normally this sort of internal advice from civil servants to ministers would not be published for at least thirty years but, unusually, this was publicly disclosed by deliberately being placed in the House of Commons library. At that time David Blunkett was Home Secretary and he was considering the correction of one of the worst nationality law injustices of the twentieth century: the treatment of the East African Asians.

Living in Africa as British subjects and citizens of the United Kingdom and Colonies, East African Asians had been assured, following the Commonwealth Citizens Act 1962, that they would be able to relocate to the UK if they needed to.[26] As newly independent governments in Kenya, then Tanzania and finally Uganda treated them increasingly harshly as the 1960s went on, ever-greater numbers started to do just that. In response, Labour Home Secretary James Callaghan passed the Commonwealth Immigrants Act 1968 in a matter of days in order to stop further arrivals. Many of the East African Asians had not acquired citizenship in their newly independent countries, meaning their own citizenship was British, but now they were prevented from entering their own country. Returning again to 2002, Blunkett had signalled during passage of the Bill that was to become the Nationality, Immigration and Asylum Act 2002, that he was sympathetic with their cause. 'We have a moral obligation to them going back a long way,' he said, 'and it is unfinished business.'[27]

Senior civil servants at the Home Office were aghast. The director of the Immigration and Nationality Policy Directorate sent Blunkett a strongly worded memorandum urging him to 'reconsider whether any action ... is really necessary'. The document stated in bold terms that 'nationality policy has been driven mainly by the immigration implications for the UK' and that it 'has, of course, been determined largely by numbers'. The idea in 1981, the director said, had been that the various lesser forms of British nationality would 'die out within a generation or two', leaving British citizenship as the sole remaining status. However, this policy had been 'eroded over time' by grants of citizenship or the creation of new forms of status following the Falklands crisis, the return of Hong Kong to China and the changing relationship with remaining British overseas territories.[28] The memorandum was full of large, estimated numbers of potentially eligible British nationals who would acquire a right to enter the United Kingdom if Blunkett got his way.

Finally, there is the racial dimension to British citizenship. This goes far beyond the modern use of citizenship-deprivation powers. Others have written more knowledgeably and eloquently than I can on the racist intent behind immigration laws in the 1960s and 1970s and the British Nationality Act 1981.[29] The history can be traced back further than that to so-called 'informal controls' in the nineteenth and early to mid-twentieth centuries. It is incontrovertible that these reforms were carried out with the intention of limiting and preventing the entry of British nationals who were non-white but who, under the British Nationality Act 1948 and previous common law, had a right of entry to and residence in the United Kingdom. When nationality laws were reformed again in 1981, the stated intention of the government was that only those with 'close ties' to the UK would gain the new status of British citizenship that was introduced with that Act.

However, the same government also planned to extend British citizenship automatically to third-generation, predominantly white emigrants in Old Commonwealth countries, such as South Africa, Canada and Australia. These were individuals whose grandparents had been born in the UK before emigrating away. Their parents had been born abroad and so had they themselves. They were citizens of independent Commonwealth countries and had no conceivable 'close ties' to the United Kingdom other than through their parentage, or, to put it another way, through their race. Meanwhile, automatic citizenship was to be denied to the predominantly black Commonwealth residents who had entered as British subjects and sometimes as citizens of the United Kingdom and Colonies, who were physically living and working in the United Kingdom at the time the law was passed. They would be able to register as British citizens if they met certain conditions, they were told, but a time limit of five years' UK residence was imposed and a fee was payable. As it turned out, many did not register and those who did not were later caught out by the hostile environment and were to become the Windrush generation. The contrasting approach to the two groups was condemned for being racist and the government was forced to amend its plans, so the rule on inheritance of British citizenship would apply only to second-generation emigrants. Defeated but unbowed, the government then created the UK Ancestry visa to enable migration to the United Kingdom for these mainly white individuals, a visa which inexplicably persists to this day. 'Close ties' did not mean meaningful physical ties, it seemed, it meant 'white parentage'.

Race was also relevant to the ending of what is legally termed *jus soli* or birth-right citizenship. Before the 1981 Act, a child born in the United Kingdom was automatically born British. This approach to the conferral of citizenship offers the twin benefits that, firstly, no children born in the country may end up with insecure status, and secondly, integration for migrant families is promoted. Critics of such laws argue that birth-right citizenship laws inappropriately confer citizenship on the children even of temporary visitors, as the child concerned may well leave the country after birth and have no real connection to it afterwards. It also, they say, rewards unauthorised migration by enabling immigrants to establish links to the country. Whether intentional or not, one of the effects of *jus soli* citizenship is that it tends to broaden the ethnic diversity of a body of citizens. The alternative form of transmitting citizenship is referred to as *jus sanguinis*, meaning blood citizenship or citizenship by descent. Under this model, parentage (and therefore ethnicity) matters as well as or instead of place of birth. As Hiroshi Motomura observes, 'Both *jus sanguinis* and restrictive naturalisation laws reflect the knowledge – and perhaps the intent – that citizenship laws preserve the ethnic origins of the population.'[30] And that was precisely what law-makers achieved with the reforms of 1981.

If it ever really was, citizenship is no longer seen as any meaningful tool for integration, and successive governments have been content to first create and then later allow the further growth of a sizeable population of long-term resident non-citizens. The purpose behind British citizenship laws and policy is to restrict the numbers of new citizens and preserve the existing ethnic origins of the already established citizenry.

CONCLUSION: WHAT NOW?

We like to think of Paddington Bear as being quintessentially British, yet we also know he is Peruvian. He is informally adopted by the Brown family almost immediately after their fortuitous meeting at the left luggage department of his eponymous railway station, but author Michael Bond, perhaps understandably, somewhat glosses over the precise details of how Paddington becomes legally resident; perhaps he never does. Whatever his legal status, he adapts to life with the Brown family and they adapt to him – a clear example of two-way integration. That Paddington never quite loses his observer status – one of the features of the books that makes them such a triumph – injects a note of melancholy with which many migrants will be familiar. Nevertheless, given that Paddington's migration story is such a success story, it is sobering to think that in Britain today we deliberately make the heart-warming tale so impossible to recreate for modern migrants.

Any system of citizenship and immigration laws inherently discriminates between insiders like the Browns and outsiders like Paddington. This is not the place to discuss whether such laws should or should not exist. The fact is that they do and will do for the foreseeable future. My concern is how to try to make those laws as fair as possible, both to the insiders and the outsiders alike. Current citizenship and immigration laws are fair to neither. Migrants are treated as if they are disposable beasts of burden and this affects not just 'them' but also 'us'. As British citizens we have few if any rights specific to that status. Thousands of us are prevented from living with our own family members and a large, unauthorised, exploitable population has been allowed to grow around us. Our society and economy depend heavily on having these migrants in our midst and they are an indelible part of our community – yet they, and sometimes their children too, have no realistic route to equality, settlement or citizenship. None of this is desirable in a healthy democracy.

American academic Hiroshi Motomura has outlined three different ways of conceptualising immigration laws: as contract, as affinity and as transition to citizenship.[1] On a contractual analysis, a migrant in effect signs up to pre-determined terms of entry and stay. This implies that a migrant need not be treated as an equal of existing citizens, that they need not be offered a route to settlement or citizenship and that the terms of entry may be harsh. A migrant signals acceptance by entering on the terms offered. As long as notice is given, any terms would seem to be fair on this contract-based analysis. Where migration routes are based on the ties that a migrant acquires, this is considered the affinity-based approach. Via this method, migrants earn increasing equality over time because it is considered unfair to disrupt the ties they have acquired in this way. Where the deportation of a migrant is characterised as unreasonable because of her residence, family links or similar, it is the affinity approach that is being applied. The final approach, seeing migrants as citizens-in-waiting, is a potentially very different way of thinking in which migrants are treated as potential citizens from the start, preferably with rights equivalent to fully-fledged citizens.

These three perspectives are not mutually exclusive. One route of entry might be contractual, a route to remain might be based on acquired affinity with the host society and throughout the migrant might be regarded as a potential future citizen. Motomura advocates in favour of treating migrants as citizens-in-waiting on the basis that this is the least discriminatory approach. He argues that doing so allows for the maintenance of a bounded society in which meaningful versions of equality can flourish, but where those granted admission are treated respectfully and as peers.

If we apply Motomura's different lenses to the treatment of migrants by British citizenship and immigration laws, the prevailing approach appears to be that of a very strict, tightly defined contract.[2] Generally, the broad qualifying criteria for settlement at the point of entry will be preserved for those migrants who have then entered, even if the rules are changed for future entrants. Breaches of the explicit or implicit conditions of entry, for example by working without permission or committing a criminal offence, lead to a voiding of the contract and draconian enforcement action. The same approach applies to breaches of the specified procedures that are set out in fine print in various annexes to the main contract.

But, in reality, there is none of the fair dealing you would expect to find in a consensual contractual relationship. One of the terms of the contract to which migrants purportedly agree through their very entry is that the United Kingdom can unilaterally increase the costs imposed by the contract (in the form of application fees), change the procedures for extensions of the contract and even alter the terms on which an extension might be sought, as Dr Odelola discovered to her cost.[3] If this were a contract, it would be the model of one we would expect to be struck down as unfair in the commercial courts. It is certainly no way for the two parties to build a constructive, long-term working relationship with one another. There are affiliation-based routes in existence today, but they are generally weak. For example, it will normally take twenty years for a migrant with any period of unlawful residence to become eligible to remain on the basis of ties, and a further ten years after that to be eligible for settlement. To the extent that migrants are seen as citizens-in-waiting, this is often considered undesirable. Since 2010, government policy has been to weaken not reinforce the link between migration, and settlement and citizenship has deliberately been made unattainable for more and more migrants.

CITIZENS-IN-WAITING

Given our unenviable starting point, how might the current system be improved? Since so much else flows from it and since politicians across the spectrum are potentially persuadable on this issue – it is overtly about what happens to migrants after they arrive and stay rather than how many should be admitted in the first place – I would suggest beginning with a rethink of British citizenship policy. A less exclusionary and more inclusive approach is needed in which it is seen as desirable for migrants to become citizens. Integration is a potentially problematic word meaning different things to different people. Personally, I understand it as a two-way process in which the migrant and the host society mutually and respectfully adapt to one another. Whatever it means, though, politicians of all hues would surely agree that the acquisition of citizenship is a significant aspect of migrant integration. Clarifying the rights attached to citizenship and attaching concrete benefits to it would reassure existing citizens that their status has value, while simultaneously outlining to potential citizens the value proposition of joining the political community as full members.

It would be a mistake to punish migrants for failing to become citizens by, for example, taking away their existing rights to access the social safety net. There may be many reasons why some migrants chose not to become citizens, and some may not be able to, for instance because they cannot pass the written citizenship exam. To take away their social rights would be retrograde. However, the same does not necessarily apply to civic rights. The right to vote in parliamentary elections could be re-examined and the faster route to citizenship for those married to a British citizen could be revived, having been rendered redundant by changes to settlement criteria wrought in 2012. Perhaps controversially but in a similar vein, citizens could be given preferential rights of family reunion over settled migrants. The criteria for and use of citizenship-stripping powers should be reviewed and the social effects of implicitly designating citizens of migrant parents as second-class, conditional citizens need to be both carefully considered and publicly discussed.

Treason laws are undoubtedly problematic and there is a clear risk of their being deployed disproportionately against certain racialised or religious groups, but it is worth discussing whether a revival of treason laws might be preferable to and more principled than citizenship deprivation. While it is hard to see law-makers relaxing the statutory criteria for acquiring citizenship, there is much that could easily be done to make citizenship more accessible without any need for new legislation. Reducing the sky-high fees is an essential start. A more nuanced approach to the good character test could also be adopted that is less punitive of minor, past immigration law breaches and more forgiving of criminal offences committed by children and young people.

THE HOSTILE ENVIRONMENT AND UNAUTHORISED MIGRANTS

Even where migrants are currently denied a route to citizenship, they are often permitted to remain physically present in the country, sometimes lawfully and sometimes unlawfully. The boundary between 'lawful' and 'unlawful' sounds clear enough, but it is porous in both directions. As we saw in Chapter 3, it is all too easy for an authorised migrant to become unauthorised by mistake. It is also possible, though considerably harder, for an unauthorised migrant to become authorised.

Unauthorised migrants are a tolerated group. Asylum seekers whose claims are rejected, for example, find themselves unauthorised but not removed and the same is true of other migrants who somehow enter illegally or overstay their visas. The hostile environment policies do enough to make their lives marginal and exploited by denying regular employment, good-quality accommodation, healthcare, banking services and the social safety net, but in the end all these measures are insufficient to persuade them to 'self-deport'. Some will inevitably form friendships and relationships with citizens or authorised migrants, thereby exposing a much wider group to the insecurity of their existence; it is unimaginably hard when your partner or one of your parents is suddenly deported. Some will be children and young people and will probably, eventually, be allowed to remain through one of the weak affiliation-based immigration routes. Yet, to deny these children further and higher education, as we do at present, is to cause them permanent disadvantage. It is also a good example of a self-defeating policy: further and higher education are not a pointless drain on public resources; they are good for society and the economy as a whole as they increase productivity and future GDP growth. To deny a particular individual this benefit on the grounds of limited resources is to fly in the face of good economics.

Law-makers have several options available to them and doing nothing is not one of them. While inaction might have been a justifiable position to adopt in previous years, it is hard to see how a rational and responsible politician could reach this conclusion today,

given that the estimated size of the unauthorised migrant population in the UK today is between 600,000 and 1.2 million. Further
deterrent policies should also be ruled out as a way forward; even if
it was desirable to force the existing population to 'self-deport', there
is no evidence that deterrent policies would achieve such a result
anyway. Many members of the unauthorised migrant population,
having been tolerated for many years, are now deeply embedded in
our society and entirely estranged from their country of origin. One
way forward would be to offer improved routes to regularisation, and
subsequently citizenship, with a view to gradually diminishing the
size of the group, rather than allowing it to grow further and further.
The current twenty-year wait for regularisation is simply too long,
and even then, it only puts a migrant on a ten-year route to settlement. As with the Deferred Action for Children Arrivals (DACA)
initiative in the United States, new regularisation routes could initially be targeted at the least controversial groups, such as children and
young people. However, the drawback of narrowly targeted measures
is that it would take many years even for the existing unauthorised
population to become authorised. This would pointlessly prolong
unauthorised status in the meantime, for migrants who would eventually be offered regularisation anyway. Any children born during
this time would be born without British citizenship and would face
precarious futures.

A more effective alternative would be to offer a more comprehensive regularisation programme, often referred to as an amnesty. This
would have the virtue of providing a more complete and rapid solution to the sheer number of unauthorised migrants currently residing
in the UK. There are several precedents for similar programmes in
the United Kingdom, including a 2003 regularisation programme for
families and a 'legacy backlog clearance exercise' that was carried out

between 2006 and 2010. Some would be concerned that an amnesty rewards past illegal behaviour and might even act as a 'pull' factor for future unauthorised migrants, who might rationally expect a further similar exercise at some point in the future. Neither of these reasons seems sufficient to justify inaction now, given that the current situation is unfair on citizen and non-citizen alike and no credible politician or public figure could propose the mass-scale detention and deportation of up to 1.2 million migrants.

Regularisation, whether piecemeal or comprehensive, could be combined with improvements to the existing Assisted Voluntary Returns programme for those who are not eligible for that route. The Home Office has been funding this programme since 1999 but so far it has met with mixed success. Run for years by the International Organization for Migration, which runs many such schemes globally, it was taken over by charity Refugee Action in 2011 and then brought in-house at the Home Office in 2015. Essentially, migrants are offered resettlement assistance, including cash, if they leave. Effective programmes do not rely entirely on money, but that is all that is available from the Home Office at present. On a purely financial analysis, voluntary returns are far cheaper than detention and enforced removal. On a moral and social level, they are surely far preferable to dawn raids – and if done well can promote international development. The number of assisted returns has fallen in recent years, but think tank the Social Market Foundation reviewed the operation of the programme in a report in December 2019 and proposed various ways in which it could be rebooted and revitalised, including through expansion and outsourcing to an independent body capable of building international partnerships.[4]

In the United States the quid pro quo that campaigners for regularisation have been willing to accept is enhanced border security, intended to prevent the growth of a replacement unauthorised population. Here in the United Kingdom, though, that is not really an option; it is hard to see how the border could be made even more secure than it already is. A rational trade-off in our context, based on the supposition that it is in no one's interests for an unauthorised population to be allowed to grow again, might be acceptance of a system of identity cards.

It is doubtful that the introduction of identity cards would have a significant deterrent effect on future unauthorised migrants. There is no evidence that country-specific deterrent policies have any impact on the decision-making of migrants. Identity cards would, though, reduce the provable harm done by hostile environment measures to citizens and settled migrants who are black and minority ethnic. As we saw in Chapter 3, the hostile environment encourages discrimination against those perceived as potentially foreign. This is because financial penalties are only imposed when a service is provided to a person who does not have legal status. Evidence suggests that skin colour influences whether service providers think a given person might be foreign or not and therefore whether their immigration status needs to be checked. Identity cards would work in a different way, as penalties would be imposed for failing to check the identity of any person, irrespective of their immigration status. This would be more inconvenient for white, middle-class, middle-aged, home-owning, self-employed men like me, who as things stand are rarely subject to immigration checks. But it would be less discriminatory towards people who are black or minority ethnic, female, young, old, casually employed, disabled, sick or poor. It also involves employers and others asking less of their employees, as to ask to see a citizen's identity card as part of a mandatory check is less challenging and offensive than to ask them to prove their immigration status. This is not to underestimate the political and practical difficulties of implementing an identity card system. But to do so would, to my mind, be defensible in a way that the present hostile environment system simply is not.

THE LIMITS OF DETERRENCE

Even if citizenship laws are not to be reformed, it would be helpful for law-makers to recognise that many migrants are future citizens. When migrants are seen in this way, many of our present immigration rules seem unwise, particularly those that intend yet fail to deter immigration in the first place. For instance, detaining unauthorised migrants – and thereby causing them huge distress, trauma and mental suffering – before releasing over half of them back into the community, where many attain lawful status and perhaps eventually citizenship, looks like very poor policy indeed. The abysmal treatment of refugees who arrive by illicit means, even though more than half are allowed lawfully to remain, belongs to another era. The sky-high immigration application fees amount to double taxation for migrants and their families, who as a result have significantly less disposable income than their peers and are therefore socially disadvantaged. The unforgiving approach to minor technical breaches of immigration procedures also leads to terrible hardship for those affected, but it does not necessarily result in departure from the United Kingdom. The raft of policies that constitute the hostile environment cause race discrimination against citizens and settled migrants who are black and minority ethnic. The harsh family rules we considered in Chapter 5 do not prevent mixed nationality families from forming but they do punish and break apart some of those that do form, with lasting consequences for the implicated children.

All such policies are intended to make migration to the United Kingdom a less attractive proposition. The whole point of them is to cause social and financial disadvantage to migrants and their families. This approach urgently needs to be rethought. There is no evidence and there never has been any evidence that the policies do actually deter migration, but we do know that they genuinely cause disadvantage to those affected, often of a lasting nature. In so doing they must surely also cause resentment, which is entirely incompatible with the integration that politicians purport to desire, making it virtually impossible. The policies disproportionately affect black and minority ethnic migrants, future citizens and actual citizens; whether or not politicians think of it this way, these immigration policies amount to discrimination, not just sanctioned but actively imposed by the state.

FAMILY IMMIGRATION

The family migration routes need reform. With as many as 40 per cent of workers earning less than £18,600, the minimum earnings rule for sponsoring a spouse or partner visa catches far too many families. The impact on them is a disaster, not just for the adults involved but also for their children and wider society. The £18,600 figure was found by the Migration Advisory Committee to be 'the annual gross pay at which no income-related benefits would be received (in a two-adult family), assuming that the family pays rent of £100 per week'.[5] The experts were clear that this recommendation was based on a purely economic analysis that did not consider the moral or social impact of splitting affected families apart, nor the longer-term positive contribution to public finances that a family would make over its lifetime if permitted to remain and flourish in the United Kingdom.

Other options were presented to the government, including setting the threshold for family sponsorship at the equivalent of a person earning the national minimum wage, which would have worked out as £12,600 in 2011. It is not just the headline figure of £18,600 that is problematic; six months of earnings are required to qualify, setting up a further significant obstacle, and the alternative route of showing sufficient savings requires an absurdly high bank balance of £62,500 for a person with no qualifying UK earnings. No minister has ever suggested what affected families are supposed to do or how they should respond. It has also never been said that the existence of the rule has a deterrent effect on the formation of mixed-nationality families, if that was supposed to be one of the purposes behind the rule. The implicit position is clearly that affected mixed-nationality families should either separate or leave the United Kingdom altogether, both of which are grossly disproportionate responses. In order to begin fixing this problem, the level of earnings required for sponsorship should at the very least be reduced to the national minimum wage, proper allowance should be made for families relocating from abroad and the impact on children should be a meaningful factor to be considered if the income rule is not met.

Both the outdated Immigration Rules relating to children and the cruel rules that effectively prevent the entry of parents and grand-parents need to be revised. The number of migrants entering under these family routes has never been very significant compared to, say, economic or EU immigration, but the impact on affected families can be disproportionately vicious. Migration is not a purely econom-ic matter and if migrant integration is to be promoted then both they and their families must be treated with respect and humanity. The family immigration rules fail miserably by these measures.

ASYLUM

There is no prospect of any voluntary reduction in the security of the external border that the United Kingdom has constructed over the past twenty years. Any such move would be deeply unpopular with the general public. If the external UK border in France has to be repatriated following Brexit, this and its consequences are likely to cause considerable concern. Politicians would be on the hunt for alternative means of making themselves look as if they are in control. A similar reaction may follow the UK's withdrawal from the EU's Common European Asylum System and in particular the so-called Dublin arrangements, which allow for removal of asylum seekers from the UK to their first point of entry into the European Union. The next few years could be a dangerous time for asylum policy.

Nevertheless, pressure to expand the refugee resettlement scheme should be maintained and there may be scope for changes to the awful reception to which refugees are subjected once they have arrived. Given that more than half of refugees eventually secure status, policy needs to be adjusted so they are not traumatised and for ever handicapped by the way they were treated when they first arrived. This includes better support and accommodation, improving family reunion rights and funding DNA tests and travel for refugee families, particularly for separated children, who currently have to be taken into local authority care.

Refugees should also be permitted to work if their applications are not decided quickly and the absurd ban on voluntary work by refugees should be scrapped. Politicians and officials should recognise that genuine refugees do not often behave in the preordained ways that the authorities would like. Genuine refugees who would suffer persecution if returned to their home country do travel through safe third countries, do have economic and social needs as well as safety needs, do struggle to provide a clear narrative of what happened to them, are not always able to explain why they left when they did and do sometimes lie to protect themselves. Proper workplace therapy should be made available to Home Office officials, who should be strongly encouraged to make use of it. Charities like Freedom from

Torture and the Helen Bamber Foundation, which offer support and counselling to torture survivors, are acutely aware of the risk of secondary trauma for their staff; the risks are no less for asylum officials. Above all, refugees need to be seen as people not problems.

IMMIGRATION FOR WORK

The economic migration routes for working in the United Kingdom also need revision, particularly given the United Kingdom's departure from the European Union and the end of free movement rules. In previous years, the economic case in favour of immigration was made in such starkly and exclusively utilitarian terms that it harmed migrants' rights and alienated members of the public who did not think in purely economic terms. If we go back to first principles, there are broadly three reasons to support and promote economic migration. The first is that economic migration can benefit the existing population as well as the migrants, for example through filling labour shortages and promoting economic growth, productivity and tax take. In particular, migrants can bring skills and investment into the economy that would otherwise be absent. Secondly, migration brings less concrete but still tangible benefits, such as enhanced consumer choice and cultural diversity. Thirdly, economic migration can be seen as a form of international development, as migrants can export their income through remittances and their skills through re-migration. This should not be underestimated: remittances sent home by migrant workers dwarf international aid budgets and there is strong evidence to suggest that such money is invested far more beneficially than aid money. On this last point, it might well also be argued that the United Kingdom, given its legacy of empire, has a moral duty to promote economic development in the countries from which it extracted so much wealth in the past. Economic migration is one way for us to do that.

If evaluated against these criteria, some of the existing economic migration routes might be found wanting. As the Migration Advisory Committee reported in 2014, 'The underlying policy objective of the Tier One (investor) route is not readily apparent.'[6] What it does do, essentially, is to allow wealthy individuals to buy visas. Similarly, the policy rationale for the UK Ancestry visa is unclear. It almost exclusively benefits white entrants from Old Commonwealth countries, such as Australia, Canada, South Africa and New Zealand, and it is hard to see how this route is justified today. However, there is surely a strong case for enabling skilled migrants to undertake roles that cannot be filled by the existing workforce, enabling wealthy migrants the opportunity to invest usefully in new or existing businesses and enabling some other migrants to move temporarily, for cultural exchanges, training, work experience and economic development.

The first function for skilled migrants is currently performed adequately but imperfectly by the Tier Two route. The principle that skilled migration should be employer-led could be retained, routes could be considerably simplified and the conditions could be loosened and made more respectful to migrants themselves, for example by allowing for changes of job more straightforwardly and providing a reasonably secure route to permanent residence and then citizenship. The second function of investment is currently performed woefully inadequately by the relatively new innovator and start-up routes. In the first six months of operation, these routes together attracted just fourteen applications, compared to nearly 1,000 for the predecessor visa types in the same period of the previous year. A substantial rethink is needed. The third function, of exchange and economic development, is currently performed very badly and only in incomplete fashion by the existing Tier Five routes. The youth mobility visa, for instance, is numerically capped at a low level and is also limited only to certain already economically developed countries. Worse, Australians and New Zealanders only take up around 30 per cent of their allocated 31,000 and 14,000 respective Tier Five visas, whereas the 1,000 visas allocated each to Hong Kong, Taiwan and Japan are fully subscribed and now allocated by a lottery system.[7] This certainly looks racist and it is hard to see how this can be justified today. The cultural exchange elements of Tier Five can be seen as minimalist tokens rather than meaningful contributions to economic development. A major rethink is required on this front. The lottery system could be expanded to other, new countries that are not currently included in the scheme and incentives to depart at the end of temporary work visas could be explored and tested.

For the past twenty years, the discussion of economic migration has centred around skilled migration. However, with the end of European Union free movement rules following Brexit, the next twenty years may focus more on how to meet the needs of the British economy for unskilled labour. At the time of writing, just as the coronavirus pandemic was starting, the unemployment rate was approaching an historic low of just 3.8 per cent. With workers therefore in short supply, failing to provide a lawful source of labour to fill low-skilled vacancies could result in driving up wages (and therefore prices) or increasing productivity or both. Such an omission would also create demand for unauthorised migrants in the shadow economy. In the 2019 general election, the Conservative Party proposed to meet this demand by introducing temporary worker visas tied to specific employers for specific jobs.[8] These would be issued for limited, short periods and would be non-renewable. Such visas are clearly not respectful to migrants and would only cement the perception that migrants are an exploitable natural resource.

With EU free movement rights and general work visas like those issued under the UK Ancestry route, a migrant who is badly treated by one employer can move down the road and work for another. Tied visas, which do not permit the worker to change employer or even job, encourage abuse by employers. The social impact of significant numbers of temporary migrants continuously passing through areas to which they have no connection, rather than settling down with families, has not necessarily been thought through. It is also inevitable that some migrants issued with such visas will not leave the country at the end of their allotted time. The disparity in available income that led a migrant to apply for such a visa in the first place will be too great a temptation for some. Law-makers will know that this is an inevitable consequence of the system and are therefore responsible for what follows. Temporary tied visas are a good example of an extreme version of the contractual approach to immigration: proponents argue the migrant knows what he or she is signing up to. To my mind, though, the power and wealth imbalance present in such systems makes this arrangement the epitome of imposing unfair contractual terms.

Shortly before the economic shutdown caused by coronavirus, the government seemed to have changed its mind. It was announced that the temporary work visas would only exist for agricultural workers. The uncertainties of Brexit and the eventual, probably very slow and painful, recovery from the pandemic make it impossible to predict the future. Historically, immigration has been an indicator of economic success: migrants come for the work generated by a booming economy. The converse is also true: an economic crash would normally be expected to reduce immigration, and it may be that there are so many unemployed British citizens that there is a plentiful supply of domestic labour for the foreseeable future, rendering redundant any discussion of a need for low-skilled work visas. It may be that a deep global economic crisis causes increased survival migration, as citizens of some countries feel they have no choice but to seek food or work outside the borders of their own countries. Or it may be that politicians and the public become more cognisant of the vital social and economic role of workers traditionally seen as low-skilled, and therefore become more responsive to the idea that attracting and retaining such workers requires their terms of entry as migrants to be less exploitative than the temporary tied worker scheme the government had previously mooted.

If temporary work routes are introduced, they should be designed, as far as possible, to recognise that those who apply for such visas are not 'just' workers; they are people. As a bare minimum, the ability to switch to alternative employers and other immigration routes should be permitted if the person qualifies.

DEPORTATION

When a non-citizen breaks the law, a careful judgement is needed about whether she should lose her right to live in the country and be deported. Public opinion and faith in the immigration system need to be weighed on one side of the scales against the effect on the individual, her family, friends and community and the role of British society in shaping her on the other. At the moment, the law on deportation is anything but careful. The reforms introduced in the wake of the 2006 deportation scandal at the Home Office, and then following Theresa May's obsession with foreign criminals, have entirely excised judgement from the decision-making process. Instead, we have hard-and-fast rules that, in practice, are almost impossible for anyone to meet. As a result, we see non-citizens who were brought to the United Kingdom as children or who were even born in the country being uprooted from everything they know and exiled to an effectively foreign land.

The automatic deportation provisions of the UK Borders Act 2007 need to be scrapped, as do the narrow rules imposed by the

Immigration Act 2014. These rules were initially introduced for short-term political reasons, but they cause real damage to effectively British individuals and their families, friends and communities.

STRUCTURAL CHANGE

In the introduction I outlined what I see as the central defining features of the current system of citizenship and immigration laws: an exclusionary approach to citizenship, a concomitant exclusionary approach to immigration, a secure and external border, extensive deployment of domestic deterrent policies, the growth of a significant unauthorised migrant population and a highly centralised system governed by unchecked executive discretion. The past two decades have also seen two major trends in the operationalisation of immigration laws, which only accentuate these negative defining features. The first is the automation or pseudo-automation of decision-making, for example under the points-based system, Appendix FM family routes, the deportation rules, the 'risk assessment' tool used in visa applications and the EU Settlement Scheme algorithm. The second is the reduction in direct contact between officials and migrants through privatisation, whether through the use of detention centres, the outsourced visa application process or, most ubiquitously, indirect enforcement through third parties. All of these approaches fundamentally dehumanise migrants. Officials are isolated from the consequences of their actions and encouraged to see migrants as logistical problems rather than real people, leading to crises like that of the Windrush scandal.

If there is one thing that might gradually mitigate and perhaps gradually reverse some of this, it is a proper role for Parliament in the making and oversight of immigration law and policy. If the government was forced to allow meaningful votes on new rules by Members of Parliament this would, for one thing, preclude frequent changes to the law and therefore require more care when changes are made. The associated increased oversight and accountability would also, hopefully, introduce a wider range of considerations into the policy-making process and improve both citizenship and immigration law over time. Yet, even aside from the fact the Immigration Act 1971 would need to be replaced, which is unlikely for the foreseeable future, the British parliamentary system does not lend itself to meaningful scrutiny. Immigration and citizenship issues can cut across party lines but a government with a strong parliamentary majority (as we currently have with Boris Johnson's Conservative leadership) is essentially able to do what it wants. However, governments rarely surrender executive powers voluntarily, and drastic changes to the architecture of immigration law seem far-fetched at present.

The current system has developed because migrants have consistently been regarded as a threat by politicians and policy-makers. There is a significant strand of thinking that sees migrants as an opportunity, but too often proponents of this view discuss those migrants as if they were a natural resource to be exploited, whose rights, if they have any at all, only flow from their economic utility. Neither view of immigration is conducive to treating migrants with respect or as future citizens. It is unrealistic to expect politicians, who owe their position to the portrayal of migrants as a threat, to climb down significantly from that position. I do wish that they would, but realistically it just is not going to happen, at least not in the short or medium term. Nevertheless, mainstream politicians of any political persuasion could bring about useful changes by simplifying the system, revisiting family immigration rules, reviewing citizenship laws and reconsidering the effectiveness and long-term consequences of deterrent policies. Ultimately, migrants must be treated as humans. Seeing them as citizens-in-waiting would be a good start.

ACKNOWLEDGEMENTS

This book is the product of experience. Not just my own experience but the experience of my clients and their friends and families, of my fellow lawyers who over the years generously took the time to train me and explain to me, of the contributors to my immigration law website freemovement.org.uk and of all those whose articles and books I have drawn on in my own writing. I am very grateful indeed to all those who knowingly or otherwise helped me in these ways.

I want to single out CJ McKinney, Caroline Wintersgill, Helena Wray, Bridget Anderson and my wife for their comments on an earlier draft and their support and encouragement during the writing process. David Owen is to blame for the idea of writing this in the first place and I am very grateful to Olivia Beattie and the team at Biteback for taking the book on. Lucy Stewardson's editorial comments were invaluable, and the final draft is very much improved as a result. I am profoundly grateful to all of them. I also want to thank Denny Pencheva and Lara Farrell for their help with some of the research on the asylum and detention chapters; Nick Nason for his, as ever, entertaining original write-up of the case with which I open the chapter on work migration; Diego Acosta for recommending Hiroshi Motomura's work; and the couples who agreed to be interviewed for the chapter on family migration. Some of their names have been changed. Simon Cox's information on the origins of the benefits tourist was illuminating, as was Amelia Gentleman's full account of the evolution of the Windrush scandal in her own book.

I cannot sufficiently thank my wife for keeping the show on the road when I took time out to write this, and my parents for their support and love over the years.

Flaws in this book, of which there are many, are my own. I have tried to steer a course between academic writing, for which I am not qualified, and accessible writing, for which I am not trained. Researching and writing the book has been a voyage of discovery for me and I am acutely conscious there is much about race, policy and advocacy that I only partially understand. I am only a lawyer, when it comes down to it.

You can follow Colin at **@colinyeo1** on Twitter
and read more of his writing on immigration
law and policy at **freemovement.org.uk**.

NOTES

INTRODUCTION

1 *Odelola v Secretary of State for the Home Department* [2009] UKHL 25. https://www.bailii.org/uk/cases/UKHL/2009/25.html

2 See 'Europe's Unauthorized Immigrant Population Peaks in 2016, Then Levels Off', Pew Research, 13 November 2019, and Andy Jolly, Siân Thomas and James Stanyer, 'London's children and young people who are not British citizens: A profile', 2020, available at: https://www.london.gov.uk/what-we-do/communities/migrants-and-refugees/londons-children-and-young-people-who-are-not-british-citizens

3 'System "not fit for purpose", says Reid', *The Guardian*, 23 May 2006.

4 Maya Goodfellow, *Hostile Environment: How Immigrants Became Scapegoats* (London: Verso, 2019), pp. 162–7.

5 For those interested in a very readable and more comprehensive treatment of the history of immigration to the United Kingdom, I would highly recommend Robert Winder's excellent *Bloody Foreigners: The Story of Immigration to Britain* (London: Abacus, 2013).

CHAPTER 1: WELCOME TO BRITAIN

1 See Winder, *Bloody Foreigners*, pp. 279–81 and 'Nicholas Winton, Rescuer of 669 Children from Holocaust, Dies at 106', *New York Times*, 1 July 2015.

2 See for example Randell Hansen, *Citizenship and Immigration in Post-War Britain* (Oxford: Oxford University Press, 2000) and Goodfellow, *Hostile Environment*.

3 See Will Somerville, *Immigration under New Labour* (Bristol: Policy Press, 2007), p. 14 and Winder, *Bloody Foreigners*, pp. 330–31.

4 'Papers released under 30-year rule reveal full force of Thatcher's fury', *The Guardian*, 30 December 2009.

5 Winder, *Bloody Foreigners*.

6 Hansen, *Citizenship and Immigration in Post-War Britain*, pp. 57, 59.

7 Ibid.

8 Gary Freeman, writing in Cornelius, Tsuda, Martin and Hollifield (eds), *Controlling Immigration: A Global Perspective* (Stanford: Stanford University Press, 1994).

9 See for example 'Dutch woman with two British children told to leave UK after 24 years', *The Guardian*, 28 December 2016.

CHAPTER 2: NET MIGRATION: THE ACCIDENTAL TARGET

1 Bridget Anderson, *Us and Them: The Dangerous Politics of Immigration Control* (Oxford: Oxford University Press, 2013), p. 51.

2 'International Passenger Survey: quality information in relation to migration flows', Office for National Statistics (accessed 9 February 2020).

3 Dr Carlos Vargas-Silva and Robert McNeil, 'The Net Migration Target and the 2017 Election', Migration Observatory, 4 May 2017.

4 'Statement from the ONS on the reclassification of international migration statistics', Office for National Statistics, 21 August 2019.

5 Hansen, 'The Decline of an Ideal: Conservatives and Immigration, 1958–1960', in *Citizenship and Immigration in Post-War Britain*, pp. 80–99.

6 Ibid., pp. 119, 150.

7 Its formal title is the '1951 UN Convention Relating to the Status of Refugees and its 1967 Protocol'.

8 "'I fear for my grandchildren" says former Archbishop of Canterbury, as he calls for Christian values to be defended', *Daily Mail*, 7 January 2010.

9 Available at: https://youtu.be/ADJ4BLqN6Vo

10 'How Cameron's jobs miracle ate his immigration target', *The Spectator*, 26 February 2015.

11 'David Cameron: net immigration will be capped at tens of thousands', *Daily Telegraph*, 10 January 2010.

12 Conservative Party election manifesto, 2005, available at: http://news.bbc.co.uk/1/shared/bsp/hi/pdfs/11_04_05_conservative_manifesto.pdf

13 'No obvious limit to immigration, says Blunkett', *Daily Telegraph*, 14 November 2003.

14 David Cameron speech, 29 October 2007, available at: http://news.bbc.co.uk/1/hi/uk_politics/7067500.stm

15 The Conservative Manifesto 2010, available at: https://www.conservatives.com/~/media/Files/Manifesto2010

16 David Cameron speech, 14 April 2011, available at: https://www.bbc.com/news/uk-politics-13083781

17 'A shortcut to hitting net migration target?', BBC News, 3 June 2014.

18 The Conservative Party Manifesto 2015, available at: http://ucrel.lancs.ac.uk/wmatrix/ukmanifestos2015/localpdf/Conservatives.pdf

19 The Conservative and Unionist Party Manifesto 2017, available at: https://s3.eu-west-2.amazonaws.com/conservative-party-manifestos/Forward+Together+-+Our+Plan+for+a+Stronger+Britain+and+a+More+Prosperous.pdf

CHAPTER 3: HOSTILE ENVIRONMENT: PAPERS, PLEASE

1 'Lib Dem MP attacks coalition's plans for immigration reform', *The Guardian*, 13 July 2013.

2 *Baker v Abellio London Ltd* [2017] UKEAT 0250_16_0510.

3 See part 6a of the Immigration Rules, entitled 'The points-based system', available at: https://www.gov.uk/guidance/immigration-rules/immigration-rules-part-6a-the-points-based-system

4 Figures compiled from Home Office migration transparency data, available at: https://www.gov.uk/government/collections/migration-transparency-data

5 'London Met wins back foreign student licence', BBC News, 9 April 2013.

6 "'It was a fake meeting": Byron Hamburgers staff on immigration raid', *The Guardian*, 28 July 2016.

7 'Pressure on law chief after fine', BBC News, 22 September 2009.

8 'Lady Scotland's former cleaner convicted of fraud', *The Guardian*, 9 April 2010.

9 'Border police arrest cleaner at heart of Mark Harper immigration row', *The Guardian*, 18 July 2014.

10 Collated from Freedom of Information requests and Home Office transparency data, available at: https://www.gov.uk/government/collections/migration-transparency-data

11 Anderson, *Us and Them*. Although the book pre-dates the Immigration Act 2014, this is very much the thrust of her argument, as I understand it.

12 'Theresa May interview: "We're going to give illegal migrants a really hostile reception"', *Daily Telegraph*, 25 May 2012.

13 'Impact Assessment: Tackling Sham Marriage', Home Office, 11 September 2013.

14 On data-sharing see Gracie Mae Bradley, 'Care Don't Share', Liberty, 2018.

15 Aneurin Bevan, *In Place of Fear* (London: William Heinemann, 1952).

16 'NHS Charges for Overseas Visitors', House of Commons Library, no. 3015, 11 October 2019.

17 'Health tourism: what's the cost?', Full Fact, 21 December 2016.

18 Memorandum of understanding between Health and Social Care Information Centre, the Home Office and the Department of Health, 29 January 2019. This has now been withdrawn.

19 'NHS hands over patient records to Home Office for immigration crackdown', *The Guardian*, 24 January 2017.

20 'Home Office scraps scheme that used NHS data to track migrants', *The Guardian*, 12 November 2018.

21 'We won! DfE are ending the nationality school census!', Against Borders for Children, 10 April 2018.

22 'Immigration Offences: Trends in Legislation and Criminal and Civil Enforcement', Migration Observatory, 12 October 2016.

23 'The Tories Are Risking Decades of Progress in Policing', Huffington Post, 17 March 2016.

24 'Woman reports rape to police – and is arrested on immigration charges', Politics.co.uk, 28 November 2017.

25 'The round-up: rough sleeper immigration raids and charity collaboration', Corporate Watch, 7 March 2017.

26 *R (Gureckis) v Secretary of State for the Home Department* [2017] EWHC 3298 (Admin).

27 Diane Taylor and Mattha Busby, 'Home Office pays religious groups to help deport rough sleepers', *The Guardian*, 5 November 2019.

28 David Cameron speech, 10 October 2011, available at: https://www.gov.uk/government/speeches/prime-ministers-speech-on-immigration

29 Quoted in 'An Inspection of the Intelligence Functions of Border Force and Immigration Enforcement', Independent Chief Inspector of Borders and Immigration, July 2016.

30 'The new border guards: MP tip-offs to the Home Office escalate', Politics.co.uk, 23 September 2019.

31 Paul Daly, 'The "hostile environment" and the overenforcement of immigration law', Administrative Law Matters, 23 April 2018.

32 'David Cameron: The prime mover behind Britain's hostile environment, who escaped the blame', *The Independent*, 8 June 2019.

33 Wendy Williams, 'Windrush Lessons Learned Review', 19 March 2020, p. 210.

34 'Evaluation of the Right to Rent scheme', Home Office, 20 October 2015.

35 David Cameron speech, 21 May 2015, available at: https://www.gov.uk/government/speeches/pm-speech-on-immigration

36 'Passport Please: The impact of the Right to Rent checks on migrants and ethnic minorities in England', Joint Council for the Welfare of Immigrants, February 2017.

37 *R (on the Application of Joint Council for the Welfare of Immigrants) v Secretary of State for the Home Department* [2019] EWHC 452 (Admin).

38 Quoted in 'The Go Home Office: how the department of Windrush could harm EU nationals next', *Prospect*, 7 October 2019.

39 'Home Office "go home" texts sent to people with right to remain', *Daily Telegraph*, 18 October 2018.

40 'Inspection report of hostile environment measures', Independent Chief Inspector of Borders and Immigration, October 2016.

41 As will be discussed in Chapter 12, before the British Nationality Act 1981 there was no such thing as a 'British citizen', and as such, only those known as 'citizens of the United Kingdom and the colonies'.

42 Fiona Bawdon, 'Chasing Status: if not British then what am I?', Legal Action Group, October 2014. The names were changed for the purposes of the report, which is available at: https://www.lag.org.uk/about-us/policy/campaigns/chasing-status

43 'Tighter immigration laws catching out long-term legal migrants – report', *The Guardian*, 15 October 2014.

44 See Amelia Gentleman, *The Windrush Betrayal: Exposing the Hostile Environment* (London: Guardian Faber, 2019) for the full account.

45 '"Shameful": widespread outrage over man denied NHS cancer care', *The Guardian*, 12 March 2018.

46 See Gentleman, *The Windrush Betrayal*.

47 Michael Gove, Boris Johnson, Priti Patel and Gisela Stuart, 'Restoring public trust in immigration policy – a points-based non-discriminatory immigration system', Vote Leave, 1 June 2016.

48 'Unsettled Status? Which EU Citizens are at Risk of Failing to Secure their Rights after Brexit?', Migration Observatory, 12 April 2018.

49 'Asylum seeker denied cancer treatment by Home Office dies', *The Guardian*, 19 September 2019.

50 See for example 'Thousands of asylum seekers and migrants wrongly denied NHS healthcare', *The Independent*, 16 April 2017, and 'Pregnant women without legal status "too afraid to seek NHS care"', *The Guardian*, 20 March 2017.

51 'Briefing: what is the hostile environment, where does it comes from, who does it affect?', Free Movement, 1 May 2018.

52 'Inspection report of hostile environment measures', Independent Chief Inspector of Borders and Immigration, October 2016.

53 'An inspection of the "Right to Rent" scheme', Independent Chief Inspector of Borders and Immigration, March 2018.

54 Williams, 'Windrush Lessons Learned Review', pp. 241–2.

55 'Inspection report of hostile environment measures', Independent Chief Inspector of Borders and Immigration, October 2016.

CHAPTER 4: COMPLEXITY AND COST: NO WAY TO RUN A WHELK STORE

1 *MA (Nigeria) v Secretary of State for the Home Department* [2009] EWCA Civ 1229.

2 Tom Bingham, *The Rule of Law* (London: Allen Lane, 2010).

3 Catherine Baksi, 'Immigration judge bemoans "worse than useless" Home Office officials', Legal Hackette's Brief, 8 November 2017.

4 Martha Bozic, Caelainn Barr and Niamh McIntyre, with additional reporting by Poppy Noor, 'Revealed: immigration rules in UK more than double in length', *The Guardian*, 27 August 2018.

5 Lord Neuberger, 'Welcome address to the Australian Bar Association Biennial Conference', 3 July 2017.

6 *R (on the application of New London College Ltd) v Secretary of State for the Home Department* [2013] UKSC 51.

7 *Pokhriyal v Secretary of State for the Home Department* [2013] EWCA Civ 1568.

8 *Sapkota v Secretary of State for the Home Department* [2011] EWCA Civ 1320.

9 *Secretary of State for the Home Department v Khan* [2016] EWCA Civ 137.

10 *Khan v Secretary of State for the Home Department* [2017] EWCA Civ 424.

11 *Mudiyanselage v Secretary of State for the Home Department* [2018] EWCA Civ 65.

12 *Hossain & Ors v Secretary of State for the Home Department* [2015] EWCA Civ 207.

13 Darren Stevenson, 'The absolute state of the UK visa application system', Free Movement, 2 May 2019.

14 'Normality is a luxury: How limited leave to remain is blighting young lives', Let Us Learn, 31 July 2019.

15 Oral evidence of Amber Rudd to Home Affairs Committee, published 17 October 2017, available at: http://data.parliament.uk/writtenevidence/committeeevidence.svc/evidencedocument/home-affairs-committee/the-work-of-the-home-secretary/oral/71645.html

16 See 'Simplifying the Immigration Rules', Law Commission, January 2020, and 'Simplifying the Immigration Rules: a response', Home Office, March 2020.

17 *R v Mohammed and Osman* [2007] EWCA Crim 2332.

18 'Syrian asylum seekers without passports to appeal UK convictions', The Justice Gap, 23 April 2015.

19 'The lawyer who takes the cases no one wants', *The Guardian*, 14 April 2016.

CHAPTER 5: FAMILIES AND FRIENDS: YOU CANNOT HUG SKYPE

1 'Impact assessment: Changes to Family Migration Routes', Home Office, 12 June 2012.

2 The precise level of savings necessary is calculated using a complex formula of (X multiplied by 2.5) plus £16,000, where X is the difference between provable, eligible income and £18,600. A person with no eligible income therefore has to show £18,600 multiplied by 2.5, which is £46,500, plus £16,000, which is a total of £62,500.

3 'The Minimum Income Requirement for Non-EEA Family Members in the UK', Migration Observatory, 27 January 2016.

4 'Skype Families: The effects on children of being separated from a mum or dad because of recent Immigration Rules', Children's Commissioner, 9 September 2015.

5 The Home Office impact assessment of 12 June 2012, cited in Note 1 above, estimated that between 13,600 and 17,800 couples per year would be affected, with a mid-point of 15,700 per year.

6 'How many people have been prevented from bringing a partner to the UK due to the £18,600 minimum income requirement?', Migration Observatory, 14 December 2018.

7 This is always automatic for a child born in the UK itself and is true for the first generation born abroad to a British citizen, but the rules are more complex for second and subsequent generations born abroad.

8 'Judge tells mother she cannot take son to Hong Kong as father "can't hug son over Skype"', *Daily Telegraph*, 27 February 2015.

9 'Partners, divorce and dissolution', Home Office, 2 August 2019.

10 Helena Wray, *Regulating Marriage Migration into the UK: A Stranger in the Home* (London: Routledge, 2011).

11 'Impact assessment: Tackling Sham Marriage', Home Office, 11 September 2013.

12 Ibid.

13 'The implementation of the 2014 "hostile environment" provisions for tackling sham marriage: report', Chief Inspector of Borders and Immigration, 15 December 2016.

14 'Family Policy: Family life (as a partner or parent), private life and exceptional circumstances', Home Office, version 5.0, 10 December 2019.

15 'Immigration Directorate Instructions', Chapter 8, Section 5a, Annex M, Children, Home Office, July 2012.

16 'Oxford professor's children refused visas to join her in UK', *The Guardian*, 1 October 2019. The decision was later reversed, but the legal basis for the new decision was not clear. The original conclusion appeared, on the basis of the media reports, to be a correct application of the harsh rules.

17 'Home Office reverses visa decision for Egyptian GP', *The Guardian*, 15 October 2019.

18 'An inspection of how the Home Office considers the "best interests" of unaccompanied asylum seeking children', paragraph 9.22, Chief Inspector of Borders and Immigration, 28 March 2018.

19 'Inspection report of applications to enter, remain and settle in the UK', paragraph 7.15, Chief Inspector of Borders and Immigration, 24 January 2013.

20 'A re-inspection of the Home Office's application of the good character requirement in the case of young persons who apply for registration as British citizens', paragraph 3.8, Chief Inspector of Borders and Immigration, 4 April 2019.

21 'Home Office ordered to pay £50,000 after child separated from father', *The Guardian*, 11 July 2018.

22 'Children's Voices: The Wellbeing of Children Subject to Immigration Controls in England', Children's Commissioner, 8 November 2017.

23 Numbers taken from *R (on the application of Britcits) v Secretary of State for the Home Department* [2016] EWHC 956 (Admin).

24 See paragraph E-ECDR.2.5 of the Immigration Rules.

25 *Ribeli v Entry Clearance Officer, Pretoria* [2018] EWCA Civ 611.

26 'How many people come to the UK each year (including visitors)?', Home Office, 28 November 2019, and Melanie Gower, 'Abolition of family visitor visa appeal rights', House of Commons Library, 5 July 2013.

27 'An inspection of entry clearance processing operations in Croydon and Istanbul', Chief Inspector of Borders and Immigration, July 2017.

28 'AI system for granting UK visas is biased, rights group claim', *The Guardian*, 29 October 2019.

29 'Entry Clearance Decision-Making: A Global Review', Independent Chief Inspector of Borders and Immigration, December 2011.

30 Tony Blair, Hansard, House of Commons debate, vol. 213, col. 43, 2 November 1992.

31 Rosie Winterton, Hansard, House of Commons debate, vol. 380, col. 65, 12 February 2002.

32 Freedom of Information request 30396, 10 March 2014.

33 'Deportation of Lebanese man with Down's "inhumane" – Vince Cable', *The Guardian*, 6 November 2014.

34 See https://twitter.com/SoniaL77/status/1179014890519855105

35 Joe Owen, Maddy Thimont Jack, Adela Iacobov and Elliott Christensen, 'Managing migration after Brexit', Institute for Government, 8 March 2019, p. 28.

36 *MM and others v Secretary of State for the Home Department* [2017] UKSC 10.

37 *Surinder Singh*, C-370/90.

38 David Cameron speech, 22 January 2010, available at: https://conservative-speeches.sayit. mysociety.org/speech/601543

CHAPTER 6: ASYLUM: SANDBANKS AND CROCODILES

1 Alasdair Mackenzie, 'No Reason At All', 1995. This is still available online, rather quaintly preserved as a scanned copy of a report typed up on a typewriter: http://repository. forcedmigration.org/pdf/?pid=fmo:3261

2 'Quality Integration Project: First Report to the Minister', UNHCR Representative to the United Kingdom, August 2010.

3 'Home Office told asylum seeker his claim was "pants"', *The Guardian*, 16 December 2000.

4 'Border staff humiliate and trick asylum seekers – whistleblower', *The Guardian*, 2 February 2010.

5 Kenneth Baker, Hansard, House of Commons debate, 2 July 1991, vol. 194, col. 165.

6 'Blair targets huge asylum cuts', *The Guardian*, 8 February 2003.

7 Theresa May speech to Conservative Party conference, 6 October 2015, available at: https:// www.independent.co.uk/news/uk/politics/theresa-may-s-speech-to-the-conservative-party-conference-in-full-a6681901.html

8 See for example William Allen and Scott Blinder, 'Migration in the News: Portrayals of Immigrants, Migrants, Asylum Seekers and Refugees in National British Newspapers, 2010–2012', Migration Observatory, 2013.

9 Helen Baillot, Sharon Cowan and Vanessa E. Munro, 'Second-hand Emotion? Exploring the Contagion and Impact of Trauma and Distress in the Asylum Law Context', *Journal of Law and Society*, vol. 40, no. 4, November 2013, pp. 509–40.

10 A classic question all barristers have been asked is, 'How do you represent clients you do not believe?' Our normal answer is that it is not our job to believe or disbelieve our clients. Our job is to present their case in court. It is the job of the judge or the jury to believe or disbelieve. Where a client actually tells us that they are lying, it is different; we are not permitted knowingly to mislead a judge or jury. In the case I mention here, I had to cease representing the client and he was left without a lawyer.

11 'Myth buster: "memories of trauma are engraved on the brain"', Centre for the Study of Emotion and Law, Free Movement, 21 June 2016.

12 Colin Yeo, 'Questions to a bisexual asylum seeker in detention', Free Movement, 24 January 2014.

13 'Gay asylum seekers face "humiliation"', *The Guardian*, 8 February 2014.

14 'Missing the mark: decision-making on Lesbian, Gay (Bisexual, Trans and Intersex) asylum claims', UK Lesbian and Gay Immigration Group, September 2013.

15 'Fleeing Persecution: Asylum Claims in the UK on Religious Freedom Grounds', All Party Parliamentary Group for International Freedom of Religion or Belief, 7 June 2016.

16 '120 leading philosophers say "appalling" Home Office humanism test "makes no sense"', Humanists UK, 25 January 2018.

17 *MST and Others (national service – risk categories (CG))* [2016] UKUT 443 (IAC).

18 For references see Nick Nason, 'The Curious Case of the Eritrean Country Guidance', Free Movement, 14 February 2017.

19 'An inspection of family reunion applications', Chief Inspector of Borders and Immigration, 14 September 2016.

20 Asylum and Immigration (Treatment of Claimants etc.) Act 2004, Sections 2 and 8.

21 Vaughan Robinson and Jeremy Segrott, 'Understanding the decision-making of asylum seekers', Home Office Research Study 243, July 2002.

22 'Figures at a glance', UNHCR, available at: https://www.unhcr.org/uk/figures-at-a-glance.html

23 Anderson, *Us and Them?*

24 *R v Immigration Officer at Prague Airport, ex parte European Roma Rights Centre* [2005] 2 AC 1.

25 'The man who fell to earth', *The Guardian*, 18 July 2001.

26 'The final episode of a stowaway's story', BBC News, 7 January 2014.

27 'Heathrow stowaway who fell to death identified as Mozambican migrant', *The Guardian*, 10 January 2016.

28 'Kenya Airways stowaway: Mystery of the man who fell from the sky', BBC News, 15 November 2019.

29 'Lonely death of migrant who tried to swim the Channel', *Sunday Times*, 22 September 2019.

30 '"We were not as brave": Woman drowned in Channel trying to save baby and fellow migrants', Sky News, 8 October 2019.

31 See https://missingmigrants.iom.int/

32 See more at www.lastrights.net. Catriona and Syd do amazing work.

33 See for example David Blunkett speech to Labour Party conference on 2 October 2003, available at: https://www.theguardian.com/politics/2003/oct/02/labourconference.labour9

34 Speech by Theresa May to Conservative conference on 6 October 2015, available at: http://www.ein.org.uk/news/home-secretary-use-conservative-party-conference-speech-warn-uk-needs-have-immigration-limit#speech

35 Sunder Katwala, Steve Ballinger and Matthew Rhodes, 'How To Talk About Immigration', British Future, 2014, p. 17.

36 See for example Jonathan Portes, 'And so the appalling human consequences of the austerity experiment become clear', *Prospect*, 25 March 2020.

37 'David Cameron: The prime mover behind Britain's hostile environment, who escaped the blame', *The Independent*, 8 June 2019.

38 'UK Public Opinion toward Immigration: Overall Attitudes and Level of Concern', Migration Observatory, 20 January 2020.

39 Rob Ford, 'Acceptable and Unacceptable Immigrants: How Opposition to Immigration in Britain is Affected by Migrants' Region of Origin', *Journal of Ethnic and Migration Studies* (2011), vol. 37, no. 7, pp. 1017–37.

40 Helen Dempster and Karen Hargrave, 'Understanding public attitudes towards refugees and migrants', Overseas Development Institute and Chatham House, 2017.

41 'Global Views on Immigration and the Refugee Crisis', Ipsos MORI, 2016 and 2017.

42 Don Flynn, '"Tough As Old Boots"? Asylum, immigration and the paradox of New Labour policy', Joint Council for the Welfare of Immigrants, 2003.

43 Robert Maclennan, Hansard, House of Commons debate, 2 July 1991, vol. 194, col. 171.

44 Michael Howard, Hansard, House of Commons debate, 20 November 1995, vol. 267, col. 335.

45 'Migration to the UK: Asylum and Resettled Refugees', Migration Observatory, 8 November 2019.

46 See Anthea Vogl, 'Telling Stories from Start to Finish: Exploring the demand for narrative in refugee testimony', *Griffith Law Review* (2013), vol. 22, no. 1, pp. 63–86.

47 Section 8 of the Asylum and Immigration (Treatment of Claimants etc.) Act 2004 is the most notorious example of this wishful thinking made law.

48 William McLennan, 'Are migrants who cross the Channel sent back?', BBC News, 20 January 2020.

49 Colin Yeo and Susan Reardon-Smith, 'The Impact of Brexit on UK Asylum Law', *Journal of Immigration, Asylum and Nationality Law* (2018), vol. 32, no. 3.

50 Jonathan Portes, *What Do We Know and What Should We Do About Immigration?* (London: Sage, 2019).

51 'Home Office policy leaving refugees homeless within days of being granted asylum, report finds', *The Independent*, 5 June 2018.

CHAPTER 7: ECONOMIC MIGRATION: POINTS MEAN PRIZES

1 'Britain's curry houses disappearing – 50 per cent to close within 10 years', *Daily Telegraph*, 23 February 2017.

2 *R (on the Application of Imam) v Secretary of State for the Home Department* [2019] EWCA Civ 1760.

3 Will Somerville, *Immigration under New Labour* (Bristol: Policy Press, 2007).

4 Erica Consterdine, *Labour's Immigration Policy: The Making of the Migration State* (London: Palgrave Macmillan, 2018).

5 'Selective Admission: Making Migration Work for Britain', Home Office, 2006.

6 'Australia's points system is more liberal than you think', *Financial Times*, 3 June 2016.

7 'Quarterly Immigration Statistics Year Ended September 2019', Home Office.

8 'The UK's points-based system for immigration', House of Commons Library, 9 July 2018.

9 Figures taken from 'Simplifying the Immigration Rules: Consultation Paper No 242', Law Commission, January 2019.

10 *Alvi* [2012], UKSC 33 and *Munir* [2012] UKSC 32.

11 'Immigration: the Points Based System – Work Routes', National Audit Office, 15 March 2011.

12 There were two separate cases, the second of which includes a summary of the first: *R (on the application of HSMP Forum (UK) Ltd) v Secretary of State for the Home Department* [2009] EWHC 711 (Admin).

13 'Analysis of the Points-Based System – Tier 1', Migration Advisory Committee, 2009, p. 84.

14 Theresa May, Hansard, House of Commons debate, 23 November 2010, vol. 519, col. 169.

15 *R (on the application of HSMP Forum (UK) Ltd) v Secretary of State for the Home Department* [2009] EWHC 711 (Admin).

16 See Chapter 8 on students.

17 'Home Office "wrongly tried to deport 300 skilled migrants"', *The Guardian*, 23 November 2018.

18 Williams, 'Windrush Lessons Learned Review', p. 115.

19 'A Points-Based System: Making Migration Work for Britain', Home Office, CM 6741, March 2006.

20 Goodfellow, *Hostile Environment*.

CHAPTER 8: STUDENTS: AWESOME OR BOGUS?

1 *R (on the application of Joshi & Anor) v Secretary of State for the Home Department* [2016] EWHC 216 (Admin).

2 *Bhandari v Secretary of State for the Home Department* [2019] EWCA Civ 129.

3 'Peer pressure, perks, or pounds: what makes overseas students violate visa laws?', Asian Image, 2 January 2020.

4 See discussion of the loss of London Metropolitan University's licence in Chapter 3.

5 'Tier 4 of the Points-Based System: Guidance for Sponsors Document 2: Sponsorship Duties Version 04/2016', Home Office.

6 'Bogus Colleges, Eleventh Report of Session 2008–09', Home Affairs Committee, 14 July 2009.

7 Theresa May, Hansard, House of Commons debate, 22 March 2011, vol. 525, col. 855.

8 David Cameron, speech on immigration, 14 April 2011, available at: https://www.theguardian.com/politics/2011/apr/14/david-cameron-immigration-speech-full-text

9 Data from Higher Education Statistics Agency.

10 'International students in the UK', Migration Advisory Committee, 11 September 2018.

11 'Investigation into the response to cheating in English language tests', National Audit Office, 24 May 2019.

12 'English language tests for overseas students: One Hundred and Sixteenth Report of Session 2017–19', Public Accounts Committee, 9 September 2019.

13 Theresa May, speech to Conservative Party conference 2015, 6 October 2015, available at https://www.independent.co.uk/news/uk/politics/theresa-may-s-speech-to-the-conservative-party-conference-in-full-a6681901.html

14 See Cameron's 14 April 2011 speech above and Theresa May, 'A borderless EU harms everyone but the gangs that sell false dreams', *Sunday Times*, 29 August 2015.

15 'International student migration research update: August 2017', Office for National Statistics.

16 'Second report on statistics being collected under the exit checks programme', Home Office, August 2017.

17 'International students in the UK', Submission of Universities UK to Migration Advisory Committee, 11 September 2018.

18 'International students in the UK', Migration Advisory Committee, 11 September 2018.

CHAPTER 9: FREE MOVEMENT: AUF WIEDERSEHEN, PET

1 'Brits abroad: how many people from the UK live in other EU countries?', Full Fact, 1 February 2018.

2 Robert Saunders, *Yes to Europe! The 1975 Referendum and Seventies Britain* (Cambridge: Cambridge University Press, 2018).

3 Margaret Thatcher, Speech to the College of Europe ('The Bruges Speech'), 20 September 1988.

4 'The making of blue Peter', *The Independent*, 3 April 1994.

5 'The road to Brexit was paved with Boris Johnson's Euromyths', *The Guardian*, 15 July 2016.

6 With thanks to Kate Lyons, 'The 10 best Euro myths – from custard creams to condoms', *The Guardian*, 23 June 2016.

7 Consterdine, *Labour's Immigration Policy*, pp. 147–8.

8 See Consterdine, 'Do Parties Matter? Party Ideology and Party Competition', in ibid., pp. 119–60.

9 Michael Howard, speech delivered in Burnley on 19 February 2004, available at: http://news.bbc.co.uk/1/hi/uk_politics/3502573.stm

10 Dustmann et al., 'The Impact of EU Enlargement on Migration Flows Home Office Report 25/03', 2005, available at: https://discovery.ucl.ac.uk/id/eprint/14332/1/14332.pdf

11 See Chapter 2 on the net migration target.

12 Robert Ford and Matthew Goodwin, *Revolt on the Right: Explaining Support for the Radical Right in Britain* (London: Routledge, 2014).

13 David Cameron, Bloomberg speech on 23 January 2013, available at: https://www.gov.uk/government/speeches/eu-speech-at-bloomberg

14 'David Cameron: we will keep out EU benefit tourists', *Daily Telegraph*, 6 January 2013.

15 'Benefits Britain here we come! Fears as migrant flood begins', *Daily Express*, 1 January 2014.

16 'We're building an immigration system that puts Britain first', *Daily Telegraph*, 28 July 2014.

17 David Cameron, Chatham House speech, 10 November 2015, available at: https://www.gov.uk/government/speeches/prime-ministers-speech-on-europe

18 'We'll halt EU dole tourists: David Cameron set for showdown over new immigrant arrivals', *The Sun*, 18 February 2013.

19 Figures quoted by Lord Russell, Hansard, House of Lords debate, 30 April 1996, vol. 571, col. 1545.

20 'Speak English or lose benefits: Cameron to stop payouts to immigrants who use taxpayer-funded translators', *Mail on Sunday*, 18 January 2014.

21 *Ahmad v Secretary of State for the Home Department* [2014] EWCA Civ 988.

22 'Using the minimum earnings threshold to determine who is a "worker"', Free Movement, 18 March 2014.

23 See *St Prix*, C-507/12 and *Dakneviciute*, C-544/18.

24 Charlotte O'Brien, *Unity in Adversity: EU Citizenship, Social Justice and the Cautionary Tale of the EU* (London: Hart, 2017).

25 See Chapter 3 on the hostile environment.

26 Home Office quarterly statistics, year ended December 2019.

27 'Why we lost the Brexit vote', Politico, 20 October 2016.

28 Sources abound for this point, but for a recent and comprehensive analysis see 'The Fiscal Impact of Immigration on the UK: A report for the Migration Advisory Committee', Oxford Economics, June 2018.

29 'The inside story of how David Cameron drove Britain to Brexit', *Prospect*, 25 November 2017.

30 'Why we lost the Brexit vote', Politico, 20 October 2016.

31 O'Brien, *Unity in adversity*. Names were changed in this work.

32 Michael Gove, Boris Johnson, Priti Patel and Gisela Stuart, 'Restoring public trust in immigration policy – a points-based non-discriminatory immigration system', Vote Leave, 1 June 2016.

33 'Unsettled Status? Which EU Citizens are at Risk of Failing to Secure their Rights after Brexit?', Migration Observatory, 12 April 2018.

CHAPTER 10: DEPORTATION, EXILE AND MODERN TRANSPORTATION

1 'This Man Faces Deportation For Carrying Cannabis Despite Living In Britain Since He Was 4', BuzzFeed, 31 May 2019.

2 *Akinyemi v Secretary of State for the Home Department* [2019] EWCA Civ 2098.

3 'Home Office Resource Accounts 2004–05 and follow-up on returning failed asylum applicants, Sixtieth Report of Session 2005–06', House of Commons Committee of Public Accounts, 21 July 2006.

4 'Managing and removing foreign national offenders', National Audit Office, 17 October 2014, p. 17.

5 'Annual Report 2019', Independent Chief Inspector of Borders and Immigration, June 2019, p. 10.

6 Tony Blair, Hansard, House of Commons debate, 3 May 2006, vol. 445, col. 961.

7 *Lee v Secretary of State for the Home Department* [2011] EWCA Civ 348.

8 Tribunal Quarterly Statistics, available at: https://www.gov.uk/government/collections/tribunals-statistics

9 Theresa May speech on 4 October 2011, available at: https://www.politics.co.uk/comment-analysis/2011/10/04/theresa-may-speech-in-full

10 'Catgate: another myth used to trash human rights', *The Guardian*, 4 October 2011.

11 'Theresa May put on the spot over Human Rights cat', Full Fact, 4 October 2011.

12 'Judges who allow foreign criminals to stay in Britain', *Daily Telegraph*, 16 June 2012.

13 'Judge who let Taliban soldier remain in Britain now allows refugee who raped girl, 12, stay in UK', *Daily Mail*, 14 July 2012.

14 See Paragraph 2 of the full determination, available at: https://www.freemovement.org.uk/judge-hung-out-to-dry/

15 'Criminality: Article 8 ECHR cases', Home Office, available at: https://www.gov.uk/government/publications/criminality-guidance-in-article-8-echr-cases

16 *R (Kiarie and Byndloss) v Secretary of State for the Home Department* [2017] UKSC 42.

17 'An Inspection of the Emergency Travel Document Process', Chief Inspector of Borders and Immigration, March 2014.

18 'Managing and removing foreign national offenders', National Audit Office, 17 October 2014, p. 32.

19 'An inspection of the Home Office's management of non-detained Foreign National Offenders' and 'An inspection of the Home Office's Reporting and Offender Management processes', Chief Inspector of Borders and Immigration, November 2017.

20 'A re-inspection of the Home Office's Reporting and Offender Management processes and of its management of non-detained Foreign National Offenders', Chief Inspector of Borders and Immigration, March 2019.

CHAPTER 11: IMMIGRATION DETENTION: ENFORCING CONTROL

1 'Report on an unannounced inspection of Harmondsworth Immigration Removal Centre', HM Chief Inspector of Prisons, January 2014.

2 'Harmondsworth death: who was Alois Dvorzac?', *Channel 4 News*, 16 January 2014.

3 See Phil Miller's articles at: https://www.opendemocracy.net/search/?query=Alois+Dvorzak

4 Amrit Wilson writing in *The Guardian* and quoted in Mary Bosworth, *Inside Immigration Detention* (Oxford: Oxford University Press, 2014), p. 39.

5 Bosworth, *Inside Immigration Detention*, p. 10.

6 *Xue v Secretary of State for the Home Department* [2015] EWHC 825 (Admin).

7 *R (on the Application of MD) v Secretary of State for the Home Department* [2014] EWHC 2249 (Admin).

8 'Deaths of immigration detainees', Inquest, available at: https://www.inquest.org.uk/deaths-of-immigration-detainees

9 P. Sen, J. Arugnaseelan, E. Connell, C. Katona, A. A. Khan, P. Moran et al., 'Mental health morbidity among people subject to immigration detention in the UK: A feasibility study', *Epidemiology and Psychiatric Sciences* (2018), vol. 27, no. 6, pp. 628–37.

10 Mary Bosworth, 'Affect and Authority in Immigration Detention', available at: https://ora.ox.ac.uk/objects/uuid:497bf576-d284-4869-a29f-9b70eb1f7197/download_file?file_format=pdf&safe_filename=Mary%2BBosworth%252C%2BAuthority%2Band%2Baffect%2Bin%2Bimmigration%2Bdetention.pdf&type_of_work=Journal+article. The names used by Bosworth are pseudonyms.

11 'G4S: "What I saw when I went undercover"', BBC News, 4 September 2017.

12 'Detained forever? Foreign prisoners and indefinite detention', Free Movement, 7 March 2011.

13 *R (Hardial Singh) v Governor of Durham Prison* [1983] EWHC 1 (QB).

14 Asylum Information Database, available at: https://www.asylumineurope.org/reports

15 Directive 2008/115/EC.

16 Detention tables, 'Table dt_14_q: Top 20 longest lengths of detention of people in detention by sex', Home Office Immigration Statistics.

17 Bosworth, *Inside Immigration Detention*, pp. 43–4.

18 Ibid., p. 3.

19 Ibid., pp. 13–14.

20 Oakington closed in 2010 and The Cedars, Dover, Haslar, Campsfield and The Verne have all closed in recent years.

21 'Profile: Yarl's Wood Detention Centre', *The Guardian*, 15 February 2002.

22 'Immigration detention: Fourteenth Report of Session 2017–19', cited in Home Affairs Committee, 12 March 2019, p. 7.

23 'Annual Report and Accounts 2018–19', Home Office, 6 June 2019.

24 *R (Gureckis) v Secretary of State for the Home Department* [2017] EWHC 3298 (Admin).

25 'The effectiveness and impact of immigration detention casework: A joint thematic review by HM Inspectorate of Prisons and the Independent Chief Inspector of Borders and Immigration', 2012, available at: https://www.justiceinspectorates.gov.uk/hmiprisons/wp-content/uploads/sites/4/2014/04/immigration-detention-casework-2012.pdf

26 M. von Werthern, K. Robjant, Z. Chui et al., 'The impact of immigration detention on mental health: a systematic review', *BMC Psychiatry*, vol. 18, no. 382 (2018).

27 Freedom of Information request, available at: https://www.whatdotheyknow.com/request/489809/response/1182364/attach/3/FOI%2048932%20Scott.pdf

28 'Europe's Unauthorized Immigrant Population Peaks in 2016, Then Levels Off', Pew Research, and Jolly, Thomas and Stanyer, 'London's children and young people who are not British citizens: A profile'.

29 Hiroshi Motomura, *Immigration Outside the Law* (Oxford: Oxford University Press, 2014), p. 26.

30 'The effectiveness and impact of immigration detention casework', HM Inspectorate of Prisons and the Independent Chief Inspector of Borders and Immigration, 2012, paragraph 4.6.

31 'Growing concerns about "incompetent" legal advice for immigration detainees', The Justice Gap, 30 May 2019.

32 'The immigration detainees held in prisons rather than detention centres', Free Movement, 21 January 2020.

33 Figures provided by Bail for Immigration Detainees via a Freedom of Information request.

34 Stephen Shaw, 'Review into the welfare in detention of vulnerable persons', 14 January 2016, available at: https://www.gov.uk/government/publications/review-into-the-welfare-in-detention-of-vulnerable-persons

35 Mark Harper, Hansard, House of Commons debate, 5 September 2013, vol. 567, col. 584.

36 'Man died in immigration detention after staff "dismissed" stroke as sign he had taken spice', The Independent, 12 November 2019.

37 'Report on an unannounced inspection of Heathrow Immigration Removal Centre Harmondsworth site', HM Chief Inspector of Prisons, 13 March 2018.

38 Stephen Shaw, 'Assessment of government progress in implementing the report on the welfare in detention of vulnerable persons', July 2018.

39 'Immigration detention: Fourteenth Report of Session 2017–19', Home Affairs Committee, 12 March 2019.

40 *Mohammed v The Home Office* [2017] EWHC 2809 (QB).

41 Chapter 12 in 'Fairer, Faster and Firmer: A modern approach to immigration and asylum', Home Office, 1999.

42 'Secure Borders, Safe Haven: Integration with Diversity in Modern Britain', Home Office, 2002, paragraph 4.73.

43 'Blunkett tells asylum seekers to go home', *Daily Telegraph*, 18 September 2002.

44 Speech by Tony Blair to Labour Party conference on 16 September 2004, available at: http://www.britishpoliticalspeech.org/speech-archive.htm?speech=183

45 'Thirty-fourth report: Returning Failed Asylum Applicants', Public Accounts Committee, 14 March 2006.

46 'Quarterly Immigration Statistics', Home Office, September 2019.

47 Shaw, 'Assessment of government progress in implementing the report on the welfare in detention of vulnerable persons', 2018, p. 8.

48 'How the US built the world's largest immigrant detention system', *The Guardian*, 24 September 2019.

CHAPTER 12: CITIZENSHIP, NATIONALITY AND INTEGRATION

1 Freedom of Information request, available at: https://www.whatdotheyknow.com/request/number_of_valid_british_passport#incoming-765591

2 See Chapter 3 on the hostile environment, for example.

3 'Commonwealth migrants arriving before 1971, year ending June 2017', Migration Observatory. Data available at: https://migrationobservatory.ox.ac.uk/commonwealth-migrants-arriving-1971-year-ending-june-2017/

4 Jolly, Thomas and Stanyer, 'London's children and young people who are not British citizens: A profile'.

5 Hiroshi Motomura, *Americans in Waiting: The Lost Story of Immigration and Citizenship in the United States* (Oxford: Oxford University Press, 2006), pp. 151 and 166.

6 Jolly, Thomas and Stanyer, 'London's children and young people who are not British citizens: A profile'.

7 See for example Thom Brooks, *Becoming British: UK Citizenship Examined* (London: Biteback Publishing, 2016) and 'The Ties that Bind: Citizenship and Civic Engagement in the 21st Century', House of Lords Committee on Citizenship and Civic Engagement, 18 April 2018.

8 'Life in the UK Test Pass Rates', Garuda Publications, 5 March 2017.

9 'The Deprivation of Citizenship in the United Kingdom: A Brief History', *Journal of Immigration, Asylum and Nationality Law* (2014), vol. 28.4, no. 326.

10 See for example 'HM Government Transparency Report 2018: Disruptive and Investigatory Powers', CM 9609.

11 'Shamima Begum: Isis Briton faces move to revoke citizenship', *The Guardian*, 19 February 2019.

12 'Shamima Begum would face death penalty in Bangladesh, says minister', *The Guardian*, 4 May 2019.

13 For example see 'Thank God, Sajid Javid grasped Shamima Begum is the one person uniting Britain – against her', *Daily Telegraph*, 19 February 2019.

14 For example see 'Britain needs a new treason law to tackle returning jihadis', *Daily Telegraph*, 17 February 2019, and 'The evil of Shamima Begum', Spiked Online, 11 February 2019.

15 'Secure Borders, Safe Haven Integration with Diversity in Modern Britain', CM 5387, Home Office, February 2002.

16 Sajid Javid, speech to Conservative Party conference on 2 October 2018, available at: https://blogs.spectator.co.uk/2018/10/full-text-sajid-javids-conservative-conference-speech/

17 House of Commons debate, 12 July 1918, quoted in Gibney, *The Deprivation of Citizenship in the United Kingdom*.

18 Lord Mackay of Clashfern, Hansard, House of Lords debate, 23 July 1981, vol. 423, col. 448.

19 Jacqui Smith, Hansard, House of Commons debate, 4 December 2008, vol. 485, col. 162.

20 Lord West of Spithead, Hansard, House of Lords debate, 9 December 2008, vol. 706, col. 273.

21 David Davies MP on 20 February 2008, Chris Grayling MP on 2 June 2009 and Damian Green MP on 14 July 2009.

22 'Immigration Bill Fact Sheet: Deprivation of Citizenship (Clause 60)', Home Office, January 2014.

23 '1 million new British citizens under Blair', *Daily Telegraph*, 24 May 2006.

24 'The great passport giveaway: Up to 250,000 foreigners to get UK citizenship every year', *Daily Mail*, 21 February 2008.

25 'We Want to Be Like Eu: Thousands of EU citizens rush to get their hands on a British passport before Brexit, new figures reveal', *The Sun*, 9 May 2017.

26 Hansen, 'The Kenyan Asians Crisis of 1968', *Citizenship and Immigration in Post-War Britain*, pp. 153–78.

27 David Blunkett, Hansard, House of Commons debate, 24 April 2002, vol. 384, col. 354.

28 Lodged in House of Commons Library HDep 2006/336, dated 19 June 2002, available at: https://publications.parliament.uk/pa/ld200506/ldlwa/60503wa1.pdf

29 For recent examples see Goodfellow, *Hostile Environment*, and Nadine El-Enany, *(B)ordering Britain: Law, Race and Empire* (Manchester: Manchester University Press, 2020).

30 Hiroshi Motomura, *Americans in Waiting*, p. 146.

CONCLUSION: WHAT NOW?

1 Motomura, *Americans in Waiting* and *Immigration Outside the Law*.

2 I should add for legal readers that the courts in the United Kingdom have declined to analyse immigration from the perspective of actual contract law. Immigration is considered a matter of public law, not contract law. See for example *R (on the application of HSMP Forum (UK) Ltd) v Secretary of State for the Home Department* [2009] EWHC 711 (Admin). Judges at times lean on broad, popular notions of contract in expressing their reasons, but this is more as a matter of rhetorical flourish.

3 See Introduction.

4 'Between a rock and a hard place: AVR 2.0: the case for rebooting Assisted Voluntary Return in the UK's immigration control regime', Social Market Foundation, December 2019.

5 'Review of the minimum income requirement for sponsorship under the family migration route', Migration Advisory Committee, 16 November 2011.

6 'Tier 1 (Investor) route: Investment thresholds and economic benefits', Migration Advisory Committee, 2014.

7 Home Office quarterly statistics, year ended September 2019.

8 'The Conservative plan for immigration after Brexit', Free Movement, 13 December 2019.

INDEX